A Season in Hell
and Other Works

Une saison en enfer
et œuvres diverses

A Season in Hell and Other Works

Une saison en enfer et œuvres diverses

ARTHUR RIMBAUD

A Dual-Language Book

Edited and Translated by
STANLEY APPELBAUM

DOVER PUBLICATIONS, INC.
Mineola, New York

Bibliographical Note

This Dover edition, first published in 2003, includes unabridged texts of *Une saison en enfer* (first published in 1873), *Illuminations* (first published in 1886), and a selection of verse poems (see Introduction for dating, and further bibliographical data in general) from standard French editions. The French texts are accompanied by new English translations by Stanley Appelbaum, who also wrote the Introduction and provided explanatory footnotes in English.

Library of Congress Cataloging-in-Publication Data

Rimbaud, Arthur, 1854–1891.
    [Saison en enfer. English & French]
    A season in hell and other works = Une saison en enfer et oeuvres diverses : a dual-language book / Arthur Rimbaud ; edited and translated by Stanley Appelbaum.
        p. cm.
    Includes index.
    ISBN 0-486-43087-1 (pbk.)
    1. Rimbaud, Arthur, 1854–1891—Translations into English. I. Title: Saison en enfer et oeuvres diverses. II. Appelbaum, Stanley. III. Title.

PQ2387.R5S313 2003
841'.8—dc21

                      2003055309

Manufactured in the United States of America
Dover Publications, Inc., 31 East 2nd Street, Mineola, N.Y. 11501

Contents

---

1. Including the verse poem "Le loup criait sous les feuilles" (The wolf was howling below the leaves).

Poésies choisies / Selected Poems in Verse   102/103

INTRODUCTION

Biography

THE WORKS in this volume, known to only a few kindred spirits at the time they were written by a boy between age fifteen and age twenty, soon became a rallying point of the poetic avant-garde in France and elsewhere, and have remained a source of wonder and inspiration to this day for their eternally youthful rebellious spirit and for their unmatched verbal magic.

Jean Nicolas Arthur Rimbaud was born on October 20, 1854, in Charleville, a small manufacturing town in the Ardennes region of northeastern France. His father was an infantry captain who deserted his family in 1860. His mother, from a well-to-do farming family, was strict, puritanical, and overly protective, perhaps as a result of her own hard experiences. At school, Rimbaud was a star pupil, skipping grades and excelling in French and Latin composition. He started writing both prose and verse very early, and by 1869 he was regularly submitting material to magazines (only three poems were printed during his creative period). He also corresponded with a few mentors, sending them drafts of poems and formulating his theories, but he failed to interest the reigning Parnassian poets. (This poetic "school," well established by 1866 and including Leconte de Lisle, Banville, Gautier, Coppée, and Heredia, believed in art for art's sake and, though often depicting exotic locales, was characterized by restraint, smoothness of technique, and precise descriptiveness.)

Though apparently fascinated by the artisans and laborers in Charleville, and certainly charmed by the forests and fields outside of town and around his mother's farm, Rimbaud felt increasingly stifled

by the rural backwardness and the smug petty-bourgeois existence of those late–Second Empire days. His schooling, and his whole life, were disrupted by the Franco-Prussian War, disastrous to France, which broke out in July 1870. In August he ran away from home, taking a train to Paris, where he was briefly arrested for having no ticket; a friendly former teacher brought him to a safe haven in Douai (northern France) before the boy returned home. In early October, after barely ten days in Charleville, Rimbaud ran away again, hiking to Douai, with stops in Charleroi (Belgium) and Brussels. In November he was back home. The fighting came close to him: at the end of the year Charleville's twin town, Mézières, was bombarded, and on New Year's Day of 1871 Charleville was occupied (armistice came on January 28).

Late in February 1871, Rimbaud spent a couple of weeks in Paris, and returned there in the second half of April. By that time, the Commune (March–May), a proletarian insurrection in Paris, was in full swing. Rimbaud was undoubtedly sympathetic to the Communards, but there is no proof of his participation in street fighting; he was back home before the movement was cruelly and bloodily repressed. But by September he was back in Paris by invitation: that of the poet Paul Verlaine (1844–1896), a so-called decadent who had already published three important volumes, including the influential *Fêtes galantes* (1869); Verlaine had responded enthusiastically to Rimbaud's letters of self-introduction.

In Paris, Rimbaud was a precocious and obnoxious member of Verlaine's socially marginal coterie of absinthe- and hashish-swilling poets. Back in Charleville for most of March and April of 1872, he returned to Paris in May, and soon began his travels with Verlaine (who was thus abandoning his wife and baby): to Brussels in July, to London (where there was a glut of French left-wing émigrés and existence was very difficult for the odd couple) in September. Rimbaud returned home at the end of November.

1873: with Verlaine in London and Ostend, January to early April; then some time on his mother's farm, where he may have begun *Une saison en enfer*. Late May, back with Verlaine, and off to Belgian cities and London; then another separation. The stormy relationship (apparently Rimbaud was much more aloof, and devastatingly sarcastic) ended with a bang in Brussels on July 10, when Verlaine, dead drunk, fired a pistol at Rimbaud, wounding him in the wrist. This led to a brief hospitalization for Rimbaud, but two years' incarceration for Verlaine. Rimbaud continued working on *Une saison en enfer*, which

was issued as a vanity publication in October. In 1874 he was back in London, this time with another, much less famous French poet.

Work on *Illuminations,* and a few poetic scraps, may have extended into 1874 and even 1875, but after that Rimbaud renounced creative writing and made a show of having lost interest in his earlier productions (though it is unsafe to say, as so many biographers and critics do, that he had lost his talent and/or never again even thought about his remarkable gifts). From 1875 on, the history of his physical person and that of his œuvre diverge.

In 1875 Rimbaud was a tutor in Stuttgart (where Verlaine, out of jail, paid him a last visit) and journeyed to Italy. In 1876 he joined the Dutch colonial army, but deserted in Batavia (now Jakarta), Java, and returned home. In 1877 he visited Germany, Sweden, and Denmark. In 1878 and 1879 he was on Cyprus, foreman of a quarry. The final phase of his career began in 1880, where he frequented Red Sea ports before accepting a job trading coffee and hides (later on, ivory–and, according to dark rumors, drugs and slaves) in Harrar (Hārer), Ethiopia (under Egyptian rule until 1887). He was chiefly in Harrar until 1890, though in 1882–83 he explored the Ogaden region between Ethiopia and Somalia (his dry, commercially oriented report was published in a Cairo journal) and in 1886–87 he was an unsuccessful gunrunner during the fighting for Harrar. In 1891 he entered a Marseilles hospital with a knee tumor; an amputation failed to halt the progress of his cancer, or syphilis, and he died on November 10, his relatives assuring the world that he departed as a good, repentant Christian.

Meanwhile, with no help from him, his work was attracting attention (Verlaine and others interested in Rimbaud's fame possessed numerous manuscripts). As early as 1878, but more frequently from 1883 on, poems received their first publication in magazines, and Verlaine made his former lover's work widely known in his 1884 book *Poètes maudits* (Accursed Poets). Volumes of Rimbaud's writings began to appear in 1886 and continued through the 1890s. The Symbolist "school" (Mallarmé, Laforgue, Verhaeren, Moréas, and others) acclaimed him (this group, established by 1886, stood for a poetry of nuance, musicality, sensations, and obscurity of metaphor, and cultivated free verse and prose poems). Rimbaud's œuvre has influenced (in technique and/or in content and outlook) such figures as Claudel, the Imagists in America, the Surrealists, and the "beat" poets, and has generated an unbelievably vast amount of criticism and scholarship.

Works

Since only three poems and *Une saison en enfer* were published under Rimbaud's supervision, there is no canonically fixed text (or sequence within volumes) for most of his work. This Dover volume contains the prose *Une saison en enfer* and the prose-poem collection *Illuminations*, both complete and unabridged (though chronologically later, they precede the verse poems here because they are more famous and the verse poems represent only a selection of the œuvre in that form), followed by 46 (out of some 60-odd) verse poems, in more or less chronological order of composition.

Other items not included here are: juvenilia in prose and verse (already exhibiting Rimbaud's gift for parody, spirit of rebellion, anticlericalism, and leaning toward scatology), including school exercises in Latin verse; a scattering of verse fragments; his contributions to the manuscript *Album zutique* (Damn-It-All Album) compiled by Verlaine's coterie (parodies of establishment poets and erotic or pornographic verses concerning love both straight and gay); a few brief prose pieces, including "Les déserts de l'amour" (The Deserts of Love); and his voluminous correspondence.

Une saison en enfer. First conceived as a "pagan" or "African" book of "agonizing stories," and written (if Rimbaud's own dating is accurate) from April to August of 1873, this work was published that October by the vanity press Alliance Typographique (M. J. Poot et Compagnie) in Brussels. Apparently paid only a small deposit, the publisher released only a few copies to Rimbaud, who gave them to friends. The bulk of the 500-copy edition was discovered in storage in 1901, though the event wasn't made public until 1914. (The text was more widely known, from later editions, by the 1890s.)

In the first section of the work, "Jadis, si je me souviens bien . . . ," the narrator is already in hell, addressing Satan. He now distrusts his childhood joys and wonders whether love has redemptive powers; the theme of escape appears.

In "Mauvais sang," he says that his inheritance is one of vice, that his kind has been of inferior stock throughout the history of France and Christianity, and that this inferiority is now universal; he is impatient with earned livelihoods and with modern technology; hope lies in a new paganism and departure from Europe; he admires the intractability of hardened criminals, and prizes amorality and freedom of thought. Rimbaud recollects the hardships of his runaway treks, and includes one of his recurring performing-arts images: life is the

farce that everyone must act out. He also introduces the major subject of European colonization of "underdeveloped" countries.

In "Nuit de l'enfer"—originally called "Fausse conversion" (False Conversion)—he is being punished by burning in hell (the "poison" he has taken is associated in *Illuminations* with his drug habit), but he wouldn't be there if he hadn't been raised as a Christian; he is thirsty (a frequent theme); he is a master of mysteries.

In "Délires I: Vierge folle," a fellow sufferer speaks. (Most scholars agree that the "foolish virgin" is Verlaine, and the "terrible husband" is Rimbaud; this sarcastic review of their relationship, with all the older man's complaints, is full of scorn for Verlaine's sentimental religiosity.) The "husband" says that love must be reinvented, because women are inadequate partners, and that life must be changed. There is a reminiscence of the couple's wretched existence as refugees in London. The mention of adventures out of children's books is typical of Rimbaud, and the "little girl at catechism" recalls his verse poem "Les premières Communions."

In "Délires II: Alchimie du verbe," Rimbaud expresses dissatisfaction with his own earlier poetry. He quotes, or misquotes, several poems reprinted elsewhere in this Dover volume[1] from other sources closer to their original wording (some of the differences here go beyond quoting from a faulty memory, and must be deliberate, sarcastic distortions); for the poem "Le loup criait sous les feuilles . . ." there is no other source, and it is not repeated in the verse-poem section of this volume. In two important statements, Rimbaud reveals his inspiration from popular art and literature (including children's books and fairy tales), with his concomitant love of the "unlovely"; and his belief that, in people's search for happiness, other lives are "owed to them" (metempsychosis). He discusses enchantment and hallucinations (from alcohol and drugs?), and probably recalls the wartime bombardments.

"L'impossible" concerns the escape from stifling everyday life, contrasting the purity of the ancient East with the horrors of the Occident and Christianity; the mind must remain alert.

In "L'éclair," he states that toil and science provide no answer; one must be idle and imaginative. The mention of the hospital bed is most likely associated with the shooting on July 10, 1873.

"Matin," with its yearning for childhood joys and the possibility of

---

1. Explanatory footnotes to these poems are supplied only in the "Selected Poems" section of this Dover volume.

their return, marks the end of his stay in hell. Rimbaud's political views are reflected in the statement that the new world he awaits must be free of tyrants.

In "Adieu," autumn has come (does this indicate the actual time of writing, like the hot weather mentioned earlier?), the memory of hell is fading, and imagination must be replaced by an acceptance of "rugged reality"; it is the eve of a new day, and a level head is needed for entering the "resplendent cities" (an echo of a similar phrase in the poem "Soleil et chair"). There is another recollection of his London sufferings. This final section of *Une saison en enfer* was long regarded as Rimbaud's final abjuration of creative writing (making this his last work), but most scholars now agree that at least parts of *Illuminations* were written in 1874 (or even a bit later), and some Rimbaud editions include poetic scraps presumably written in 1875. (With regard to Rimbaud's later years, all that can be said with certainty is that no creative writing has *survived.*)

Illuminations. Rimbaud may have been writing prose poems by November 1870, but it cannot be proved that any material in *Illuminations* precedes 1873; the composition proceeded through 1874 and may have extended until February 1875. The general title is first found in an 1878 letter of Verlaine, who explains it as the equivalent of *enluminures,* gaudily colored popular prints (although other, more ethereal, interpretations are obvious). Most of the pieces were first published in the new Symbolist magazine *La vogue* in May and June issues in 1886; they appeared in volume form, with some poems, later that year, with the Vogue imprint. The pieces "Fairy," "Guerre," "Génie," "Jeunesse I," and "Solde" were discovered later and were not published until the 1895 edition of Rimbaud's works, *Poésies complètes d'Arthur Rimbaud* (Vanier, Paris). Modern editions, based on sources without Rimbaud's "imprimatur," vary noticeably in wording and in sequence of items.

The prose-poem genre may have begun with *Gaspard de la nuit* (published posthumously 1842, probably written by 1836) by Aloysius Bertrand (1807–1841); it was consecrated by Baudelaire (1821–1867) in his *Petits poëmes en prose* (aka *Le spleen de Paris;* published posthumously in 1869). Rimbaud's pieces in *Illuminations* (some of which may be the pinnacle of his achievement) are much less descriptive and discursive; they are flights of fancy that transmute his experiences into coruscating verbal marvels.

"Après le déluge" picks up the motif of the cleansing, world-altering flood that had already appeared in some verse poems and is

echoed in "Soir historique" (later on in *Illuminations*), with its vision of the destruction of the bourgeois world, as well as in "Mouvement." "Après le déluge" also contains the theme of fairy tales (here, Bluebeard) and the motif of the hotel, which recurs in "Promontoire." "Enfance" recalls Rimbaud's boredom at home, like living in a tomb with just a faint hopeful ray of light.

"Conte" is an actual fairy tale, with homoerotic overtones; Rimbaud himself is the prince who longs for a revolution in love and finds that his actions are futile.

"Parade" exemplifies Rimbaud's performing-arts imagery, which recurs in "Ornières" (coupled with fairy-tale imagery), "Villes (II)" (dramas in shops), "Fêtes d'hiver" (comic opera), and "Scènes" (mingled with images of a city on a body of water).

"Antiquité" reflects Rimbaud's school studies of Greco-Roman civilization, as does "Villes (II)."

The title of "Being Beauteous" (which has military imagery at the end, like "À une raison") is from Longfellow's poem "Footsteps of Angels" (from his 1839 volume *The Voices of the Night*), in which it refers to a sweetheart of the poet's youthful days who is now dead.

"Vies" recounts a number of prior existences (the other lives "owed" to people; see "Délires II" in *Une saison en enfer*).

"Départ" clearly expresses Rimbaud's constant craving for something new (entailing his wanderlust and his progressive disavowal of his own creations).

"Royauté" is a utopian vision, with a promising young couple who may be the same as the one surviving the flood at the end of "Mouvement."

Both "À une raison" and "Matinée d'ivresse" are concerned with new life and love, the hope for a new order of the world. In the latter piece, "poison" is associated with hashish.

"Phrases," and "Fragments," once thought to be part of "Phrases," are brief oddments.

In "Ouvriers," in which suburbs are polluted by cities, one of the chief subjects of *Illuminations* appears: the disquieting phenomenon of the big city (many clues indicate that Rimbaud's repeated long sojourns in London were the inspiration for much of this material). The subject recurs in "Les ponts" (a geometrical cityscape with an intertwining of musical imagery), "Ville," "Villes (II)," "Villes (I)," and "Métropolitain" (in which the inn that won't open may be a nostalgic reminiscence of the Cabaret-Vert in Charleroi; see the verse poem "Au Cabaret-Vert").

"Vagabonds," in which Rimbaud quotes Verlaine's complaints about

him (as in "Délires I" of *Une saison en enfer*), reflects the two poets' difficulties in London and elsewhere.

"Veillées," probably reflecting the wild thoughts of sleepless nights, contains boat-at-sea imagery, like "Mouvement" and the verse poem "Le bateau ivre."

"Mystique," like the end of *Une saison en enfer*, combines a hope for progress with bad memories.

"Aube" and "Fleurs," like many of the verse poems, celebrate Rimbaud's love of nature.

"Nocturne vulgaire" is a dream of a coach journey at night.

"Marine," a highly influential free-verse piece, is a remarkable blend of seaside with forest-and-moor imagery.

In "Angoisse," the hope of personal and universal happiness appears to be just as illusion.

"Solde" calls for a renewal of mentality and society, a theme also touched on in "Jeunesse" (of which the section called "Sonnet" apparently just happened to be written in fourteen lines on the manuscript).

"Promontory" concerns seaside architecture and luxury hotels.

"Bottom" narrates magical transformations, like those in *A Midsummer Night's Dream* and *The Golden Ass* (*Metamorphoses*) of Apuleius.

"H" is probably a veiled reference to masturbation.

In "Mouvement" (which is visually organized like verse) and "Démocratie," the colonizers of "Mauvais sang" (in *Une saison en enfer*) return, brutally cynical in the latter piece. Here, and in his other works about exotic travel, Rimbaud is prefiguring his own future.

"Dévotion," like many anticlerical verse poems, mocks Christianity.

"Génie" is one of Rimbaud's most programmatic statements, hopeful and utopian; one's own personality must be one's guide, replacing the tenets of established religion and social norms.

("Barbare," "Fairy," and "Guerre" are abstruse pieces that all but defy interpretation.)

Selected Poems. Of the verse poems written before 1872, only about a dozen and a half are omitted in this volume, generally speaking because they are weaker examples or because they are too topical (such as most of the poems concerning politics, the Franco-Prussian War, and its aftermath). On the other hand (except for the *Album zutique* items), *all* the 1872 poems, with their important experimentation, are included.

"Les étrennes des orphelins" was written late in 1869. The next 13 poems included[2] were all written in 1870: the first three by May (the dating is derived from Rimbaud's letters or other clues) and the rest by October (the last four on the autumn hike to Charleroi, Brussels, and Douai). "Les corbeaux" was written late in 1870 or early in 1871; "Mes petites amoureuses," "Accroupissements," and "Le cœur volé," by May 1871; "Les poètes de sept ans" and "Les pauvres à l'église," by June 1871; "Les assis," "Tête de faune," "Voyelles," and "Les premières Communions," by September 1871; "Oraison du soir" and "Le bateau ivre," by October 1871; and "Les chercheuses de poux," between 1870 and 1872. All the rest (sometimes grouped as "Derniers vers" [Last Verses] in modern editions) are usually assigned to 1872 (from "Larme" through "Âge d'or," plus "Qu'est-ce pour nous, mon cœur . . ." and possibly "Mémoire," in the first half of the year; there is no evidence outside the manuscripts of the poems). "Qu'est-ce pour nous, mon cœur . . ." may have been written late in 1871; "Honte," early in 1873.

Some of the verse poems were published in magazines before appearing in volumes. The chief pre-1900 volume publications[3] (referred to, after this paragraph, by their years of publication) were: the 1886 *Illuminations* volume; *Le reliquaire,* Genonceaux, Paris, 1891; *Poésies complètes d'Arthur Rimbaud,* Vanier, Paris, 1895; and *Œuvres de J.-A. Rimbaud,* Mercure de France, Paris, 1898. Individual publication dates, in magazines where applicable (all the French-language magazines were published in Paris), and in the first (only!) volumes, follow.

"Les étrennes des orphelins": *La revue pour tous,* Jan. 2, 1870; vol., 1898. "Sensation": *La revue indépendante,* Jan.–Feb. 1883; vol., 1891. "Soleil et chair": vol., 1891 (minus 36 lines). "Ophélie": vol., 1891. "À la musique": *La revue indépendante,* Jan.–Feb. 1889; vol., 1891. "Vénus anadyomène": *Mercure de France,* Nov. 1, 1891; vol., 1895. "Les effarés": *Lutèce,* Oct. 19, 1883; vol., 1891 (the poem had already appeared with the title "Petits pauvres" [Poor Children] in the London *Gentleman's Magazine,* Jan. 1878). "Roman": vol., 1891. "Rêvé pour l'hiver": vol., 1891. "Le dormeur du val": vol., 1891. "Au Cabaret-Vert": *La revue d'aujourd'hui,* Mar. 15, 1890; vol., 1891. "La maline": vol., 1891. "Le buffet": vol., 1891. "Ma Bohème": *La revue*

---

2. All thirteen, with nine others not in this Dover volume, were copied into two notebooks (the "cahiers de Douai"), probably with a view toward a publication that never came to pass.   3. Not including the various editions of Verlaine's *Poètes maudits,* and other multiauthor anthologies.

indépendante, Jan. 1889; vol., 1891. "Les corbeaux," *Renaissance littéraire et artistique,* Sept. 14, 1872; vol., 1891. "Les assis": *Lutèce,* Oct. 12–19, 1883; vol., 1891. "Tête de faune": *La vogue,* June 7–14, 1886; vol., 1891. "Oraison du soir": *Lutèce,* Oct. 5–12, 1883; vol., 1891. "Mes petites amoureuses": vol., 1891. "Accroupissements": vol., 1891. "Les poètes de sept ans": vol., 1891. "Les pauvres à l'église": vol., 1891. "Le cœur volé": *La vogue,* June 7–14, 1886; vol., 1891. "Les mains de Jeanne-Marie": *Littérature,* June 1919. "Voyelles": *Lutèce,* Oct. 5–12, 1883; vol., 1891. "Les premières Communions": *Lutèce,* Nov. 2–9, 1883; vol., 1891. "Les chercheuses de poux": *Lutèce,* Oct. 19–26, 1883; vol., 1891. "Le bateau ivre": *Lutèce,* Nov. 2–9, 1883; vol., 1891. "Larme": *La vogue,* June 21–27, 1886; vol., 1886. "La rivière de Cassis": *La vogue,* June 21–27, 1886; vol., 1886. "Comédie de la soif": *La vogue,* June 7–13, 1886; vol., 1886. "Bonne pensée du matin": vol., 1891. "Bannières de mai": *La vogue,* June 7–13, 1886; vol., 1886. "Chanson de la plus haute tour," "L'éternité," and "Âge d'or": data exactly like "Bannières de mai." "Jeune ménage": vol., 1895. "Platesbandes d'amarantes . . .": *La vogue,* June 14–20, 1886; vol., 1886. "Est-elle almée? . . .": vol., 1895. "Fêtes de la faim": vol., 1895. "Qu'est-ce pour nous, mon cœur . . .": *La vogue,* June 7–14, 1886; vol., 1886. "Entends comme brame . . .": vol., 1891. "Michel et Christine": *La vogue,* June 14–20, 1886; vol., 1886. "Honte": *La vogue,* June 14–20, 1886; vol., 1886. "Mémoire": parts IV and V, *L'ermitage,* Sept. 19, 1892; complete in vol., 1895. "O saisons, ô châteaux . . .": *La vogue,* June 21–27, 1886; vol., 1886.

In technique, the verse poems develop from straightforward handling of traditional forms (especially alexandrines in couplets or quatrains) to alexandrines with more dislocated rhythms and colloquial sonnets, and finally to a bold variety of forms with vocabulary of very mixed levels and occasional assonance in place of rhyme. In content, the poems are at first completely lucid, whether they are descriptive or theoretical (the earlier ones full of Greco-Roman mythology, and clearly influenced by the Romantics and Parnassians); then the poems become more and more personal expressions until they finally become obscure and hermetic, and Rimbaud abandons verse for prose. (A ceaseless experimenter, he repeatedly claimed to be dissatisfied with his earlier work, and finally entered a long creative silence.)

Major themes in the verse poems (many also occurring in the prose works) are: a need for love; a concern for childhood (his own was not remotely distant) and for children's literature, especially fairy tales; an appreciation of the simple, quiet natural phenomena of the country-

side; an active pursuit of ugliness and the repellent (including scatology); a longing for escape and travel; sympathy (but not unqualified!) for the downtrodden; adolescent sex of all kinds; liberal politics and war; anticlericalism; a thirst for drink; and an anarchic wish for destruction of the present world, coupled with a utopian yearning for a new, better one (most often, a second universal flood is the agency of the change). A few selected comments on individual poems follow.

"Les étrennes des orphelins": very traditional in form, and very sentimental for Rimbaud (though his later callousness—more like teenage cockiness—was often just a pose).

"Soleil et chair": not a great poem (too much rhetoric and erudition), but a significant manifesto of views restated more subtly (and obscurely) in *Une saison en enfer:* the ancient Greeks understood that love is natural; the poet rejects the current garden variety of love, as well as both Christianity and modern science, and prefers to be a pagan; mankind has a great future, but is plagued by doubt.

"À la musique": a satire on the bourgeoisie, amorous adventures with "little sweethearts"; boldness in syntax and modes of thought.

"Vénus anadyomène": the manifesto of the "beauty of ugliness"; contempt for women.

"Les effarés": some editions print a significantly different version based on another manuscript.

"Le dormeur dans le val": the only war poem included here (though "Les corbeaux" is a poem of mourning for the victims of the war, or of the Commune, or both).

"Les assis": a virulent attack on the Charleville municipal librarians, who balked at finding unusual books for the precocious poet.

"Oraison du soir": the calls of nature elicit blasphemy and a revolt against pretty versemaking.

"Les poètes de sept ans": autobiographical; an urge for freedom (with sailing-ship metaphors); hypocrisy; a liking for laborers; very early sex adventures; the outhouse as a refuge from hard-to-tolerate summer heat (the "seat" of Rimbaud's scatology?).

"Les pauvres à l'église": even the poor can be unpleasant.

"Le cœur volé": two other versions exist, one called "Le cœur supplicié" (The Tortured Heart) and the other, "Un cœur de pitre" (A Clown's Heart). The word *pioupiesques* leads one to believe that the words *caporal* and *général,* though used in other senses, are to be associated with military ranks, as well. Some commentators believe that this poem records a rape of the poet by soldiers.

"Les mains de Jeanne-Marie": the only proletarian, Communard, political poem included here.

"Voyelles": countless theories, many irresponsible, have been put forward to "explain" this sonnet, which appears to be a personal expansion of the synaesthesia in Baudelaire's stupendous sonnet "Correspondances" (in *Les fleurs du mal*, 1857).

"Les premières Communions": probably inspired by the first Communion of the poet's sister on May 14, 1871; in this anticlerical piece, it's the lovesick young girl who takes refuge in the outhouse.

"Le bateau ivre": probably Rimbaud's greatest achievement in verse, said to have been written shortly before the first meeting with Verlaine, as literary "credentials" to be presented in Paris; in this extremely musical and imaginative poem, the escape is thrilling but eventually goes wrong, and he poet longs for home and cherishes the memory of his childhood in humble, everyday surroundings.

"Comédie de la soif": here again (as in "Métropolitan" in *Illuminations*), the "green inn" probably evokes the pleasant memory of the Cabaret-Vert (Maison Verte) in October 1870.

The four poems "Bannières de mai," "Chanson de la plus haute tour," "L'éternité," and "Âge d'or" are often printed with a common heading, "Fêtes de la patience" (Celebrations of Patience).

The six poems "Larme," "Bonne pensée du matin," "Chanson de la plus haute tour," "L'éternité," "Fêtes de la faim," and "O saisons, ô châteaux . . ." reappear in variant versions in the "Délires II" section of *Une saison en enfer*. The poem "Le loup criait sous les feuilles . . ." occurs *only* there, and is not included in the verse-poem section of this Dover volume.

"Jeune ménage": generally seen as a reference to the housekeeping of the couple Verlaine and Rimbaud, reflecting Verlaine's discomfort and complaints; a fairy-tale atmosphere pervades the poem.

"Plates-bandes d'amarantes . . .": Rimbaud's enjoyment of Brussels before the shooting; one of his numerous references to theatrical scenes.

"Michel et Christine": was this the *titre de vaudeville* (the title of a light comedy [by Scribe]) by which Rimbaud was allegedly awestruck? (See "Délires II" in *Une saison en enfer*.)

"Honte": here, as in "Délires I" of *Une saison en enfer* and "Vagabonds" in *Illuminations*, Rimbaud is reporting, with frankness but with irony, the bad things that others say about him.

The Nature of This Edition

Since 1939, when the first critical edition of Rimbaud appeared, it has been editorial practice to base the text not so much on earlier printed editions (except for *Une saison en enfer,* which the poet supervised) as on the mass of manuscripts (not necessarily definitive versions, many being in hands other than Rimbaud's), so that recent editions differ among themselves in numerous big and small ways. The French text in this volume reflects one tradition, with a very good pedigree. A sampling of important variant readings (only a sampling!—more are supplied for *Illuminations* than for the verse poems) is given in some of the footnotes. The rest of the footnotes provide a variety of aids to the immediate comprehension of the text (with a few intentional exceptions, the footnotes do not explain Greco-Roman mythology, references to the Bible, readily accessible terms from geography and history, or English technical terms, especially in natural history, that are exact equivalents of the corresponding French words).

The translation is as accurate as the translator could make it. Though not in verse, it follows the verse poems line for line (to the extent that the differences between French and English syntax allow), making it easier for the reader to follow along. The difficulties involved in translating Rimbaud are considerable. His vocabulary is vast, ranging from scientific terms to slang, and including regional terms from the Ardennes and words he made up himself. His language is highly idiomatic (a glance at the boners in some translations will reveal the pitfalls), and some of the idioms are further disguised by the unusual word order that French prosody permits. Many French words, moreover, have a wide variety of meanings, and, whereas in everyday prose the context normally supplies the correct choice, Rimbaud's contexts are often ambiguous or obscure. The present translator cannot claim with confidence that he has solved every problem, when even French scholars disagree on many issues. In general, he has supplied in each case just one of the possible equivalents of the French, the one that seemed most appropriate.

This Dover edition, to save space and thus to include more material, omits the dates (derived from manuscripts) that follow the verse poems in most editions; it has been shown that these dates usually indicate when the particular clean copy was made, not when the poem was first written.

A Season in Hell
and Other Works

Une saison en enfer
et œuvres diverses

UNE SAISON EN ENFER

Jadis, si je me souviens bien, ma vie était un festin où s'ouvraient tous les cœurs, où tous les vins coulaient.

Un soir, j'ai assis la Beauté sur mes genoux. — Et je l'ai trouvée amère. — Et je l'ai injuriée.

Je me suis armé contre la justice.

Je me suis enfui. O sorcières, ô misère, ô haine, c'est à vous que mon trésor a été confié!

Je parvins à faire s'évanouir dans mon esprit toute l'espérance humaine. Sur toute joie pour l'étrangler j'ai fait le bond sourd de la bête féroce.

J'ai appelé les bourreaux pour, en périssant, mordre la crosse de leurs fusils. J'ai appelé les fléaux, pour m'étouffer avec le sable, le sang. Le malheur a été mon dieu. Je me suis allongé dans la boue. Je me suis séché à l'air du crime. Et j'ai joué de bons tours à la folie.

Et le printemps m'a apporté l'affreux rire de l'idiot.

Or, tout dernièrement m'étant trouvé sur le point de faire le dernier *couac!* j'ai songé à rechercher la clef du festin ancien, où je reprendrais peut-être appétit.

La charité est cette clef. — Cette inspiration prouve que j'ai rêvé!

«Tu resteras hyène, etc . . . ,» se récrie le démon qui me couronna de si aimables pavots. «Gagne la mort avec tous tes appétits, et ton égoïsme et tous les péchés capitaux.»

Ah! j'en ai trop pris: — Mais, cher Satan, je vous en conjure, une prunelle moins irritée! et en attendant les quelques petites lâchetés en retard, vous qui aimez dans l'écrivain l'absence des facultés descriptives ou instructives, je vous détache ces quelques hideux feuillets de mon carnet de damné.

A SEASON IN HELL

In the past, if my memory serves me, my life was a banquet at which every heart expanded, at which every wine flowed.

One evening, I sat Beauty on my lap.—And I found it bitter.—And I insulted it.

I armed myself against justice.

I ran away. O witches, O poverty, O hatred, it was to you that my treasure was entrusted!

I succeeded in making all human hope vanish from my mind. In order to throttle every joy, I pounced on it noiselessly as wild animals do.

I summoned the executioners so that, as I perished, I could bite their rifle butts. I summoned plagues in order to smother myself with sand, with blood. Unhappiness was my god. I stretched out in the mud. I dried myself off in the air of crime. And I played some good tricks on madness.

And springtime brought me the idiot's hideous laughter.

Now, quite recently finding myself at the point of emitting my last squawk,[1] I thought about searching for the key to that former banquet, at which I might perhaps regain my appetite.

That key is charity.[2]—This inspiration proves that I was dreaming!

"You will remain a hyena, etc.," exclaims the demon who garlanded me with such charming poppies. "Obtain death with all your appetites, and your selfishness and all the deadly sins."

Ah, I've taken too much of it:—But, Satan dear, I beseech you, look on me with eyes less angry! And, while waiting for the few miserable items that I'm late with,[3] you who like writers to be lacking in descriptive or instructive powers, for you I detach this handful of loathsome leaves from my doomed man's notebook.

---

1. Either a death rattle or a badly produced note on a wind instrument.   2. With an emphasis on the cardinal virtue *caritas,* true Christian love.   3. Perhaps a reference to the texts later assembled as *Illuminations*.

Mauvais sang

J'ai de mes ancêtres gaulois l'œil bleu blanc, la cervelle étroite, et la maladresse dans la lutte. Je trouve mon habillement aussi barbare que le leur. Mais je ne beurre pas ma chevelure. Les Gaulois étaient les écorcheurs de bêtes, les brûleurs d'herbes les plus ineptes de leur temps.

D'eux, j'ai: l'idolâtrie et l'amour du sacrilège; — oh! tous les vices, colère, luxure, — magnifique, la luxure; — surtout mensonge et paresse.

J'ai horreur de tous les métiers. Maîtres et ouvriers, tous paysans, ignobles. La main à plume vaut la main à charrue. — Quel siècle à mains! — Je n'aurai jamais ma main. Après, la domesticité mène trop loin. L'honnêteté de la mendicité me navre. Les criminels dégoûtent comme des châtrés: moi, je suis intact, et ça m'est égal.

Mais! qui a fait ma langue perfide tellement qu'elle ait guidé et sauvegardé jusqu'ici ma paresse? Sans me servir pour vivre même de mon corps, et plus oisif que le crapaud, j'ai vécu partout. Pas une famille d'Europe que je ne connaisse. — J'entends des familles comme la mienne, qui tiennent tout de la déclaration des Droits de l'Homme. — J'ai connu chaque fils de famille!

———————

Si j'avais des antécédents à un point quelconque de l'histoire de France!

Mais non, rien.

Il m'est bien évident que j'ai toujours été de race inférieure. Je ne puis comprendre la révolte. Ma race ne se souleva jamais que pour piller: tels les loups à la bête qu'ils n'ont pas tuée.

Je me rappelle l'histoire de la France fille aînée de l'Église. J'aurais fait, manant, le voyage de terre sainte, j'ai dans la tête des routes dans les plaines souabes, des vues de Byzance, des remparts de Solyme; le culte de Marie, l'attendrissement sur le crucifié s'éveillent en moi parmi les mille féeries profanes. — Je suis assis, lépreux, sur les pots cassés et les orties, au pied d'un mur rongé par le soleil. — Plus tard, reître, j'aurais bivaqué sous les nuits d'Allemagne.

Ah! encore: je danse le sabbat dans une rouge clairière, avec des vieilles et des enfants.

Bad Blood[4]

From my Gallic ancestors I have inherited my pale blue eyes, my narrow skull, and my clumsiness in fighting. I find my own clothing as barbarous as theirs. But I don't butter my hair.

The Gauls were the most inept skinners of animals and burners of herbs in their day.

From them I've inherited: idolatry and love of sacrilege;—oh, all the vices, wrath, lechery—lechery is wonderful!—and especially lying and laziness.

I abhor all occupations. Masters and their workmen, all are peasants and base. The hand that wields the pen is just as bad as the hand that wields the plow.—What an era this one is for hands!—I'll never hold a winning hand. Beyond that, a servant's life goes too far. The respectability of a beggar's life reduces me to tears. Criminals are just as disgusting as castrated men; as for me, I'm intact, and I don't care.

But! Who made my tongue so perfidious that it has guided and protected my laziness up till now? Without using even my body to live on, and idler than a toad, I've lived everywhere. Not one family in Europe that I don't know.—I mean families like mine, who derived everything they own from the Declaration of the Rights of Man.[5]—I've met every man of good family!

———————

If only I had antecedents at any given point in the history of France! But I don't; none.

It's quite clear to me that I've always been of inferior stock. I can't understand rebellion. My breed never rose up except to pillage: like wolves gorging on an animal they didn't kill themselves.

I recall the history of France, "eldest daughter of the Church." I would have been a commoner making the journey to the Holy Land, I have in my mind highways across the Swabian plains, views of Byzantium, of the ramparts of Salem;[6] the worship of the Virgin, tender feelings for Christ crucified awaken in me alongside the thousands of secular marvels.—I'm a leper sitting on potsherds and nettles at the foot of a wall corroded by the sun's heat.—In a later era, I would have been a mercenary bivouacking at night in Germany.

Ah, there's more: I'm dancing at a witches' sabbath in a red-lit clearing, along with old women and children.

4. The French expression can connote "bad temper, crossness" and denote inferior ancestry.   5. This Revolutionary Decree of 1789 established the power of the bourgeoisie in France.   6. Jerusalem.

Je ne me souviens pas plus loin que cette terre-ci et le christianisme. Je n'en finirais pas de me revoir dans ce passé. Mais toujours seul; sans famille; même, quelle langue parlais-je? Je ne me vois jamais dans les conseils du Christ; ni dans les conseils des Seigneurs, — représentants du Christ.

Qu'étais-je au siècle dernier: je ne me retrouve qu'aujourd'hui. Plus de vagabonds, plus de guerres vagues. La race inférieure a tout couvert — le peuple, comme on dit, la raison; la nation et la science.

Oh! la science! On a tout repris. Pour le corps et pour l'âme, — le viatique, — on a la médecine et la philosophie, — les remèdes de bonnes femmes et les chansons populaires arrangées. Et les divertissements des princes et les jeux qu'ils interdisaient! Géographie, cosmographie, mécanique, chimie! . . .

La science, la nouvelle noblesse! Le progrès. Le monde marche! Pourquoi ne tournerait-il pas?

C'est la vision des nombres. Nous allons à l'*Esprit*. C'est très certain, c'est oracle, ce que je dis. Je comprends, et ne sachant m'expliquer sans paroles païennes, je voudrais me taire.

Le sang païen revient! L'Esprit est proche, pourquoi Christ ne m'aide-t-il pas, en donnant à mon âme noblesse et liberté. Hélas! l'Évangile a passé! l'Évangile! l'Évangile.

J'attends Dieu avec gourmandise. Je suis de race inférieure de toute éternité.

Me voici sur la plage armoricaine. Que les villes s'allument dans le soir. Ma journée est faite; je quitte l'Europe. L'air marin brûlera mes poumons; les climats perdus me tanneront. Nager, broyer l'herbe, chasser, fumer surtout; boire des liqueurs fortes comme du métal bouillant, — comme faisaient ces chers ancêtres autour des feux.

Je reviendrai, avec des membres de fer, la peau sombre, l'œil furieux: sur mon masque, on me jugera d'une race forte. J'aurai de l'or: je serai oisif et brutal. Les femmes soignent ces féroces infirmes retour des pays chauds. Je serai mêlé aux affaires politiques. Sauvé.

Maintenant je suis maudit, j'ai horreur de la patrie. Le meilleur, c'est un sommeil bien ivre, sur la grève.

On ne part pas. — Reprenons les chemins d'ici, chargé de mon vice, le vice qui a poussé ses racines de souffrance à mon côté, dès l'âge de raison — qui monte au ciel, me bat, me renverse, me traîne.

I can't think farther back than this country and Christianity. I could go on and on remembering myself in that past. But always alone; without a family; in fact, what language did I speak? I never see myself among the councillors of Christ; nor among the councillors of mighty lords—the representatives of Christ.

What was I last century? It's only the present day that I find myself in. No more vagabonds, no more vague wars. The inferior breed has spread over everything—"the people," as the saying goes; reason; the nation and science.

Oh, science! Everything has been readapted. For the body and the soul—the last sacrament—we have medical knowledge and philosophy—old wives' nostrums and a new arrangement of old folk songs. And the amusements of princes and the merriment they used to prohibit! Geography, cosmography, mechanics, chemistry! . . .

Science, the new nobility! Progress. The world is on the march! So why shouldn't it rotate?

It's the vision of numbers. We are heading for Spirit. What I'm saying is a sure thing, it's an oracle. I understand and, unable to give an explanation without using pagan words, I prefer to be silent.

Pagan blood is returning! The Spirit is near, why doesn't Christ help me by lending my soul nobility and liberty? Alas! The Gospel has had its day! The Gospel, the Gospel.

I await God greedily. I have been of inferior stock from all eternity.

Here I am on the beach in Brittany. Let the cities turn on their lights in the evening. My day is over; I'm leaving Europe. The sea air will burn my lungs; remote climes will tan my skin. To swim, to tread the grass down, to hunt, especially to smoke; to imbibe drinks as strong as molten metal—as my beloved ancestors did around their bonfires.

I shall return with steely limbs, my skin dark, fury in my eyes: by the look of my face, people will judge me to be of a strong breed. I shall have gold: I shall be idle and brutal. Women take good care of those ferocious invalids who have come back from hot countries. I shall dabble in political affairs. I shall be saved.

Now I'm accursed, I abhor my native land. The best thing is a dead-drunk stupor, on the shore.

There will be no departure.—Let me return to the local roads, laden with my vice, that vice which has struck roots of suffering in my side, ever since the age of reason—which rises to the sky, beats me, knocks me over, and drags me.

La dernière innocence et la dernière timidité. C'est dit. Ne pas porter au monde mes dégoûts et mes trahisons.

Allons! La marche, le fardeau, le désert, l'ennui et la colère.

À qui me louer? Quelle bête faut-il adorer? Quelle sainte image attaque-t-on? Quels cœurs briserai-je? Quel mensonge dois-je tenir? — Dans quel sang marcher?

Plutôt, se garder de la justice. — La vie dure, l'abrutissement simple, — soulever, le poing desséché, le couvercle du cercueil, s'asseoir, s'étouffer. Ainsi point de vieillesse, ni de dangers: la terreur n'est pas française.

— Ah! je suis tellement délaissé que j'offre à n'importe quelle divine image des élans vers la perfection.

O mon abnégation, ô ma charité merveilleuse! ici-bas, pourtant!

De profundis Domine, suis-je bête!

Encore tout enfant, j'admirais le forçat intraitable sur qui se referme toujours le bagne; je visitais les auberges et les garnis qu'il aurait sacrés par son séjour; je voyais *avec son idée* le ciel bleu et le travail fleuri de la campagne; je flairais sa fatalité dans les villes. Il avait plus de force qu'un saint, plus de bon sens qu'un voyageur — et lui, lui seul! pour témoin de sa gloire et de sa raison.

Sur les routes, par des nuits d'hiver, sans gîte, sans habits, sans pain, une voix étreignait mon cœur gelé: «Faiblesse ou force: te voilà, c'est la force. Tu ne sais ni où tu vas ni pourquoi tu vas, entre partout, réponds à tout. On ne te tuera pas plus que si tu étais cadavre.» Au matin j'avais le regard si perdu et la contenance si morte, que ceux que j'ai rencontrés *ne m'ont peut-être pas vu.*

Dans les villes la boue m'apparaissait soudainement rouge et noire, comme une glace quand la lampe circule dans la chambre voisine, comme un trésor dans la forêt! Bonne chance, criais-je, et je voyais une mer de flammes et de fumée au ciel; et, à gauche, à droite, toutes les richesses flambant comme un milliard de tonnerres.

Mais l'orgie et la camaraderie des femmes m'étaient interdites. Pas même un compagnon. Je me voyais devant une foule exaspérée, en face du peloton d'exécution, pleurant du malheur qu'ils n'aient pu comprendre, et pardonnant! — Comme Jeanne d'Arc! — «Prêtres, professeurs, maîtres, vous vous trompez en me livrant à la justice. Je

The final innocence and the final timidity. That's firm. I resolve not to carry my loathings and my betrayals into the world.

Let's go! Walking, the burden, the desert, boredom and anger.

To whom shall I hire myself out? What beast should I worship? What holy image is to be attacked? What hearts shall I break? What lie must I hold fast to?—What blood am I to wade through?

Rather, I must beware of justice.—A hard life, simple brutishness—to raise the coffin lid with my shriveled fist, to sit down, to stifle. And so, no old age, no dangers: terror is un-French.

—Ah, I'm so all alone that I offer to any divine image whatsoever a striving for perfection.

O my abnegation, O my wonderful charity! In this world below, however!

De profundis Domine,[7] how stupid I am!

While still a small child, I admired the intractable galley slave on whom the prison gates close again and again; I used to visit the inns and furnished rooms that he might have hallowed by staying there; *through his eyes* I saw the blue sky and the blossoming rural labors; I nosed out his doom in the towns. He had more strength than a saint, more good sense than a traveler—and he had himself, himself alone, as a witness to his glory and his reason.

On the highways on winter nights, without a lodging, without proper clothing, without bread, a voice gripped my frozen heart: "Weakness or strength: there you are, it's strength. You know neither where you're going nor why you're going; enter every door, answer every question. People won't kill you any more than if you were a corpse." In the morning I had such a lost look in my eyes, and my bearing was so dead, that the people I met *possibly didn't see me.*

In the towns the mud suddenly looked red and black to me, like a mirror when a lamp is moving around in the next room, like a treasure in the forest! "Good luck!" I'd shout, and I'd see an ocean of flames and smoke in the sky; and to the left, to the right, all riches blazing like a billion thunderbolts.

But orgies and the friendship of women were forbidden to me. Not even a male companion. I found myself in front of a provoked crowd, facing a firing squad, weeping with sadness because they were unable to understand, and forgiving them!—Like Joan of Arc!—"Priests, professors, masters, you are mistaken when you hand me over to the law. I

---

7. "Out of the depths, Lord"; Psalm 130 in the Latin version.

n'ai jamais été de ce peuple-ci; je n'ai jamais été chrétien; je suis de la race qui chantait dans le supplice; je ne comprends pas les lois; je n'ai pas le sens moral, je suis une brute: vous vous trompez . . .»

Oui, j'ai les yeux fermés à votre lumière. Je suis une bête, un nègre. Mais je puis être sauvé. Vous êtes de faux nègres, vous maniaques, féroces, avares. Marchand, tu es nègre; magistrat, tu es nègre; général, tu es nègre; empereur, vieille démangeaison, tu es nègre: tu as bu d'une liqueur non taxée, de la fabrique de Satan. — Ce peuple est inspiré par la fièvre et le cancer. Infirmes et vieillards sont tellement respectables qu'ils demandent à être bouillis. — Le plus malin est de quitter ce continent, où la folie rôde pour pourvoir d'otages ces misérables. J'entre au vrai royaume des enfants de Cham.

Connais-je encore la nature? me connais-je? — *Plus de mots.* J'ensevelis les morts dans mon ventre. Cris, tambour, danse, danse, danse, danse! Je ne vois même pas l'heure où, les blancs débarquant, je tomberai au néant.

Faim, soif, cris, danse, danse, danse, danse!

Les blancs débarquent. Le canon! Il faut se soumettre au baptême, s'habiller, travailler.

J'ai reçu au cœur le coup de la grâce. Ah! je ne l'avais pas prévu!

Je n'ai point fait le mal. Les jours vont m'être légers, le repentir me sera épargné. Je n'aurai pas eu les tourments de l'âme presque morte au bien, où remonte la lumière sévère comme les cierges funéraires. Le sort du fils de famille, cercueil prématuré couvert de limpides larmes. Sans doute la débauche est bête, le vice est bête; il faut jeter la pourriture à l'écart. Mais l'horloge ne sera pas arrivée à ne plus sonner que l'heure de la pure douleur! Vais-je être enlevé comme un enfant, pour jouer au paradis dans l'oubli de tout le malheur!

Vite! est-il d'autres vies? — Le sommeil dans la richesse est impossible. La richesse a toujours été bien public. L'amour divin seul octroie les clefs de la science. Je vois que la nature n'est qu'un spectacle de bonté. Adieu chimères, idéals, erreurs.

Le chant raisonnable des anges s'élève du navire sauveur: c'est l'amour divin. — Deux amours! je puis mourir de l'amour terrestre,

have never been one of this populace; I have never been a Christian; I am of the breed that used to sing under torture;[8] I don't understand the laws; I have no sense of morality, I'm a brute beast; you're mistaken. . . ."

Yes, my eyes are closed to your light. I'm an animal, a Negro.[9] But I can be saved. You are fake Negroes, you ferocious and miserly maniacs. Merchant, you are a Negro; magistrate, you are a Negro; general, you are a Negro; emperor, you old mange, you are a Negro: you have drunk of a liquor free of luxury tax, one distilled by Satan.—This populace is inspired by fever and cancer. Invalids and the aged are so highly respected that they just cry out to be boiled.—The smartest thing is to leave this continent, where folly prowls about in order to furnish these wretched creatures with hostages. I am entering the true kingdom of the children of Ham.

Do I still know nature? Do I know myself?—*No more words.* I bury the dead in my belly. Shouts, drumming, dancing, dancing, dancing, dancing! I can't even foresee the time when the white men land and I shall plummet into nothingness.

Hunger, thirst, shouts, dancing, dancing, dancing, dancing!

The whites land. Their ship's cannon! We must submit to baptism, we must wear clothes and work.

I've received the touch of Grace in my heart. Oh, I hadn't expected that!

I've done no evil. My days will rest lightly on my shoulders, I'll be spared repentance. I won't have felt the torments of the soul that is almost dead to goodness, in which there rises a light as harsh as that of funeral tapers. The fate of the man of good family, a premature coffin covered with limpid tears. No doubt debauchery is stupid, vice is stupid; rottenness must be discarded. But the clock will not have succeeded in any longer striking any hour but that of pure sorrow! Shall I be abducted like a child, to play in Paradise, all unhappiness forgotten?

Quick! Are there other lives?—To slumber amid wealth is impossible. Wealth has always been public property. Only divine love grants the keys to knowledge. I see that Nature is merely a spectacle of goodness. Farewell to chimeras, ideals, delusions.

The rational song of angels emanates from the redemptive ship: it is divine love.—Two loves! I can die of earthly love, die of devoutness.

---

8. The meaning may be: of the breed of criminals who confess their crimes only under torture, having exulted in them up to then.   9. Though this term is not "politically correct" at the moment of this writing, it is the most appropriate choice, given the date and implications of Rimbaud's text.

mourir de dévouement. J'ai laissé des âmes dont la peine s'accroîtra de mon départ! Vous me choisissez parmi les naufragés, ceux qui restent sont-ils pas mes amis?

Sauvez-les!

La raison m'est née. Le monde est bon. Je bénirai la vie. J'aimerai mes frères. Ce ne sont plus des promesses d'enfance. Ni l'espoir d'échapper à la vieillesse et à la mort. Dieu fait ma force, et je loue Dieu.

———————

L'ennui n'est plus mon amour. Les rages, les débauches, la folie, dont je sais tous les élans et les désastres, — tout mon fardeau est déposé. Apprécions sans vertige l'étendue de mon innocence.

Je ne serais plus capable de demander le réconfort d'une bastonnade. Je ne me crois pas embarqué pour une noce avec Jésus-Christ pour beau-père.

Je ne suis pas prisonnier de ma raison. J'ai dit: Dieu. Je veux la liberté dans le salut: comment la poursuivre? Les goûts frivoles m'ont quitté. Plus besoin de dévouement ni d'amour divin. Je ne regrette pas le siècle des cœurs sensibles. Chacun a sa raison, mépris et charité: je retiens ma place au sommet de cette angélique échelle de bon sens.

Quant au bonheur établi, domestique ou non . . . non, je ne peux pas. Je suis trop dissipé, trop faible. La vie fleurit par le travail, vieille vérité: moi, ma vie n'est pas assez pesante, elle s'envole et flotte loin au-dessus de l'action, ce cher point du monde.

Comme je deviens vieille fille, à manquer du courage d'aimer la mort!

Si Dieu m'accordait le calme céleste, aérien, la prière, — comme les anciens saints. — Les saints! des forts! les anachorètes, des artistes comme il n'en faut plus!

Farce continuelle! Mon innocence me ferait pleurer. La vie est la farce à mener par tous.

———————

Assez! voici la punition. — *En marche!*

Ah! les poumons brûlent, les tempes grondent! la nuit roule dans mes yeux, par ce soleil! le cœur . . . les membres . . .

Où va-t-on? au combat? Je suis faible! les autres avancent. Les outils, les armes . . . le temps! . . .

I have abandoned souls whose pain will be increased by my departure! You single me out among the shipwrecked; aren't those who remain my friends?

Save them!

Reason has been born in me. The world is good. I shall bless life. I shall love my brothers. These are no longer childish promises. Or the hope of escaping old age and death. God is my strength, and I praise God.

Ennui is no longer my sweetheart. Rage, debauch, folly, all of whose impulses and disasters I know—all my burden is laid down. Let us appraise without giddiness the extent of my innocence.

I would no longer be capable of asking consolation of a beating. I don't believe that I am voyaging toward a wedding with Jesus Christ as father-in-law.

I am not the prisoner of my reason. I mean: God. I want freedom within salvation: how am I to pursue it? Frivolous likings have left me. No more need for devoutness or divine love. I don't miss the century of sensitive hearts.[10] Every man has his own rationality, contempt, and charity: I retain my place at the top of this angelic ladder of good sense.

As for established happiness, domestic or otherwise . . . no, it's beyond me. I'm too dissipated, too weak. Life blossoms through work, an ancient truth; as for me, my life doesn't weigh enough, it flies away and hovers far above action, that central point dear to the world.

See how I'm becoming an old maid, lacking the courage to love death!

If God only granted me aerial, celestial calm, prayer—as He did to the saints of yore! The saints! Strong characters! Anchorites, artists such as are no longer needed!

A continual farce! My innocence could make me cry. Life is the farce that everyone must act out.

Enough! Here is the punishment.—*Forward march!*

Ah, my lungs are burning, my temples are aching! Night circulates in my eyes, amid all this sunshine! My heart . . . my limbs . . .

Where am I headed? To combat? I'm weak! The others advance. Utensils, weapons, . . . time! . . .

---

10. This has been taken to mean the eighteenth century.

Feu! feu sur moi! Là! ou je me rends. — Lâches! — Je me tue! Je me jette aux pieds des chevaux!

Ah!...

— Je m'y habituerai.

Ce serait la vie française, le sentier de l'honneur!

Nuit de l'enfer

J'ai avalé une fameuse gorgée de poison. — Trois fois béni soit le conseil qui m'est arrivé! — Les entrailles me brûlent. La violence du venin tord mes membres, me rend difforme, me terrasse. Je meurs de soif, j'étouffe, je ne puis crier. C'est l'enfer, l'éternelle peine! Voyez comme le feu se relève! Je brûle comme il faut. Va, démon!

J'avais entrevu la conversion au bien et au bonheur, le salut. Puis-je décrire la vision, l'air de l'enfer ne souffre pas les hymnes! C'était des millions de créatures charmantes, un suave concert spirituel, la force et la paix, les nobles ambitions, que sais-je?

Les nobles ambitions!

Et c'est encore la vie! — Si la damnation est éternelle! Un homme qui veut se mutiler est bien damné, n'est-ce pas? Je me crois en enfer, donc j'y suis. C'est l'exécution du catéchisme. Je suis esclave de mon baptême. Parents, vous avez fait mon malheur et vous avez fait le vôtre. Pauvre innocent! l'enfer ne peut attaquer les païens. — C'est la vie encore! Plus tard, les délices de la damnation seront plus profondes. Un crime, vite, que je tombe au néant, de par la loi humaine.

Tais-toi, mais tais-toi!... C'est la honte, le reproche, ici: Satan qui dit que le feu est ignoble, que ma colère est affreusement sotte. — Assez!... Des erreurs qu'on me souffle, magies, parfums faux, musiques puériles. — Et dire que je tiens la vérité, que je vois la justice: j'ai un jugement sain et arrêté, je suis prêt pour la perfection... Orgueil. — La peau de ma tête se dessèche. Pitié! Seigneur, j'ai peur. J'ai soif, si soif! Ah! l'enfance, l'herbe, la pluie, le lac sur les pierres, *le clair de lune quand le clocher sonnait douze*... le diable est au clocher, à cette heure. Marie! Sainte-Vierge!... — Horreur de ma bêtise.

Là-bas, ne sont-ce pas des âmes honnêtes, qui me veulent du bien ... Venez... J'ai un oreiller sur la bouche, elles ne m'entendent pas,

Fire! Fire at me! There! Or else I'll surrender.—Cowards!—I'll kill myself! I'll throw myself under the horses' feet!

Ah! . . .

—I'll get used to it.

That would be French life, the pathway to honor!

Hell's Night

I have swallowed a terrific mouthful of poison.—Thrice blessed be the advice that came to me!—My insides are on fire. The violence of the venom is twisting my limbs, making me shapeless, prostrating me. I'm dying of thirst, I'm choking, I can't cry out. This is hell, eternal suffering! See how the fire rises again! I'm burning good and proper. Away with you, demon!

I had glimpsed the conversion to goodness and happiness, to salvation. Can I describe the vision? The atmosphere of hell won't permit any hymns! There were millions of charming creatures, a gentle sacred concert, strength and peace, noble ambitions, who knows what else?

Noble ambitions!

And life goes on!—I'll say damnation is eternal! A man who wants to mutilate himself is good and damned, isn't he? I think I'm in hell, therefore I am there. It's the fulfillment of catechism. I'm the slave of my baptism. Parents, you caused my unhappiness and you caused your own. Pour innocent! Hell can't attack heathens.—Life goes on! Later on, the delights of damnation will be more profound. A crime, quick, so I can plummet into nothingness, in the name of human laws.

Be quiet, can't you be quiet! Here there is shame, reproach: Satan saying that the fire is ignoble, that my anger is terribly foolish.— Enough! . . . Delusions that some prompter whispers to me, acts of magic, fake perfumes, childish music.—And to think that I possess the truth, that I see justice: my judgment is sane and settled, I'm ready for perfection . . . Pride.—The skin on my head is drying out. Mercy! Lord, I'm afraid. I'm thirsty, so thirsty! Ah, childhood, grass, rain, the lake on the stones, "moonlight when the steeple bell was striking twelve"[11] . . . the devil's in the belfry at that hour. Mary! Blessed Virgin! . . .—Loathing of my stupidity.

Over yonder, aren't they honorable souls who wish me well? . . . Come . . . I have a pillow on my mouth, they don't hear me, they're

---

11. This verse, an alexandrine in the French, also occurs in a poem by Verlaine.

ce sont des fantômes. Puis, jamais personne ne pense à autrui. Qu'on
n'approche pas. Je sens le roussi, c'est certain.
  Les hallucinations sont innombrables. C'est bien ce que j'ai tou-
jours eu: plus de foi en l'histoire, l'oubli des principes. Je m'en tairai:
poètes et visionnaires seraient jaloux. Je suis mille fois le plus riche,
soyons avare comme la mer.
  Ah çà! l'horloge de la vie s'est arrêtée tout à l'heure. Je ne suis plus
au monde. — La théologie est sérieuse, l'enfer est certainement *en
bas* — et le ciel en haut. — Extase, cauchemar, sommeil dans un nid
de flammes.
  Que de malices dans l'attention dans la campagne . . . Satan,
Ferdinand, court avec les graines sauvages . . . Jésus marche sur les
ronces purpurines, sans les courber . . . Jésus marchait sur les eaux ir-
ritées. La lanterne nous le montra debout, blanc et des tresses brunes,
au flanc d'une vague d'émeraude . . .
  Je vais dévoiler tous les mystères: mystères religieux ou naturels,
mort, naissance, avenir, passé, cosmogonie, néant. Je suis maître en
fantasmagories.
  Écoutez! . . .
  J'ai tous les talents! — Il n'y a personne ici et il y a quelqu'un: je ne
voudrais pas répandre mon trésor.
  — Veut-on des chants nègres, des danses de houris? Veut-on que je
disparaisse, que je plonge à la recherche de l'*anneau*? Veut-on? Je
ferai de l'or, des remèdes.
  Fiez-vous donc à moi, la foi soulage, guide, guérit. Tous, venez, —
même les petits enfants, — que je vous console, qu'on répande pour vous
son cœur, — le cœur merveilleux! — Pauvres hommes, travailleurs! Je ne
demande pas de prières; avec votre confiance seulement, je serai heureux.
  — Et pensons à moi. Ceci me fait peu regretter le monde. J'ai de la
chance de ne pas souffrir plus. Ma vie ne fut que folies douces, c'est
regrettable.
  Bah! faisons toutes les grimaces imaginables.
  Décidément, nous sommes hors du monde. Plus aucun son. Mon
tact a disparu. Ah! mon château, ma Saxe, mon bois de saules. Les
soirs, les matins, les nuits, les jours . . . Suis-je las!
  Je devrais avoir mon enfer pour la colère, mon enfer pour l'orgueil,
— et l'enfer de la caresse; un concert d'enfers.
  Je meurs de lassitude. C'est le tombeau, je m'en vais aux vers, hor-

ghosts. Besides, no one ever thinks about anyone else. Let them keep
away. I'm sure I smack of heresy.

The hallucinations are numberless. This is surely what's always
been wrong with me: no more faith in history; principles all forgotten.
I'll keep silent on that subject: poets and visionaries would be jealous.
I'm the richest one a thousandfold, let me be as miserly as the sea.

Now this! The clock of life stopped a little while ago. I'm no longer
in the world.—Theology must be taken seriously; hell is surely
below—and heaven above.—Ecstasy, nightmare, and slumber in a
nest of flames.

How many tricks of one's attention in the country! . . . Satan,
Ferdinand,[12] runs about with wild seeds . . . Jesus walks on crimson
briars without bending them . . . Jesus used to walk on troubled wa-
ters. The magic lantern showed him to us standing, light-complex-
ioned, with dark locks, beside an emerald wave . . .

I'm going to unveil all the mysteries: mysteries of nature or of reli-
gion, death, birth, future, past, cosmogony, nothingness. I'm a master
of phantasmagoria.

Listen! . . .

I possess every talent!—There's nobody here, and yet there *is*
someone: I wouldn't like to scatter my treasures.

—Do you want African chants, houris' dances? Do you want me to
disappear, to dive in quest of the *ring*?[13] Do you want that? I shall cre-
ate gold, nostrums.

Thus, trust in me; faith comforts, guides, heals. Come, everyone—
even little children—for me to console you, to pour out my heart for
you—that wonderful heart! Poor people, laborers! I don't ask for
prayers; having nothing but your confidence, I'll be happy.

—And let's think about me. This makes me miss the world all the
less. I'm lucky not to be suffering any more. My life was comprised of
nothing but sweet follies; it's regrettable.

Bah! Let's make every imaginable grimace.

Decidedly, we're out of the world. No more sounds. My sense of
touch is gone. Ah, my château, my Saxony, my willow forest. Evenings,
mornings, nights, days . . . Am I weary!

I ought to have my hell for wrath, my hell for pride,—and the hell
of love-making; a concert of hells.

I'm dying of weariness. This is the tomb, I'm departing for the

---

12. A name given to the Devil by peasants in the region of Mme. Rimbaud's rural
property.   13. This has been seen as an allusion to the submerged treasure of the
Nibelungen.

reur de l'horreur! Satan, farceur, tu veux me dissoudre, avec tes charmes. Je réclame. Je réclame! un coup de fourche, une goutte de feu.

Ah! remonter à la vie! Jeter les yeux sur nos difformités. Et ce poison, ce baiser mille fois maudit! Ma faiblesse, la cruauté du monde! Mon Dieu, pitié, cachez-moi, je me tiens trop mal! — Je suis caché et je ne le suis pas.

C'est le feu qui se relève avec son damné.

Délires I: Vierge folle

L'époux infernal

Écoutons la confession d'un compagnon d'enfer: «O divin Époux, mon Seigneur, ne refusez pas la confession de la plus triste de vos servantes. Je suis perdue. Je suis soûle. Je suis impure. Quelle vie!

«Pardon, divin Seigneur, pardon! Ah! pardon! Que de larmes! Et que de larmes encore plus tard, j'espère!

«Plus tard, je connaîtrai le divin Époux! Je suis née soumise à Lui. — L'autre peut me battre maintenant!

«À présent, je suis au fond du monde! O mes amies! . . . non, pas mes amies . . . Jamais délires ni tortures semblables . . . Est-ce bête!

«Ah! je souffre, je crie. Je souffre vraiment. Tout pourtant m'est permis, chargée du mépris des plus méprisables cœurs.

«Enfin, faisons cette confidence, quitte à la répéter vingt autres fois, — aussi morne, aussi insignifiante!

«Je suis esclave de l'Époux infernal, celui qui a perdu les vierges folles. C'est bien ce démon-là. Ce n'est pas un spectre, ce n'est pas un fantôme. Mais moi qui ai perdu la sagesse, qui suis damnée et morte au monde, — on ne me tuera pas! — Comment vous le décrire! Je ne sais même plus parler. Je suis en deuil, je pleure, j'ai peur. Un peu de fraîcheur, Seigneur, si vous voulez, si vous voulez bien!

«Je suis veuve . . . — J'étais veuve . . . — mais oui, j'ai été bien sérieuse jadis, et je ne suis pas née pour devenir squelette! . . . — Lui était presque un enfant . . . Ses délicatesses mystérieuses m'avaient séduite. J'ai oublié tout mon devoir humain pour le suivre. Quelle vie! La vraie vie est absente. Nous ne sommes pas au monde. Je vais où il va, il le faut. Et souvent il s'emporte contre moi, *moi, la pauvre âme*. Le Démon! — C'est un Démon, vous savez, *ce n'est pas un homme*.

worms, horror of horror! Satan, you joker, you want to dissolve me with your spells. I clamor. I clamor for a shove with a pitchfork, a drop of fire!

Ah, to reascend into life! To cast our eyes on our deformities! And that poison, that kiss a thousand times accursed! My weakness, the world's cruelty! My God, mercy, hide me, my grip on myself is too weak!—I'm hidden and I'm not.

It's the fire rising up again along with the damned soul that's in it.

Deliriums I: Foolish Virgin

The Hellish Husband

Let us listen to the confession of a fellow sufferer in hell: "O divine Spouse, my Lord, do not reject the confession of the saddest of your handmaidens. I'm lost. I'm drunk. I'm impure. What a life!

"Forgive me, divine Lord, forgive me! Oh, forgive me! So many tears! And how many tears even later, I hope!

"Later on, I shall meet the divine Spouse! I was born in submission to Him.—Let the other one beat me now!

"At the moment, I'm at the bottom of the world! O my girl friends! . . . No, not my friends . . . Never were there similar deliriums or tortures . . . How stupid it is!

"Ah! I'm suffering, I cry out. I'm really suffering. And yet I'm allowed everything, laden as I am with the contempt of the most contemptible hearts.

"Finally, let me make this admission, even if I repeat it twenty more times—just as dismal, just as insignificant!

"I am a slave to the hellish Husband, the one who ruined the foolish virgins. It's that very same demon. He isn't a specter, he isn't a ghost. But I, who have lost wisdom, I who am damned and dead to the world—I won't be killed!—How to describe it to you? I don't even know how to talk any more. I'm in mourning, I weep, I'm in fear. A little coolness, Lord, if you please, if you don't mind!

"I'm a widow . . .—I was a widow . . .—Oh, yes, I was quite a serious person once, and I wasn't born to become a skeleton! . . .—He was almost a child. . . . His mysterious refinement had seduced me. I forgot all my human duties in order to follow him. What a life! True life is absent. We aren't in the world. I go where he goes: I must. And often he gets angry with me, *me, the poor soul*. The demon!—he's a demon, you know, *he isn't a human being.*

«Il dit: «Je n'aime pas les femmes. L'amour est à réinventer, on le sait. Elles ne peuvent plus que vouloir une position assurée. La position gagnée, cœur et beauté sont mis de côté: il ne reste que froid dédain, l'aliment du mariage, aujourd'hui. Ou bien je vois des femmes, avec les signes du bonheur, dont, moi, j'aurais pu faire de bonnes camarades, dévorées tout d'abord par des brutes sensibles comme des bûchers . . .»

«Je l'écoute faisant de l'infamie une gloire, de la cruauté un charme: «Je suis de race lointaine: mes pères étaient Scandinaves: ils se perçaient les côtes, buvaient leur sang. — Je me ferai des entailles par tout le corps, je me tatouerai, je veux devenir hideux comme un Mongol: tu verras, je hurlerai dans les rues. Je veux devenir bien fou de rage. Ne me montre jamais de bijoux, je ramperais et me tordrais sur le tapis. Ma richesse, je la voudrais tachée de sang partout. Jamais je ne travaillerai . . .» Plusieurs nuits, son démon me saisissant, nous nous roulions, je luttais avec lui! — Les nuits, souvent, ivre, il se poste dans des rues ou dans des maisons, pour m'épouvanter mortellement. — «On me coupera vraiment le cou; ce sera dégoûtant.» Oh! ces jours où il veut marcher avec l'air du crime!

«Parfois il parle, en une façon de patois attendri, de la mort qui fait repentir, des malheureux qui existent certainement, des travaux pénibles, des départs qui déchirent les cœurs. Dans les bouges où nous nous enivrions, il pleurait en considérant ceux qui nous entouraient, bétail de la misère. Il relevait les ivrognes dans les rues noires. Il avait la pitié d'une mère méchante pour les petits enfants. — Il s'en allait avec des gentillesses de petite fille au catéchisme. — Il feignait d'être éclairé sur tout, commerce, art, médecine. — Je le suivais, il le faut!

«Je voyais tout le décor dont, en esprit, il s'entourait; vêtements, draps, meubles: je lui prêtais des armes, une autre figure. Je voyais tout ce qui le touchait, comme il aurait voulu le créer pour lui. Quand il me semblait avoir l'esprit inerte, je le suivais, moi, dans des actions étranges et compliquées, loin, bonnes ou mauvaises: j'étais sûre de ne jamais entrer dans son monde. À côté de son cher corps endormi, que d'heures des nuits j'ai veillé, cherchant pourquoi il voulait tant s'évader de la réalité. Jamais l'homme n'eut pareil vœu. Je reconnaissais, — sans craindre pour lui, — qu'il pouvait être un sérieux danger dans la société. — Il a peut-être des secrets pour *changer la vie*? Non, il ne fait qu'en chercher, me répliquais-je. Enfin sa charité est ensorcelée, et j'en suis la prisonnière. Aucune autre âme n'aurait assez de force, — force de désespoir! — pour la supporter, — pour être protégée et

"He says: 'I don't like women. Love must be reinvented, that's well known. By now all they can wish for is a secure position in life. That position obtained, heart and beauty are set aside: all that remains today is cold disdain, the food of marriage. Or else I see women with the tokens of possible happiness, women whom *I* could have made good comrades, devoured right at the start by brutes as sensitive as heaps of logs. . . .'

"I listen to him glorifying infamy, making cruelty sound charming: 'I come from a far-off race: my fathers were Scandinavian: they pierced their sides, drank their blood.—I shall cut notches all over my body, I'll tattoo myself, I want to become as hideous as a Mongol: you'll see, I'll howl in the streets. I want to become really mad with rage. Never show me any jewels, I'd crawl and writhe on the carpet. I'd like my riches to be stained with blood all over. I'll never work. . . .' Several nights, when his demon seized me, we'd roll around, I wrestled with him!—Often at night he'll be drunk and he'll station himself in streets or in houses, to give me a mortal fright.—'I'll really be beheaded; it will be disgusting.' Oh, those days when he wants to go about with the air of a criminal!

"Sometimes he speaks, in a sort of emotional jargon, of death which brings about repentance, of the unfortunate wretches who surely exist, of painful labors, of heart-rending departures. In the dives where we got drunk, he'd cry at the sight of those around us, the livestock of poverty. He'd pick up fallen drunks in the black streets. He had the pity that a malicious mother feels for little children.—He'd go away acting as sweet as a little girl at catechism.—He'd pretend to be knowledgeable about everything, business, art, medicine.—I followed him: I have to!

"I saw all the scenery he surrounded himself with mentally; clothes, draperies, furniture: I lent him weapons, a different face. I saw everything that affected him, the way he'd have liked to create it for himself. When his mind seemed to me to be dulled, I myself would follow him in strange, complicated actions, far, whether they were good or bad: I was sure I could never enter into his world. Alongside his dear sleeping body, how many hours of the nights I lay awake, wondering why he had such a desire to escape from reality. Never did man have a similar wish. I realized—without fearing for him—that he could be a serious danger to society.—Maybe he has secret means of *changing life?* No, he's merely seeking for some, I answered myself. The long and short of it is that his charity is under a spell, and I'm its captive. No other soul would have enough strength—the strength of

aimée par lui. D'ailleurs, je ne me le figurais pas avec une autre âme: on voit son Ange, jamais l'Ange d'un autre, — je crois. J'étais dans son âme comme dans un palais qu'on a vidé pour ne pas voir une personne si peu noble que vous: voilà tout. Hélas! je dépendais bien de lui. Mais que voulait-il avec mon existence terne et lâche? Il ne me rendait pas meilleure, s'il ne me faisait pas mourir! Tristement dépitée, je lui dis quelquefois: «Je te comprends.» Il haussait les épaules.

«Ainsi, mon chagrin se renouvelant sans cesse, et me trouvant plus égarée à mes yeux, — comme à tous les yeux qui auraient voulu me fixer, si je n'eusse été condamnée pour jamais à l'oubli de tous! — j'avais de plus en plus faim de sa bonté. Avec ses baisers et ses étreintes amies, c'était bien un ciel, un sombre ciel, où j'entrais, et où j'aurais voulu être laissée, pauvre, sourde, muette, aveugle. Déjà j'en prenais l'habitude. Je nous voyais comme deux bons enfants, libres de se promener dans le Paradis de tristesse. Nous nous accordions. Bien émus, nous travaillions ensemble. Mais, après une pénétrante caresse, il disait: «Comme ça te paraîtra drôle, quand je n'y serai plus, ce par quoi tu as passé. Quand tu n'auras plus mes bras sous ton cou, ni mon cœur pour t'y reposer, ni cette bouche sur tes yeux. Parce qu'il faudra que je m'en aille, très loin, un jour. Puis il faut que j'en aide d'autres: c'est mon devoir. Quoique ce ne soit guère ragoûtant . . ., chère âme . . .» Tout de suite je me pressentais, lui parti, en proie au vertige, précipitée das l'ombre la plus affreuse: la mort. Je lui faisais promettre qu'il ne me lâcherait pas. Il l'a faite vingt fois, cette promesse d'amant. C'était aussi frivole que moi lui disant: «Je te comprends.»

«Ah! je n'ai jamais été jalouse de lui. Il ne me quittera pas, je crois. Que devenir? Il n'a pas une connaissance; il ne travaillera jamais. Il veut vivre somnambule. Seules, sa bonté et sa charité lui donneraient-elles droit dans le monde réel? Par instants, j'oublie la pitié où je suis tombée: lui me rendra forte, nous voyagerons, nous chasserons dans les déserts, nous dormirons sur les pavés des villes inconnues, sans soins, sans peines. Ou je me réveillerai, et les lois et les mœurs auront changé, — grâce à son pouvoir magique, — le monde, en restant le même, me laissera à mes désirs, joies, nonchalances. Oh! la vie d'aventures qui existe dans les livres des enfants, pour me récompenser, j'ai tant souffert, me la donneras-tu? Il ne peut pas. J'ignore son idéal. Il m'a dit avoir des regrets, des espoirs: cela ne doit pas me regarder. Parle-t-il à Dieu? Peut-être devrais-je m'adresser à Dieu. Je suis au plus profond de l'abîme, et je ne sais plus prier.

despair!—to support it—to be protected and loved by him. Besides, I never imagined him with a different soul: you can see your own angel, never someone else's angel—I think. I dwelt in his soul as if in a palace that had been emptied out in order not to see a person as ignoble as you: that's all. Alas, I was really dependent on him. But what did he want with my colorless and cowardly existence? He wasn't making me a better woman, even if he wasn't causing my death! Sad and vexed, I said to him at times: 'I understand you.' He'd shrug his shoulders.

"And so, my sorrow constantly renewing itself, and finding myself farther astray in my own eyes—as in all the eyes that might have wished to gaze at me, had I not been forever condemned to universal oblivion!—I felt greater and greater hunger for his kindness. With his kisses and his loving embraces, it was truly a heaven, a dark heaven, that I was entering, one in which I would have liked to be left, poor, deaf, mute, blind. I was already getting used to it. I saw us as being two good-natured children, free to walk about in the Paradise of sadness. We suited each other. Deeply touched, we worked together. But after a penetrating caress he'd say: 'How funny this experience of yours will seem to you after I'm gone! When you no longer have my arms under your neck, or my heart to rest on, or my lips on your eyes. Because I'll have to go away some day, very far. Besides, I have to help others: it's my duty. Though it's hardly appetizing . . . , dear soul. . . .' Suddenly I had a vision of myself after his departure; a prey to vertigo, plunged into the most horrible darkness: death. I made him promise not to desert me. He made that lover's promise twenty times. It was just as insubstantial as my saying to him: 'I understand you.'

"Ah, he's never caused me any jealousy. I don't think he'll leave me. What would become of him? He doesn't have one acquaintance; he'll never work. He wants to live like a sleepwalker. Would his kindness and charity alone give him some right to the real world? At moments I forget the pitiful state I've descended to: he will make me strong, we'll travel, we'll hunt in the wilderness, we'll sleep on the sidewalks of unknown cities, free from care, free from pain. Or else I'll wake up, and laws and customs will have changed—thanks to his magic powers—the world, though remaining the same, will leave me to my own desires, joys, lack of concern. Oh, that adventurous life which exists in children's books—will you give it to me as repayment? I've suffered so! He can't. I don't know what his ideal is. He told me he had regrets, hopes: they probably have nothing to do with me. Does he talk to God? Maybe I ought to address God. I'm at the lowest point of the abyss, and I no longer know how to pray.

«S'il m'expliquait ses tristesses, les comprendrais-je plus que ses railleries? Il m'attaque, il passe des heures à me faire honte de tout ce qui m'a pu toucher au monde, et s'indigne si je pleure.

«— Tu vois cet élégant jeune homme, entrant dans la belle et calme maison: il s'appelle Duval, Dufour, Armand, Maurice, que sais-je? Une femme s'est dévouée à aimer ce méchant idiot: elle est morte, c'est certes une sainte au ciel, à présent. Tu me feras mourir comme il a fait mourir cette femme. C'est notre sort, à nous, cœurs charitables . . .» Hélas! il avait des jours où tous les hommes agissant lui paraissaient les jouets de délires grotesques: il riait affreusement, longtemps. — Puis, il reprenait ses manières de jeune mère, de sœur aimée. S'il était moins sauvage, nous serions sauvés! Mais sa douceur aussi est mortelle. Je lui suis soumise. — Ah! je suis folle!

«Un jour peut-être il disparaîtra merveilleusement; mais il faut que je sache, s'il doit remonter à un ciel, que je voie un peu l'assomption de mon petit ami!»

Drôle de ménage!

Délires II: Alchimie du verbe

À moi. L'histoire d'une de mes folies.

Depuis longtemps je me vantais de posséder tous les paysages possibles, et trouvais dérisoires les célébrités de la peinture et de la poésie moderne.

J'aimais les peintures idiotes, dessus de portes, décors, toiles de saltimbanques, enseignes, enluminures populaires; la littérature démodée, latin d'église, livres érotiques sans orthographe, romans de nos aïeules, contes de fées, petits livres de l'enfance, opéras vieux, refrains niais, rythmes naïfs.

Je rêvais croisades, voyages de découvertes dont on n'a pas de relations, républiques sans histoires, guerres de religion étouffées, révolutions de mœurs, déplacements de races et de continents: je croyais à tous les enchantements.

J'inventai la couleur des voyelles! — A noir, E blanc, I rouge, O bleu, U vert. — Je réglai la forme et le mouvement de chaque consonne, et, avec des rythmes instinctifs, je me flattai d'inventer un

"If he explained his sadness to me, would I understand it any more than I do his mockery? He attacks me, he spends hours making me feel ashamed of everything in the world that might have touched my heart, and he gets angry if I cry.

"'—Do you see that elegant young man walking into that beautiful, calm house? His name is Duval, Dufour, Armand, Maurice, or whatever. A woman devoted her life to loving that malevolent fool: she died, she's surely a saint in heaven now.[13] You'll cause my death the way he caused that woman's death. It's our fate, we loving hearts. . . .' Alas! He had days on which all active men seemed to him like the playthings of grotesque deliriums: he'd laugh long and hideously.—Then he'd return to behaving like a young mother or a beloved[14] sister. If he were less of a savage, we'd be saved! But his gentleness is deadly, too. I'm under his thumb.—Ah, I'm insane!

"Some day, perhaps, he'll disappear miraculously; but if he's to ascend to some heaven, I've got to know about it, so I can catch a glimpse of my little sweetheart's assumption!"

A peculiar couple!

Deliriums II: Alchemy of Speech

Back to me! The story of one of my follies.

For a long time I had boasted that I possessed every imaginable landscape, and I found the celebrities of painting and modern poetry to be laughable.

I loved foolish paintings, overdoor scenes, stage sets, mountebanks' daubs, shop signs, popular colored prints; outmoded literature, Church Latin, badly spelled erotic books, the novels our grandmothers read, fairy tales, little books written for children, old operas, silly ditties, naïve rhythms.

I dreamt of crusades, voyages of discovery of which no record remained, republics without a history, wars of religion that had been aborted, revolutions in morality, the displacement of races and of continents: I believed in every kind of enchantment.

I invented the color of the vowels!—A black, E white, I red, O blue, U green.—I regulated the form and movement of every consonant and, with instinctive rhythms, I flattered myself that I had invented a

---

13. The paragraph down to here seems to allude to Alexandre Dumas the Younger's novel (1848) and play (1852) *La dame aux camélias* ("Camille"), the hero of which is Armand Duval.   14. One commentator amends *aimée* (beloved) to *aînée* (elder).

verbe poétique accessible, un jour ou l'autre, à tous les sens. Je réservais la traduction.

Ce fut d'abord une étude. J'écrivais des silences, des nuits, je notais l'inexprimable. Je fixais des vertiges.

Loin des oiseaux, des troupeaux, des villageoises,
Que buvais-je, à genoux dans cette bruyère
Entourée de tendres bois de noisetiers,
Dans un brouillard d'après-midi tiède et vert?

Que pouvais-je boire dans cette jeune Oise,
— Ormeaux sans voix, gazon sans fleurs, ciel couvert!
Boire à ces gourdes jaunes, loin de ma case
Chérie? Quelque liqueur d'or qui fait suer.

Je faisais une louche enseigne d'auberge.
— Un orage vint chasser le ciel. Au soir
L'eau des bois se perdait sur les sables vierges,
Le vent de Dieu jetait des glaçons aux mares;

Pleurant, je voyais de l'or — et ne pus boire. —

À quatre heures du matin, l'été,
Le sommeil d'amour dure encore.
Sous les bocages s'évapore
     L'odeur du soir fêté.

Là-bas, dans leur vaste chantier
Au soleil des Hespérides,
Déjà s'agitent — en bras de chemise —
     Les Charpentiers.

Dans leurs Déserts de mousse, tranquilles,
Ils préparent les lambris précieux
     Où la ville
     Peindra de faux cieux.

O, pour ces Ouvriers charmants
Sujets d'un roi de Babylone,
Vénus! quitte un instant les Amants
     Dont l'âme est en couronne.

     O Reine des Bergers,
Porte aux travailleurs l'eau-de-vie,

poetic speech accessible some day to all the senses. I reserved trans-
lation rights.

At first I experimented. I wrote down silences, nights, I noted down
the inexpressible. I captured dizzying emotions on paper.

Far from birds, flocks, village women,
what was I drinking, kneeling on this heath
that's surrounded by young hazel thickets,
in a warm, green afternoon mist?

What could I be drinking from this young Oise?
—mute young elms, flowerless turf, overcast sky!
Drinking with these yellow gourds, far from my beloved
hut? Some golden potion that brings out a sweat.

I represented a disreputable inn sign.
—A storm came and drove away the sky. In the evening
the forest waters lost themselves in the virgin sand,
God's wind was casting blocks of ice into the ponds;

Weeping, I saw gold—and was unable to drink.—

At four in the morning, in summertime,
love-slumber still lasts.
Beneath the copses the smell
    of the festive evening evaporates.

Over yonder, in their vast lumberyard
in the sunshine of the Hesperides,
the carpenters—in their shirtsleeves—
    are already bustling about.

In their mossy wilderness, tranquilly,
they are preparing the costly wainscoting
    on which the city
    will paint imitation skies.

Oh, for those charming workmen,
subjects of a king of Babylon,
Venus, for a moment leave those lovers
    whose soul is in the form of a wreath.

    O queen of shepherds,
take the brandy to the laborers,

Que leurs forces soient en paix
En attendant le bain dans la mer à midi.

La vieillerie poétique avait une bonne part dans mon alchimie du verbe.

Je m'habituai à l'hallucination simple: je voyais très franchement une mosquée à la place d'une usine, une école de tambours faite par des anges, des calèches sur les routes du ciel, un salon au fond d'un lac; les monstres, les mystères; un titre de vaudeville dressait des épouvantes devant moi.

Puis j'expliquai mes sophismes magiques avec l'hallucination des mots!

Je finis par trouver sacré le désordre de mon esprit. J'étais oisif, en proie à une lourde fièvre: j'enviais la félicité des bêtes, — les chenilles, qui représentent l'innocence des limbes, les taupes, le sommeil de la virginité!

Mon caractère s'aigrissait. Je disais adieu au monde dans d'espèces de romances:

Chanson de la plus haute tour

Qu'il vienne, qu'il vienne,
Le temps dont on s'éprenne.

J'ai tant fait patience
Qu'à jamais j'oublie.
Craintes et souffrances
Aux cieux sont parties.
Et la soif malsaine
Obscurcit mes veines.

Qu'il vienne, qu'il vienne,
Le temps dont on s'éprenne.

Telle la prairie
À l'oubli livrée,
Grandie, et fleurie
D'encens et d'ivraies,
Au bourdon farouche
Des sales mouches.

Qu'il vienne, qu'il vienne,
Le temps dont on s'éprenne.

so that their strength may be in peace
while awaiting a swim in the sea at noon.

———————————

Obsolete poetics played a large role in my alchemy of speech.

I became accustomed to simple hallucinations: quite unhesitatingly I saw a mosque in place of a factory, a drumming school conducted by angels, carriages on the highways of the sky, a parlor at the bottom of a lake; monsters, mysteries; the title of a light comedy would instill fear into me.

Then I explained my magical sophisms with the hallucination of words!

Finally I considered the disordering of my mind to be sacred. I was an idler, a prey to a strong fever: I envied the happiness of animals— the caterpillars, which represent the innocent babes in Limbo; the moles, which stand for the slumber of virgins!

My character was souring. I was bidding farewell to the world in poems that resembled songs:

Song of the Highest Tower

Let it come, let it come,
the time that one can fall in love with!

I've been patient so long
that I'm forever forgetting.
Fear and suffering
have departed for the skies.
And an unwholesome thirst
darkens my veins.

Let it come, let it come,
the time that one can fall in love with!

Like the meadow
consigned to oblivion,
grown and blossoming
with incense and darnels,
amid the fierce buzzing
of the filthy flies.

Let it come, let it come,
the time that one can fall in love with!

J'aimai le désert, les vergers brûlés, les boutiques fanées, les boissons tiédies. Je me traînais dans les ruelles puantes et, les yeux fermés, je m'offrais au soleil, dieu de feu.

«Général, s'il reste un vieux canon sur tes remparts en ruines, bombarde-nous avec des blocs de terre sèche. Aux glaces des magasins splendides! dans les salons! Fais manger sa poussière à la ville. Oxyde les gargouilles. Emplis les boudoirs de poudre de rubis brûlante . . .»

Oh! le moucheron enivré à la pissotière de l'auberge, amoureux de la bourrache, et que dissout un rayon!

Faim

Si j'ai du goût, ce n'est guère
Que pour la terre et les pierres.
Je déjeune toujours d'air,
De roc, de charbons, de fer.

Mes faims, tournez. Paissez, faims,
    Le pré des sons.
Attirez le gai venin
    Des liserons.

Mangez les cailloux qu'on brise,
Les vieilles pierres d'églises;
Les galets des vieux déluges,
Pains semés dans les vallées grises.

Le loup criait sous les feuilles
En crachant les belles plumes
De son repas de volailles:
Comme lui je me consume.

Les salades, les fruits
N'attendent que la cueillette;
Mais l'araignée de la haie
Ne mange que des violettes.

Que je dorme! que je bouille
Aux autels de Salomon.
Le bouillon court sur la rouille,
Et se mêle au Cédron.

I loved the wilderness, scorched orchards, faded shops, drinks that had become warm. I dragged myself through stinking alleys and, with eyes shut, I offered myself up to the sun, god of fire.

"General, if there's still an old cannon on your ruined ramparts, bombard us with blocks of dry earth. Into the windows of the luxurious stores! Into parlors! Make the city eat its dust. Oxidize the gutter spouts. Fill the boudoirs with a burning powder of rubies. . . ."

Oh, the horsefly intoxicated at the inn urinal, in love with borage, and dissolved in a sunbeam!

Hunger

If I have an appetite, it's for hardly
anything else than earth and stones.
I always dine on air,
rock, coals, iron.

Turn, my hungers! Graze, hungers,
        on the pasture of sounds!
Attract the merry venom
        of the bindweeds.

Eat the rocks that people break,
the old stones of churches;
the shingles left on beaches by ancient floods,
loaves sown in gray valleys.

———————

The wolf was howling below the leaves
while spitting out the beautiful feathers
from his meal of poultry:
like him I consume myself.

The salad greens, the fruits
are waiting only to be picked;
but the spider in the hedge
eats only violets.

Let me sleep! Let me boil
at the altars of Solomon.
The broth runs onto the rust,
and mingles with the Kidron.[15]

_____

15. The wadi (arroyo) between Jerusalem and the Mount of Olives.

Enfin, ô bonheur, ô raison, j'écartai du ciel l'azur, qui est du noir, et je vécus, étincelle d'or de la lumière *nature*. De joie, je prenais une expression bouffonne et égarée au possible:

Elle est retrouvée!
Quoi? l'éternité.
C'est la mer mêlée
    Au soleil.

Mon âme éternelle,
Observe ton vœu
Malgré la nuit seule
Et le jour en feu.

Donc tu te dégages
Des humains suffrages,
Des communs élans!
Tu voles selon . . .

— Jamais l'espérance.
    Pas d'*orietur*.
Science et patience,
Le supplice est sûr.

Plus de lendemain,
Braises de satin,
    Votre ardeur
    Est le devoir.

Elle est retrouvée!
— Quoi? — l'Éternité.
C'est la mer mêlée
    Au soleil.

———————

Je devins un opéra fabuleux: je vis que tous les êtres ont une fatalité de bonheur: l'action n'est pas la vie, mais une façon de gâcher quelque force, un énervement. La morale est la faiblesse de la cervelle.

À chaque être, plusieurs *autres* vies me semblaient dues. Ce monsieur ne sait ce qu'il fait: il est un ange. Cette famille est une nichée de chiens. Devant plusieurs hommes, je causai tout haut avec un moment d'une de leurs autres vies. — Ainsi, j'ai aimé un porc.

Finally, O happiness, O reason, I removed the azure, which is blackness, from the sky, and I lived as a golden spark of *natural* light. In my joy I assumed an expression that was as comical and distracted as possible:

It has been found again!
What? Eternity.
It's the sea mingled
    with the sun.

My eternal soul,
keep your vow
in spite of the lone night
and the fiery day.

Thus you detach yourself
from human approbation,
from everyday impulses!
You fly wherever you wish. . . .

—Never any hope.
    No *orietur*.[16]
Science and patience,
torture is a certainty.

No more tomorrow,
embers of satin,
    your ardor
    is duty.

It has been found again!
—What?—Eternity.
It's the sea mingled
    with the sun.

———————

I became a fabulous opera: I saw that all beings are doomed to happiness: action isn't life, but a way of squandering some strength, a nervous state. Morality is the brain's feebleness.

It seemed to me that several *other* lives were owed to each being. This gentleman doesn't know what he's doing: he's an angel. This family is a brood of dogs. Face to face with several men, I chatted out loud with a moment from one of their other lives.—In that way, I was in love with a pig.

———

16. Latin for "[the sun] shall rise."

Aucun des sophismes de la folie, — la folie qu'on enferme, — n'a été oublié par moi: je pourrais les redire tous, je tiens le système. Ma santé fut menacée. La terreur venait. Je tombais dans des sommeils de plusieurs jours, et, levé, je continuais les rêves les plus tristes.

J'étais mûr pour le trépas, et par une route de dangers ma faiblesse me menait aux confins du monde et de la Cimmérie, patrie de l'ombre et des tourbillons.

Je dus voyager, distraire les enchantements assemblés sur mon cerveau. Sur la mer, que j'aimais comme si elle eût dû me laver d'une souillure, je voyais se lever la croix consolatrice. J'avais été damné par l'arc-en-ciel. Le Bonheur était ma fatalité, mon remords, mon ver: ma vie serait toujours trop immense pour être dévouée à la force et à la beauté.

Le Bonheur! Sa dent, douce à la mort, m'avertissait au chant du coq, — *ad matutinum,* au *Christus venit,* — dans les plus sombres villes:

O saisons, ô châteaux!
Quelle âme est sans défauts?

J'ai fait la magique étude
Du bonheur, qu'aucun n'élude.

Salut à lui, chaque fois
Que chante le coq gaulois.

Ah! je n'aurai plus d'envie:
Il s'est chargé de ma vie.

Ce charme a pris âme et corps
Et dispersé les efforts.

O saisons, ô châteaux!

L'heure de sa fuite, hélas!
Sera l'heure du trépas.

O saisons, ô châteaux!

─────────────

Cela s'est passé. Je sais aujourd'hui saluer la beauté.

None of the sophisms of madness—the madness that's locked away—was forgotten by me: I could repeat them all, I possess the system.

My health was threatened. Terror was approaching. I would go to sleep for days at a time, and, when I awoke, the saddest dreams would continue. I was ripe for death, and by a road of dangers my weakness was leading me to the ends of the earth, to the borders of Cimmeria,[17] home of darkness and whirlwinds.

I had to travel, to distract the magic spells clustered in my brain. On the ocean, that ocean which I loved as if it were bound to wash away some contamination from me, I would see the consoling Cross rise. I had been damned by the rainbow. Happiness was my doom, my remorse, my worm: my life would always be too immense to be dedicated to strength and beauty.

Happiness! Its tooth, mortally sweet, was warning me at cockcrow—*ad matutinum,*[18] at the *Christus venit*[19]—in the darkest cities:

O seasons, O castles!
what soul is free of defects?

I have made the magical study
of happiness, which no one eludes.

Greetings to it, each time
that the Gallic cock crows.

Ah, I won't have any more desires:
it has assumed responsibility for my life.

This charm has taken on a soul and a body
and has scattered my efforts.

O seasons, O castles!

The hour when it runs away, alas!
will be the hour of death.

O seasons, O castles!

———————

All of that is in the past. Today I know how to greet beauty.

———————

17. In ancient Greek mythology, a remote land perpetually shrouded in fog.   18. Latin: "in the morning"; the cockcrow probably alludes to St. Peter's three denials of Christ.   19. Latin: "Christ is coming" or "Christ has come."

L'impossible

Ah! cette vie de mon enfance, la grande route par tous les temps, sobre surnaturellement, plus désintéressé que le meilleur des mendiants, fier de n'avoir ni pays, ni amis, quelle sottise c'était. — Et je m'en aperçois seulement!

— J'ai eu raison de mépriser ces bonshommes qui ne perdraient pas l'occasion d'une caresse, parasites de la propreté et de la santé de nos femmes, aujourd'hui qu'elles sont si peu d'accord avec nous.

J'ai eu raison dans tous mes dédains: puisque je m'évade!

Je m'évade!

Je m'explique.

Hier encore, je soupirais: «Ciel! sommes-nous assez de damnés ici-bas! Moi j'ai tant de temps déjà dans leur troupe! Je les connais tous. Nous nous reconnaissons toujours; nous nous dégoûtons. La charité nous est inconnue. Mais nous sommes polis; nos relations avec le monde sont très convenables.» Est-ce étonnant? Le monde! les marchands, les naïfs! — Nous ne sommes pas déshonorés. — Mais les élus, comment nous recevraient-ils? Or il y a des gens hargneux et joyeux, de faux élus, puisqu'il nous faut de l'audace ou de l'humilité pour les aborder. Ce sont les seuls élus. Ce ne sont pas des bénisseurs!

M'étant retrouvé deux sous de raison — ça passe vite! — je vois que mes malaises viennent de ne m'être pas figuré assez tôt que nous sommes à l'Occident. Les marais occidentaux! Non que je croie la lumière altérée, la forme exténuée, le mouvement égaré . . . Bon! voici que mon esprit veut absolument se charger de tous les développements cruels qu'a subis l'esprit depuis la fin de l'Orient . . . Il en veut, mon esprit!

. . . Mes deux sous de raison sont finis! — L'esprit est autorité, il veut que je sois en Occident. Il faudrait le faire taire pour conclure comme je voulais.

J'envoyais au diable les palmes des martyrs, les rayons de l'art, l'orgueil des inventeurs, l'ardeur des pillards; je retournais à l'Orient et à la sagesse première et éternelle. — Il paraît que c'est un rêve de paresse grossière!

Pourtant, je ne songeais guère au plaisir d'échapper aux souffrances modernes. Je n'avais pas en vue la sagesse bâtarde du Coran. — Mais n'y a-t-il pas un supplice réel en ce que, depuis cette déclaration de la science, le christianisme, l'homme *se joue*, se prouve les évidences, se

The Impossible

Ah, that life of my childhood, the highway in all sorts of weather, supernaturally sober, more impartial than the best of beggars, proud of not having a native region or friends, how foolish it was!—And I realize it only now!

—I was right to look down on those simpletons who would lose no opportunity for a caress, parasites of our women's cleanliness and good health, today when they are in such disagreement with us.

I was right in all my disdains: since I'm escaping!

I'm escaping!

Let me explain.

Even yesterday, I was sighing: "Heavens! Aren't there plenty of us here on earth who are damned! As for me, I've already spent so much time in their troop! I know them all. We always recognize one another; we disgust one another. Charity is unknown to us; But we're polite; our relations with society are very proper." Is it surprising? Society! The merchants, the naïve!—We aren't dishonored.—But the elect, how would *they* receive us? Now, there are ill-tempered and joyous people, the false-elect, since we need audacity or humility in order to confront them. Those are the only chosen ones. They aren't sweet talkers with empty promises!

Having found that I possessed two cents' worth of reason—how quickly it's used up!—I see that my discomfort is caused by not having reflected soon enough that we're in the Occident. The swamps of the West! Not that I think that the light is faded, that form is exhausted, that movement has gone astray. . . . Good! Now my mind absolutely wants to assume the burden of every cruel development which mind has undergone ever since the end of the Orient. . . . My mind wants it!

. . . My two cents' worth of reason is used up!—My mind is an authority, it wants me to be in the Occident. I'd have to silence it if I wanted things to turn out my way.

I was packing off to the devil the palms of the martyrs, the radiance of art, the pride of inventors, the ardor of pillagers; I was returning to the East, to primal and eternal wisdom.—It seems that that's a dream of crass laziness!

All the same, I was hardly thinking of the pleasure of escaping from modern torments. I didn't have in mind the hybrid wisdom of the Koran.—But isn't there a genuine torture in the fact that, ever since that declaration of science, Christianity, man has been *deceiving him-*

gonfle du plaisir de répéter ces preuves, et ne vit que comme cela! Torture subtile, niaise; source de mes divagations spirituelles. La nature pourrait s'ennuyer, peut-être M. Prudhomme est né avec le Christ.

N'est-ce pas parce que nous cultivons la brume! Nous mangeons la fièvre avec nos légumes aqueux. Et l'ivrognerie! et le tabac! et l'ignorance! et les dévouements! — Tout cela est-il assez loin de la pensée de la sagesse de l'Orient, la patrie primitive? Pourquoi un monde moderne, si de pareils poisons s'inventent!

Les gens d'Église diront: C'est compris. Mais vous voulez parler de l'Éden. Rien pour vous dans l'histoire des peuples orientaux. — C'est vrai; c'est à l'Éden que je songeais! Qu'est-ce que c'est pour mon rêve, cette pureté des races antiques!

Les philosophes: Le monde n'a pas d'âge. L'humanité se déplace, simplement. Vous êtes en Occident, mais libre d'habiter dans votre Orient, quelque ancien qu'il vous le faille, — et d'y habiter bien. Ne soyez pas un vaincu. Philosophes, vous êtes de votre Occident.

Mon esprit, prends garde. Pas de partis de salut violents. Exerce-toi! — Ah! la science ne va pas assez vite pour nous!

— Mais je m'aperçois que mon esprit dort.

S'il était bien éveillé toujours à partir de ce moment, nous serions bientôt à la vérité, qui peut-être nous entoure avec ses anges pleurant! . . . — S'il avait été éveillé jusqu'à ce moment-ci, c'est que je n'aurais pas cédé aux instincts délétères, à une époque immémoriale! . . . — S'il avait toujours été bien éveillé, je voguerais en pleine sagesse! . . .

O pureté! pureté!

C'est cette minute d'éveil qui m'a donné la vision de la pureté! — Par l'esprit on va à Dieu!

Déchirante infortune!

L'éclair

Le travail humain! c'est l'explosion qui éclaire mon abîme de temps en temps.

«Rien n'est vanité; à la science, et en avant!» crie l'Ecclésiaste moderne, c'est-à-dire *Tout le monde.* Et pourtant les cadavres des méchants et des fainéants tombent sur le cœur des autres . . . Ah! vite, vite un peu; là-bas, par-delà la nuit, ces récompenses futures, éternelles . . . les échappons-nous? . . .

self, proving to himself that which is obvious, swelling with the pleasure of repeating those proofs, and living in that fashion only?! A subtle, silly torture; the source of my mental wanderings. Nature might get bored; maybe Monsieur Prudhomme[20] was born at the same time as Christ.

Isn't it because we cultivate fogginess? We eat fever together with our watery vegetables. And drunkenness! And tobacco! And ignorance! And devotions!—Isn't all of that quite remote from the wise philosophy of the East, the primal homeland? What good is a modern world if similar poisons are invented?!

Churchmen will say: "We understand. You're talking about Eden. There's nothing for you in the history of Eastern nations."—It's true, I *was* thinking about Eden! What has that to do with my dream—that purity of the ancient races?!

Philosophers will say: "The world is ageless. Mankind simply moves from place to place. You're in the Occident, but free to dwell in your Orient—as ancient as you like—and to enjoy dwelling there. Don't be a loser." Philosophers, you're grounded in your Occident.

Beware, my mind. Make no hasty resolves to be saved. Train yourself!—Ah, science doesn't move fast enough for us!

—But I notice that my mind is sleeping.

If it were always wide awake from this moment on, we'd soon reach the truth, which may be all around us, its angels weeping! . . .—If it had been awake up till this moment, I wouldn't have succumbed to my harmful instincts from time immemorial! . . .—If it had always been wide awake, I'd be sailing on a sea of wisdom! . . .

O purity, purity!

It was that minute of wakefulness that afforded me the vision of purity!—By way of the mind we go to God!

Heartrending calamity!

The Lightning Flash

Human labor! It's the explosion that lights up my abyss every so often.

"Nothing is vanity; head for science, and forward march!" cries the modern Ecclesiastes—that is, *everybody*. And yet the corpses of the wicked and the idle fall upon the heart of the others. . . . Ah, quick! Step lively! Over there, beyond the night, those future, eternal rewards . . . are we to do without them? . . .

---

20. A fictional figure standing for the narrow-minded, self-satisfied bourgeois.

— Qu'y puis-je? Je connais le travail; et la science est trop lente. Que la prière galope et que la lumière gronde . . . je le vois bien. C'est trop simple, et il fait trop chaud; on se passera de moi. J'ai mon devoir, j'en serai fier à la façon de plusieurs, en le mettant de côté. Ma vie est usée. Allons! feignons, fainéantons, ô pitié! Et nous existerons en nous amusant, en rêvant amours monstres et univers fantastiques, en nous plaignant et en querellant les apparences du monde, saltimbanque, mendiant, artiste, bandit, — prêtre! Sur mon lit d'hôpital, l'odeur de l'encens m'est revenue si puissante; gardien des aromates sacrés, confesseur, martyr . . .

Je reconnais là ma sale éducation d'enfance. Puis quoi! . . . Aller mes vingt ans, si les autres vont vingt ans . . .

Non! non! à présent je me révolte contre la mort! Le travail paraît trop léger à mon orgueil: ma trahison au monde serait un supplice trop court. Au dernier moment, j'attaquerais à droite, à gauche . . .

Alors, — oh! — chère pauvre âme, l'éternité serait-elle pas perdue pour nous!

Matin

N'eus-je pas *une fois* une jeunesse aimable, héroïque, fabuleuse, à écrire sur des feuilles d'or, — trop de chance! Par quel crime, par quelle erreur, ai-je mérité ma faiblesse actuelle? Vous qui prétendez que des bêtes poussent des sanglots de chagrin, que des malades désespèrent, que des morts rêvent mal, tâchez de raconter ma chute et mon sommeil. Moi, je ne puis pas plus m'expliquer que le mendiant avec ses continuels *Pater* et *Ave Maria. Je ne sais plus parler!*

Pourtant, aujourd'hui, je crois avoir fini la relation de mon enfer. C'était bien l'enfer; l'ancien, celui dont le fils de l'homme ouvrit les portes.

Du même désert, à la même nuit, toujours mes yeux las se réveillent à l'étoile d'argent, toujours, sans que s'émeuvent les Rois de la vie, les trois mages, le cœur, l'âme, l'esprit. Quand irons-nous, pardelà les grèves et les monts, saluer la naissance du travail nouveau, la sagesse nouvelle, la fuite des tyrans et des démons, la fin de la superstition, adorer — les premiers! — Noël sur la terre!

Le chant des cieux, la marche des peuples! Esclaves, ne maudissons pas la vie.

—What can I do about it? I'm familiar with labor; and science is too slow. That prayer gallops and the light mutters . . . I see it clearly. It's too simple, and the weather's too hot; people will get along without me. I have my duty, I'll be proud of it the same way many people are, by setting it aside.

My life is worn out. Come, let's pretend, let's be idle, O mercy! And we'll live our lives having fun, dreaming of monstrous loves and fantastic universes, complaining and picking quarrels with the world's semblances, as mountebank, beggar, artist, bandit,—priest! On my hospital bed, the aroma of incense came back to me with such force; guardians of the sacred fragrances, confessor, martyr. . . .

Therein I recognize my rotten upbringing as a child. What of it?! . . . Go on living till I'm twenty, if other people reach twenty . . .

No, no! Now I rebel against death! Work seems too lightweight for my pride: my betrayal to the world would be too brief a torment. At the last moment, I'd lash out to the right of me, to the left. . . .

Then—oh!—poor dear soul, wouldn't eternity be lost to us?!

Morning

Didn't I *once* have young days that were pleasant, heroic, fabulous, worthy to be recorded on golden pages?—Too lucky! Through what crime, through what mistake, have I deserved my present weakness? You who claim that animals sob in sorrow, that sick people fall into despair, that the dead have bad dreams, try to narrate my fall and my sleep. As for me, I can no more explain myself than the beggar with his continual "Our Father" and "Hail Mary." *I don't know how to speak any more!*

And yet, today, I think I've finished the relation of my hell. It really was hell; the ancient one, the one whose gates were opened by the Son of Man.

From the same desert, in the same night, my weary eyes always awaken to the silver star, always, without the Kings of life, the three Magi, the heart, soul, and mind, being stirred up by it. When shall we go, beyond the shores and the mountains, to hail the birth of new labor, new wisdom, the taking to flight of tyrants and demons, the end of superstition, and to worship—the first to do so!—the Christ Child on earth?!

The song of the skies, the progress of nations! Slaves, let us not curse life.

Adieu

L'automne déjà! — Mais pourquoi regretter un éternel soleil, si nous sommes engagés à la découverte de la clarté divine, — loin des gens qui meurent sur les saisons.

L'automne. Notre barque élevée dans les brumes immobiles tourne vers le port de la misère, la cité énorme au ciel taché de feu et de boue. Ah! les haillons pourris, le pain trempé de pluie, l'ivresse, les mille amours qui m'ont crucifié! Elle ne finira donc point cette goule reine de millions d'âmes et de corps morts *et qui seront jugés!* Je me revois la peau rongée par la boue et la peste, des vers plein les cheveux et les aisselles et encore de plus gros vers dans le cœur, étendu parmi les inconnus sans âge, sans sentiment . . . J'aurais pu y mourir . . . L'affreuse évocation! J'exècre la misère.

Et je redoute l'hiver parce que c'est la saison du comfort!

— Quelquefois je vois au ciel des plages sans fin couvertes de blanches nations en joie. Un grand vaisseau d'or, au-dessus de moi, agite ses pavillons multicolores sous les brises du matin. J'ai créé toutes les fêtes, tous les triomphes, tous les drames. J'ai essayé d'inventer de nouvelles fleurs, de nouveaux astres, de nouvelles chairs, de nouvelles langues. J'ai cru acquérir des pouvoirs surnaturels. Eh bien! je dois enterrer mon imagination et mes souvenirs! Une belle gloire d'artiste et de conteur emportée!

Moi! moi qui me suis dit mage ou ange, dispensé de toute morale, je suis rendu au sol, avec un devoir à chercher, et la réalité rugueuse à étreindre! Paysan!

Suis-je trompé? la charité serait-elle sœur de la mort, pour moi?

Enfin, je demanderai pardon pour m'être nourri de mensonge. Et allons.

Mais pas une main amie! et où puiser le secours?

Oui, l'heure nouvelle est au moins très sévère.

Car je puis dire que la victoire m'est acquise: les grincements de dents, les sifflements de feu, les soupirs empestés se modèrent. Tous les souvenirs immondes s'effacent. Mes derniers regrets détalent, — des jalousies pour les mendiants, les brigands, les amis de la mort, les arriérés de toutes sortes. — Damnés, si je me vengeais!

Il faut être absolument moderne.

Point de cantiques: tenir le pas gagné. Dure nuit! le sang séché fume sur ma face, et je n'ai rien derrière moi, que cet horrible arbris-

Farewell

Already autumn!—But why miss eternal sunshine, when we're committed to the discovery of divine brightness—far from the people who die by the seasons?

Autumn. Our vessel, raised up in the motionless mists, is returning to the harbor of poverty, the enormous city whose sky is stained with fire and mud. Ah, the rotting tatters, the rain-soaked bread, drunkenness, the thousand loves that have crucified me! And so, she'll have no end, that ghoul who is queen of millions of souls and dead bodies, *which will be judged!* I see myself again with my skin eaten away by mud and plague, my hair and armpits full of worms, with even fatter worms in my heart, as I lie prostrate amid ageless strangers devoid of feeling. . . . I could have died there. . . . Horrible reminiscence! I detest poverty.

And I dread the winter because it's the season of creature comforts!

—At times I see in the sky endless expanses covered with joyful white nations. A large golden ship, above me, waves its many-colored flags in the morning breezes. I have created every festival, every triumph, every drama. I have tried to invent new flowers, new heavenly bodies, new kinds of flesh, new languages. I have believed that I was acquiring supernatural powers. Oh, well! I've got to bury my imagination and my memories! A fine reputation as artist and narrator swept away!

I! I who called myself a magus or angel, exempt from all morality, I am brought back down to the soil, with a duty to be sought and rugged reality to be embraced! Peasant!

Am I mistaken? Could charity be the sister of death, for me?

Finally, I shall ask forgiveness for having fed myself on lies. And on our way!

But not one friendly hand! And where to go for help?

———

Yes, my new situation is very harsh, to say the least.

For I can well say that victory has been won by me: the gnashing of teeth, the hissing of fire, the foul-smelling sighs are abating. Every unclean memory is fading away. My last regrets are decamping—envy of beggars, outlaws, friends of death, backward people of every kind.—They'd be damned if I were to take revenge!

One must be absolutely modern.

No canticles: maintain the ground I've won. Hard night! The dried blood smokes on my face, and I have nothing in back of me but that

seau! . . . Le combat spirituel est aussi brutal que la bataille d'hommes; mais la vision de la justice est le plaisir de Dieu seul.

Cependant c'est la veille. Recevons tous les influx de vigueur et de tendresse réelle. Et à l'aurore, armés d'une ardente patience, nous entrerons aux splendides villes.

Que parlais-je de main amie! Un bel avantage, c'est que je puis rire des vieilles amours mensongères, et frapper de honte ces couples menteurs, — j'ai vu l'enfer des femmes là-bas; — et il me sera loisible de *posséder la vérité dans une âme et un corps.*

Avril–août, 1873.

dreadful shrub! . . . Mental combat is just as brutal as a battle between men; but the vision of justice is the pleasure of God alone.

Meanwhile we're on the eve. Let us receive every influx of vigor and true affection. And at dawn, armed with a burning patience, we shall enter the resplendent cities.

What was I saying about a friendly hand? One real advantage is that I can laugh at my old untruthful loves and heap shame on those lying couples—I've seen the hell for women down there—and I will be permitted to *possess the truth in a soul and a body.*

April–August, 1873.

ILLUMINATIONS

Après le Déluge

Aussitôt après que l'idée du Déluge se fut rassise,

Un lièvre s'arrêta dans les sainfoins et les clochettes mouvantes et dit sa prière à l'arc-en ciel à travers la toile de l'araignée.

Oh les pierres précieuses qui se cachaient, — les fleurs qui regardaient déjà.

Dans la grande rue sale les étals se dressèrent, et l'on tira les barques vers la mer étagée là-haut comme sur les gravures.

Le sang coula, chez Barbe-Bleue, — aux abattoirs, — dans les cirques, où le sceau de Dieu blêmit les fenêtres. Le sang et le lait coulèrent.

Les castors bâtirent. Les «mazagrans» fumèrent dans les estaminets.

Dans la grande maison de vitres encore ruisselante les enfants en deuil regardèrent les merveilleuses images.

Une porte claqua, et sur la place du hameau, l'enfant tourna ses bras, compris des girouettes et des coqs des clochers de partout, sous l'éclatante giboulée. Madame*** établit un piano dans les Alpes. La messe et les premières communions se célébrèrent aux cent mille autels de la cathédrale.

Les caravanes partirent. Et le Splendide Hôtel fut bâti dans le chaos de glaces et de nuit du pôle.

Depuis lors, la Lune entendit les chacals piaulant par les déserts de thym, — et les églogues en sabots grognant dans le verger. Puis, dans la futaie violette, bourgeonnante, Eucharis me dit que c'était le printemps.

ILLUMINATIONS

After the Flood

Immediately after the vision of the Flood had been calmed,

A hare stood still in the sainfoin and the waving bellflowers and said its prayer to the rainbow across the spiderweb.

Oh, the precious stones that were in hiding—the flowers that were already looking!

In the big, dirty street the butcher stalls were set up, and the boats were pulled toward the sea, which rose in tiers up there, the way it does in engravings.

Blood flowed, in Bluebeard's house—in the slaughterhouses—in the circuses, where God's seal turned the windows pale. Blood and milk flowed.

The beavers constructed. The "mazagrans"[21] gave off steam in the bars.

In the big greenhouse still streaming with water, the children in mourning looked at the wonderful pictures.

A door slammed, and on the hamlet square, the child rotated his arms, being understood by the weather vanes and steeplecocks everywhere, beneath the glaring shower. Madame°°° installed a piano in the Alps. Mass and first Communion were celebrated at the hundred thousand altars in the cathedral.

The caravans departed. And the Hotel Splendid was built in the chaos of ice and polar night.

Since then, the moon has heard the jackals whining in the deserts of thyme—and the eclogues in wooden shoes growling in the orchard. Then, in the violet, budding woods, Eucharis[22] told me it was spring.

---

21. Coffee, either cold and diluted or spiked with brandy, or else coffee cups, without handles, according to various definitions.　22. "Good grace" in Greek; the name of a nymph in François Fénelon's *Télémaque* (1699).

47

— Sourds, étang, — Écume, roule sur le pont, et par-dessus les bois; — draps noirs et orgues, — éclairs et tonnerre, — montez et roulez; — Eaux et tristesses, montez et relevez les Déluges.

Car depuis q'ils se sont dissipés, — oh les pierres précieuses s'enfouissant, et les fleurs ouvertes! — c'est un ennui! et la Reine, la Sorcière qui allume sa braise dans le pot de terre, ne voudra jamais nous raconter ce qu'elle sait, et que nous ignorons.

Enfance

I

Cette idole, yeux noirs et crin jaune, sans parents ni cour, plus noble que la fable, mexicaine et flamande; son domaine, azur et verdure insolents, court sur des plages nommées, par des vagues sans vaisseaux, de noms férocement grecs, slaves, celtiques.

À la lisière de la forêt — les fleurs de rêve tintent, éclatent, éclairent, — la fille à lèvre d'orange, les genoux croisés dans le clair déluge qui sourd des prés, nudité qu'ombrent, traversent et habillent les arcs-en-ciel, la flore, la mer.

Dames qui tournoient sur les terrasses voisines de la mer; enfantes et géantes, superbes, noires dans la mousse vert-de-gris, bijoux debout sur le sol gras des bosquets et des jardinets dégelés — jeunes mères et grandes sœurs aux regards pleins de pèlerinages, sultanes, princesses de démarche et de costume tyranniques, petites étrangères et personnes doucement malheureuses.

Quel ennui, l'heure du «cher corps» et «cher cœur».

II

C'est elle, la petite morte, derrière les rosiers. — La jeune maman trépassée descend le perron. — La calèche du cousin crie sur le sable. — Le petit frère — (il est aux Indes!) là, devant le couchant, sur le pré d'œillets. — Les vieux qu'on a enterrés tout droits dans le rempart aux giroflées.

L'essaim des feuilles d'or entoure la maison du général. Ils sont dans le midi. — On suit la route rouge pour arriver à l'auberge vide. Le château est à vendre; les persiennes sont détachées. —

Well up, pond—foam, roll onto the bridge and over the top of the forests;—black hangings and organs—lightnings and thunders—rise up and roll;—Waters and sadnesses, rise and raise up the Floods.

Because ever since they cleared away—oh, the precious stones being covered over, and the open flowers!—it's been boring! And the Queen, the Witch who kindles her embers in the clay pot, will never be willing to recount to us what she knows, that of which we are in ignorance.

Childhood

I

This idol, with dark eyes and yellow hair, without relatives or court, nobler than fable, Mexican and Flemish; its domain, insolent azure and greenery, extends along beaches named by shipless waves with names ferociously Greek, Slavic, Celtic.

At the edge of the forest—the dream flowers tinkle, burst, illuminate—the girl with orange lips, her knees crossed in the bright flood that wells up from the pastures, a nude figure shaded, traversed, and garmented by the rainbows, the plants, the sea.

Ladies who whirl on the terraces next to the sea; girl-children and giantesses, magnificent, dark[23] in the verdigris moss, jewels standing erect on the rich soil of the copses and little thawed gardens—young mothers and big sisters with eyes full of pilgrimages, sultanas, princesses with tyrannical bearing and costume, little foreign women and gently unhappy persons.

How boring, the hour of the "dear body" and "dear heart"!

II

It's she, the dead girl, behind the rosebushes.—The young deceased mother comes down the front steps.—The cousin's carriage creaks on the sand.—The little brother—(he's in India!) there, in front of the setting sun, in the meadow of carnations.—The old people who have been buried erect in the rampart with the wallflowers.

The swarm of golden leaves encircles the general's house. They're in the south.—One followed the red road to get to the empty inn. The manor house is for sale; the shutters have become loose.—The parish priest has

---

23. Or: reading *superbes noires* (without a comma): "magnificent black women."

Le curé aura emporté la clef de l'église. — Autour du parc, les
loges des gardes sont inhabitées. Les palissades sont si hautes
qu'on ne voit que les cimes bruissantes. D'ailleurs il n'y a rien à
voir là-dedans.

Les prés remontent aux hameaux sans coqs, sans enclumes.
L'écluse est levée. O les calvaires et les moulins du désert, les îles et
les meules.

Des fleurs magiques bourdonnaient. Les talus *le* berçaient. Des
bêtes d'une élégance fabuleuse circulaient. Les nuées s'amassaient
sur la haute mer faite d'une éternité de chaudes larmes.

III

Au bois il y a un oiseau, son chant vous arrête et vous fait rougir.

Il y a une horloge qui ne sonne pas.

Il y a une fondrière avec un nid de bêtes blanches.

Il y a une cathédrale qui descend et un lac qui monte.

Il y a une petite voiture abandonnée dans le taillis, ou qui descend
le sentier en courant, enrubannée.

Il y a une troupe de petits comédiens en costumes, aperçus sur la
route à travers la lisière du bois.

Il y a enfin, quand l'on a faim et soif, quelqu'un qui vous chasse.

IV

Je suis le saint, en prière sur la terrasse, — comme les bêtes pacifiques
paissent jusqu'à la mer de Palestine.

Je suis le savant au fauteuil sombre. Les branches et la pluie se jet-
tent à la croisée de la bibliothèque.

Je suis le piéton de la grand'route par les bois nains; la rumeur des
écluses couvre mes pas. Je vois longtemps la mélancolique lessive d'or
du couchant.

Je serais bien l'enfant abandonné sur la jetée partie à la haute mer,
le petit valet, suivant l'allée dont le front touche le ciel.

Les sentiers sont âpres. Les monticules se couvrent de genêts. L'air
est immobile. Que les oiseaux et les sources sont loin! Ce ne peut être
que la fin du monde, en avançant.

probably taken away the key to the church.—Around the park, the keepers' lodges are uninhabited. The picket fences are so high that only the rustling treetops can be seen. There's nothing to see in there, anyway. The pastures rise all the way to the hamlets devoid of roosters and anvils. The sluice gate is raised. O the Stations of the Cross and mills of the desert, the islands and millstones.[24]

Magical flowers were humming. The grassy slopes were cradling *him*. Animals of fabulous elegance were moving about. The clouds were stacking up above the high sea, which was made up of an eternity of hot tears.

III

In the forest, there's a bird; its song makes you stop and blush.

There's a clock that doesn't strike.

There's a hollow with a nest of white animals.

There's a cathedral that descends and a lake that rises.

There's a little vehicle abandoned in the brush, or which goes down the path running, ribboned.

There's a troupe of little actors in costume, glimpsed on the road across the edge of the forest.

Lastly, when you're hungry and thirsty, there's someone who chases you away.

IV

I am the saint, praying on the terrace—the way that peaceful animals graze all the way to the sea of Palestine.

I am the scholar in the dark armchair. The branches and the rain hurl themselves against the library casement.

I am the man walking the highway through the dwarf woods; the noise of the sluices drowns out my footsteps. For a long time I see the melancholy golden laundry[25] of the sunset.

I would very likely be the child abandoned on the pier which has drifted out to the high seas, the little servant following the tree-lined lane whose brow touches the sky.

The paths are rough. The hillocks are covered with broom. The air is motionless. How far away the birds and fountains are! This can only be the end of the world, drawing nearer.

24. Or: "haystacks." 25. *Lessive* means both "wash(ing)" (the ensemble of laundered items) and the "lye" used to wash it. It is also a technical term in alchemy, and some commentators detect an extensive alchemical subtext in Rimbaud's oeuvre.

V

Qu'on me loue enfin ce tombeau, blanchi à la chaux avec les lignes du ciment en relief — très loin sous terre.

Je m'accoude à la table, la lampe éclaire très vivement ces journaux que je suis idiot de relire, ces livres sans intérêt.

À une distance énorme au-dessus de mon salon souterrain, les maisons s'implantent, les brumes s'assemblent. La boue est rouge ou noire. Ville monstrueuse, nuit sans fin!

Moins haut, sont des égouts. Aux côtés, rien que l'épaisseur du globe. Peut-être les gouffres d'azur, des puits de feu. C'est peut-être sur ces plans que se rencontrent lunes et comètes, mers et fables.

Aux heures d'amertume je m'imagine des boules de saphir, de métal. Je suis maître du silence. Pourquoi une apparence de soupirail blêmirait-elle au coin de la voûte?

Conte

Un Prince était vexé de ne s'être employé jamais qu'à la perfection des générosités vulgaires. Il prévoyait d'étonnantes révolutions de l'amour, et soupçonnait ses femmes de pouvoir mieux que cette complaisance agrémentée de ciel et de luxe. Il voulait voir la vérité, l'heure du désir et de la satisfaction essentiels. Que ce fût ou non une aberration de piété, il voulut. Il possédait au moins un assez large pouvoir humain.

Toutes les femmes qui l'avaient connu furent assassinées. Quel saccage du jardin de la beauté! Sous le sabre, elles le bénirent. Il n'en commanda point de nouvelles. — Les femmes réapparurent.

Il tua tous ceux qui le suivaient, après la chasse ou les libations. — Tous le suivaient.

Il s'amusa à égorger les bêtes de luxe. Il fit flamber les palais. Il se ruait sur les gens et les taillait en pièces. — La foule, les toits d'or, les belles bêtes existaient encore.

Peut-on s'extasier dans la destruction, se rajeunir par la cruauté! Le peuple ne murmura pas. Personne n'offrit le concours de ses vues.

Un soir il galopait fièrement. Un Génie apparut, d'une beauté ineffable, inavouable même. De sa physionomie et de son maintien ressortait la promesse d'un amour multiple et complexe! d'un bon-

V

May I finally be rented this tomb, whitewashed, with the lines of the cement in relief—very deep below ground!

I lean my elbows on the table; the lamp illuminates very brightly these newspapers which it's idiotic of me to reread, these books devoid of interest.

At an enormous distance above my underground parlor, the houses take root, the fogs gather. The mud is red or black. Monstrous city, endless night!

Less high up, there are sewers. Alongside, nothing but the thickness of the globe. Perhaps azure abysses, wells of fire. It's on these levels, perhaps, that moons and comets, seas and fables, meet.

At hours of bitterness I envision spheres of sapphire, of metal. I am master of silence. Why should the semblance of a skylight palely appear in the corner of the vault?

Tale

A Prince was annoyed because he had never devoted himself to anything but the perfecting of vulgar acts of generosity. He foresaw surprising revolutions in love, and he suspected that his women could do better than that obligingness embellished with heaven and luxury. He wanted to see the truth, the hour of essential desire and satisfaction. Whether or not this was a pious aberration, he wanted it. At least he possessed human powers that were sufficiently extensive.

All the women he had slept with were put to death. What a ravaging of the garden of beauty! The saber over their heads, they blessed him. He didn't send for any replacements.—The women reappeared.

He killed everyone who followed him, after the hunt or festive potations.—Everyone followed him.

He took pleasure in slaughtering costly animals. He had the palaces set ablaze. He would pounce on people and cut them to bits.—The crowd, the golden roofs, the beautiful animals still existed.

Is it possible to be enraptured by destruction, to grow young through cruelty? The populace didn't grumble. No one offered to assist with a personal opinion.

One evening he was galloping proudly. A Genie appeared, one of ineffable, indeed unavowable beauty. His features and bearing bore clear evidence of the promise of a multiple, complex love, of inde-

heur indicible, insupportable même! Le Prince et le Génie s'anéanti-
rent probablement dans la santé essentielle. Comment n'auraient-ils
pas pu en mourir? Ensemble donc ils moururent.
Mais ce Prince décéda, dans son palais, à un âge ordinaire. Le
Prince était le Génie. Le Génie était le Prince.
La musique savante manque à notre désir.

Parade

Des drôles très solides. Plusieurs ont exploité vos mondes. Sans be-
soins, et peu pressés de mettre en œuvre leurs brillantes facultés et
leur expérience de vos consciences. Quels hommes mûrs! Des yeux
hébétés à la façon de la nuit d'été, rouges et noirs, tricolores, d'acier
piqué d'étoiles d'or; des faciès déformés, plombés, blêmis, incendiés;
des enrouements folâtres! La démarche cruelle des oripeaux! — Il y a
quelques jeunes, — comment regarderaient-ils Chérubin? — pourvus
de voix effrayantes et de quelques ressources dangereuses. On les en-
voie prendre du dos en ville, affublés d'un *luxe* dégoûtant.
O le plus violent Paradis de la grimace enragée! Pas de comparai-
son avec vos Fakirs et les autres bouffonneries scéniques. Dans des
costumes improvisés avec le goût du mauvais rêve ils jouent des com-
plaintes, des tragédies de malandrins et de demi-dieux spirituels
comme l'histoire ou les religions ne l'ont jamais été. Chinois,
Hottentots, bohémiens, niais, hyènes, Molochs, vieilles démences, dé-
mons sinistres, ils mêlent les tours populaires, maternels, avec les
poses et les tendresses bestiales. Ils interpréteraient des pièces nou-
velles et des chansons «bonnes filles». Maîtres jongleurs, ils transfor-
ment le lieu et les personnes, et usent de la comédie magnétique. Les
yeux flambent, le sang chante, les os s'élargissent, les larmes et des
filets rouges ruissellent. Leur raillerie ou leur terreur dure une
minute, ou des mois entiers.
J'ai seul la clef de cette parade sauvage.

scribable, indeed unbearable happiness! The Prince and the Genie probably annihilated each other in their constitutional health. How could they help dying of it? Thus, they died together.

But this Prince passed away, in his palace, at a normal age. The Prince was the Genie. The Genie was the Prince.

Learned music is lacking to[26] our desire.

Outside Show[27]

Very sturdy fellows. Several have exploited your worlds. Without material needs, and in no hurry to put into action their brilliant talents and their experience of your consciences. What mature men! Eyes dulled like a summer night; red and black, tricolored, wearing steel spangled with gold stars; deformed, livid, pallid, burnt features; gamesomely hoarse! The cruel bearing of their tinsel!—There are a few young ones—how would they regard Cherubino?—endowed with frighting voices and a few dangerous expedients. They're sent out to strut around[28] in town, decked out in disgusting *luxury*.

Oh, the most violent Paradise of enthusiastic grimacing! No comparison with your fakirs or other stage buffoonery. In costumes improvised with the taste of bad dreams, they act out old ballads, tragedies about bandits and demigods who are wittier than history or religions have ever been. As Chinese, Hottentots, Gypsies, fools, hyenas, Molochs, crazy old men, sinister demons, they combine maternal, traditional stunts with animal-like poses and tenderness. They could interpret new plays and treacly songs. Master minstrels, they transform the locale and the characters, and employ hypnotism in their performance. Their eyes blaze, their blood sings, their bones expand, tears and red streaks trickle down. Their mockery or their terror lasts a minute, or months on end.

I alone possess the key to this savage show.

---

26. Or: "falls short of."   27. A *parade* is a sampling of the entertainment within, provided by performers in fairground shows or small popular theaters.   28. A French editor's conjecture for the unusual *prendre du dos*, which has also been taken to mean "to be chicken hustlers."

Antique

Gracieux fils de Pan! Autour de ton front couronné de fleurettes et de baies tes yeux, des boules précieuses, remuent. Tachées de lies brunes, tes joues se creusent. Tes crocs luisent. Ta poitrine ressemble à une cithare, des tintements circulent dans tes bras blonds. Ton cœur bat dans ce ventre où dort le double sexe. Promène-toi, la nuit, en mouvant doucement cette cuisse, cette seconde cuisse et cette jambe de gauche.

Being Beauteous

Devant une neige un Être de Beauté de haute taille. Des sifflements de mort et des cercles de musique sourde font monter, s'élargir et trembler comme un spectre ce corps adoré; des blessures écarlates et noires éclatent dans les chairs superbes. Les couleurs propres de la vie se foncent, dansent, et se dégagent autour de la Vision, sur le chantier. Et les frissons s'élèvent et grondent, et la saveur forcenée de ces effets se chargeant avec les sifflements mortels et les rauques musiques que le monde, loin derrière nous, lance sur notre mère de beauté, — elle recule, elle se dresse. Oh! nos os sont revêtus d'un nouveau corps amoureux.

✿ ✿ ✿

O la face cendrée, l'écusson de crin, les bras de cristal! Le canon sur lequel je dois m'abattre à travers la mêlée des arbres et de l'air léger!

Vies

I

O les énormes avenues du pays saint, les terrasses du temple! Qu'a-t-on fait du brahmane qui m'expliqua les Proverbes? D'alors, de là-bas, je vois encore même les vieilles! Je me souviens des heures d'argent et de soleil vers les fleuves, la main de la campagne sur mon épaule, et de nos caresses debout dans les plaines poivrées. — Un envol de pi-

An Antiquity

Gracious son of Pan! Around your brow garlanded with flowerets and berries, your eyes, precious spheres, move. Stained with brown lees, your cheeks are hollow. Your fangs gleam. Your chest resembles a cithara, tinklings circulate in your light-colored arms. Your heart beats in that belly where the double sex sleeps. Walk about at night, gently moving this thigh, that other thigh, and that left leg.

Being Beauteous

In front of the snow, a Beauteous Being of tall stature. Hissings of death and circles of muffled music make that adored body rise, expand, and tremble like a phantom; scarlet and black wounds burst open in its superb flesh. The colors proper to life grow deeper, dance, and detach themselves around the Vision, while work is in progress. And the shivers rise and mutter, and the frantic flavor of these effects becoming laden with the deathly hissings and the raucous music which the world, far behind us, hurls at our mother of beauty—she recoils, she holds herself erect. Oh, our bones are clothed in a new, loving body.

* * *

Oh, the ashen face, the horsehair escutcheon, the crystal arms! The cannon onto which I must swoop, through the battle of the trees and the weightless air!

Lives

I

Oh, the enormous avenues of the holy land, the terraces of the temple! What has become of the Brahman who expounded the Vedas to me? I still see even the old women of that time, of that distant place! I remember hours of silver and sunlight toward the rivers, the hand of the countryside on my shoulder, and our lovemaking as we stood in the

geons écarlates tonne autour de ma pensée. — Exilé ici, j'ai eu une scène où jouer les chefs-d'œuvre dramatiques de toutes les littératures. Je vous indiquerais les richesses inouïes. J'observe l'histoire des trésors que vous trouvâtes. Je vois la suite! Ma sagesse est aussi dédaignée que le chaos. Qu'est mon néant, auprès de la stupeur qui vous attend?

II

Je suis un inventeur bien autrement méritant que tous ceux qui m'ont précédé; un musicien même, qui ai trouvé quelque chose comme la clef de l'amour. À présent, gentilhomme d'une campagne aigre au ciel sobre, j'essaye de m'émouvoir au souvenir de l'enfance mendiante, de l'apprentissage ou de l'arrivée en sabots, des polémiques, des cinq ou six veuvages, et quelques noces où ma forte tête m'empêcha de monter au diapason des camarades. Je ne regrette pas ma vieille part de gaîté divine: l'air sobre de cette aigre campagne alimente fort activement mon atroce scepticisme. Mais comme ce scepticisme ne peut désormais être mis en œuvre, et que d'ailleurs je suis dévoué à un trouble nouveau, — j'attends de devenir un très méchant fou.

III

Dans un grenier où je fus enfermé à douze ans j'ai connu le monde, j'ai illustré la comédie humaine. Dans un cellier j'ai appris l'histoire. À quelque fête de nuit dans une cité du Nord, j'ai rencontré toutes les femmes des anciens peintres. Dans un vieux passage à Paris on m'a enseigné les sciences classiques. Dans une magnifique demeure cernée par l'Orient entier j'ai accompli mon immense œuvre et passé mon illustre retraite. J'ai brassé mon sang. Mon devoir m'est remis. Il ne faut même plus songer à cela. Je suis réellement d'outre-tombe, et pas de commissions.

Départ

Assez vu. La vision s'est rencontrée à tous les airs.
Assez eu. Rumeurs des villes, le soir, et au soleil, et toujours.
Assez connu. Les arrêts de la vie. — O Rumeurs et Visions!
Départ dans l'affection et le bruit neufs!

spicy plains.—A flight of scarlet pigeons thunders around my thought.—Exiled here, I've had a stage on which to act out the dramatic masterpieces of all literature. I could point out unheard-of riches to you. I observe the history of the treasures that you found. I see the consequences! My wisdom is disdained as much as chaos is. What is my nothingness, compared with the amazement that awaits you?

II

I'm an inventor far more deserving than all my predecessors; in fact, a musician who has found something resembling the key of love. At present, country squire of a sour rural estate with a sober sky, I attempt to become emotional when recollecting my childhood spent as a beggar, my apprenticeship or arrival wearing wooden clogs, the controversies, the five or six periods when I was a widower, and a few wedding parties at which my strong head kept me from getting as drunk as my friends. I don't miss my old share of divine joyousness: the sober air of this sour countryside provides quite lively nourishment to my atrocious skepticism. But, seeing that this skepticism can no longer be put into action, and moreover that I am dedicated to a new agitation,—I expect to become a very malevolent lunatic.

III

In an attic where I was locked up, at the age of twelve, I got to know the world; I illustrated the human comedy. In a pantry I learned history. At some nighttime party in a northern city, I met all the wives of the old painters. In an old arcade in Paris I was taught classical knowledge. In a magnificent residence encircled by the entire Orient I accomplished my immense work and spent my illustrious retirement. I stirred my blood. My duty has been remitted. I mustn't even think about it any more. I am really and truly beyond the grave, and have no errands to run.

Departure

Seen enough. The vision was met with in every atmosphere.
Had enough. Sounds of cities, in the evening, and in the sunshine, and always.
Known enough. The decrees of life.—O Sounds and Sights!
Departure in brand-new affection and noise!

Royauté

Un beau matin, chez un peuple fort doux, un homme et une femme superbes criaient sur la place publique. «Mes amis, je veux qu'elle soit reine!» «Je veux être reine!» Elle riait et tremblait. Il parlait aux amis de révélation, d'épreuve terminée. Ils se pâmaient l'un contre l'autre.

En effet ils furent rois toute une matinée où les tentures carminées se relevèrent sur les maisons, et toute l'après-midi, où ils s'avancèrent du côté des jardins de palmes.

À une raison

Un coup de ton doigt sur le tambour décharge tous les sons et commence la nouvelle harmonie.

Un pas de toi, c'est la levée des nouveaux hommes et leur en-marche.

Ta tête se détourne: le nouvel amour!

Ta tête se retourne, — le nouvel amour!

«Change nos lots, crible les fléaux, à commencer par le temps», te chantent ces enfants. «Élève n'importe où la substance de nos fortunes et de nos vœux» on t'en prie.

Arrivée de toujours, qui t'en iras partout.

Matinée d'ivresse

O *mon* Bien! O *mon* Beau! Fanfare atroce où je ne trébuche point! chevalet féerique! Hourra pour l'œuvre inouïe et pour le corps merveilleux, pour la première fois! Cela commença sous les rires des enfants, cela finira par eux. Ce poison va rester dans toutes nos veines même quand, la fanfare tournant, nous serons rendu à l'ancienne inharmonie. O maintenant, nous si digne de ces tortures! rassemblons fervemment cette promesse surhumaine faite à notre corps et à notre âme créés: cette promesse, cette démence! L'élégance, la science, la violence! On nous a promis d'enterrer dans l'ombre l'arbre du bien et du mal, de déporter les honnêtetés tyranniques, afin que nous amenions notre très pur amour. Cela commença par quelques dégoûts et cela finit, — ne pouvant nous saisir sur-le-champ de cette éternité, — cela finit par une débandade de parfums.

Royalty

One fine morning, among the people of a very gentle nation, a magnificent man and woman were calling out on the public square. "My friends, I want her to be queen!" "I want to be queen!" She was laughing and trembling. He was speaking to his friends about revelation, about a test that had been passed. They were swooning on each other.

Indeed, they were king and queen for one entire morning, during which carmine hangings were draped on the houses, and for all that afternoon, during which they proceeded in the direction of the gardens of palm trees.

To a Reason

One tap of your finger on the drum discharges all sounds and begins the new harmony.

One step that you take is a levy of new men and their march forward.

Your head turns aside: new love!

Your head turns back—new love!

"Change our lot, riddle the scourges, beginning with time," these children sing to you. "Raise to any level whatever the substance of our fortune and our wishes," people implore you.

Having arrived since the immemorial past, you shall depart for all places.

Morning of Intoxication

O *my* Good! O *my* Beautiful! Atrocious fanfare in which I don't stumble at all! Wondrous torture-rack! Hurrah for the unheard-of oeuvre and for the marvelous body, for the first time! It began to the sound of children's laughter, it will finish likewise. This poison will remain in all our veins even when the fanfare turns sour and we're sent back to the former disharmony. Oh, now, we so deserving of these tortures, let us fervently reassemble that superhuman promise given to our created body and soul: that promise, that madness! elegance, science, violence! A promise was given to us to bury in the shade the tree of good and evil, to deport all tyrannical respectability, so that we could carry on our very pure love. It began with a few unpleasant things and it finished—since we couldn't immediately lay hold of that eternity—with a general rout of fragrances.

Rires des enfants, discrétion des esclaves, austérité des vierges, horreur des figures et des objets d'ici, sacrés soyez-vous par le souvenir de cette veille. Cela commençait par toute la rustrerie, voici que cela finit par des anges de flamme et de glace.

Petite veille d'ivresse, sainte! quand ce ne serait que pour le masque dont tu nous as gratifié. Nous t'affirmons, méthode! Nous n'oublions pas que tu as glorifié hier chacun de nos âges. Nous avons foi au poison. Nous savons donner notre vie tout entière tous les jours.

Voici le temps des ASSASSINS.

Phrases

Quand le monde sera réduit en un seul bois noir pour nos quatre yeux étonnés, — en une plage pour deux enfants fidèles, — en une maison musicale pour notre claire sympathie, — je vous trouverai.

Qu'il n'y ait ici-bas qu'un vieillard seul, calme et beau, entouré d'un «luxe inouï», — et je suis à vos genoux.

Que j'aie réalisé tous vos souvenirs, — que je sois celle qui sait vous garrotter, — je vous étoufferai.

Quand nous sommes très forts, — qui recule? très gais, qui tombe de ridicule? Quand nous sommes très méchants, que ferait-on de nous?

Parez-vous, dansez, riez. — Je ne pourrai jamais envoyer l'Amour par la fenêtre.

— Ma camarade, mendiante, enfant monstre! comme ça t'est égal, ces malheureuses et ces manœuvres, et mes embarras. Attache-toi à nous avec ta voix impossible, ta voix! unique flatteur de ce vil désespoir.

[Fragments]

Une matinée couverte, en Juillet. Un goût de cendres vole dans l'air; — une odeur de bois suant dans l'âtre, — les fleurs rouies, — le

Children's laughter, slaves' discretion, virgins' austerity, abhorrence of the faces and objects here, may you be hallowed by the memory of this vigil! It began with total boorishness; here it is, finishing with angels of flame and ice.

Brief wakeful period of intoxication, you are holy, if only for the mask you bestowed on us. We affirm you, method! We don't forget that yesterday you glorified each one of our ages. We have faith in the poison. We know how to give our entire life every day.

Here is the time of the ASSASSINS.[29]

Sentences

When the world has shrunk to a single black forest in front of our four astonished eyes—to a beach for two faithful children—to a musical house for our clear mutual attraction—I shall find you.

Let there be here on earth only a single old man, calm and handsome, surrounded by "unheard-of luxury"—and I am at your feet.

Let me have fulfilled all your memories,—let me be the woman who is able to bind you firmly,—I shall smother you.

When we're very strong,—who recoils? Very cheerful, who collapses from ridicule? When we're very wicked, what would they do to us?

Adorn yourself, dance, laugh.—I'll never be able to chase Love out the window.

—My girl friend, beggar, monstrous child! How little you care about these unfortunate women and these manual laborers,[30] and my difficulties. Join yourself to us with your impossible voice, your voice, the sole deluder of this base despair.

[Fragments]

An overcast morning, in July. A taste of ashes flies in the air;—a smell of wood exuding sap in the hearth,—steeped flowers,—the plunder of

---

29. In its etymological sense of "takers of hashish." The historical assassins (Middle East, ca. 1100 A.D.) committed political murders under the influence of the drug.
30. Or: "maneuvers."

saccage des promenades, — la bruine des canaux par les champs —
pourquoi pas déjà les joujoux et l'encens?

———————

J'ai tendu des cordes de clocher à clocher; des guirlandes de fenêtre
à fenêtre; des chaînes d'or d'étoile à étoile, et je danse.

———————

Le haut étang fume continuellement. Quelle sorcière va se
dresser sur le couchant blanc? Quelles violettes frondaisons vont
descendre?

———————

Pendant que les fonds publics s'écoulent en fêtes de fraternité, il
sonne une cloche de feu rose dans les nuages.

———————

Avivant un agréable goût d'encre de Chine, une poudre noire pleut
doucement sur ma veillée. — Je baisse les feux du lustre, je me jette
sur le lit, et, tourné du côté de l'ombre, je vous vois, mes filles! mes
reines!

Ouvriers

O cette chaude matinée de février. Le Sud inopportun vint relever nos
souvenirs d'indigents absurdes, notre jeune misère.

Henrika avait une jupe de coton à carreau blanc et brun, qui a dû
être portée au siècle dernier, un bonnet à rubans, et un foulard de
soie. C'était bien plus triste qu'un deuil. Nous faisions un tour dans la
banlieue. Le temps était couvert, et ce vent du Sud excitait toutes les
vilaines odeurs des jardins ravagés et des prés desséchés.

Cela ne devait pas fatiguer ma femme au même point que moi.
Dans une flache laissée par l'inondation du mois précédent à un sen-
tier assez haut elle me fit remarquer de très petits poissons.

La ville, avec sa fumée et ses bruits de métiers, nous suivait très
loin dans les chemins. O l'autre monde, l'habitation bénie par le ciel
et les ombrages! Le sud me rappelait les misérables incidents de mon
enfance, mes désespoirs d'été, l'horrible quantité de force et de sci-
ence que le sort a toujours éloignée de moi. Non! nous ne passerons
pas l'été dans cet avare pays où nous ne serons jamais que des or-
phelins fiancés. Je veux que ce bras durci ne traîne plus *une chère
image*.

promenades,—the drizzle of canals in the fields—why not toys and incense, as well?

I have stretched ropes from steeple to steeple; garlands from window to window; golden chains from star to star, and I'm dancing.

The pond in its lofty situation gives off vapor continually. What witch is going to hold herself erect against the white sunset? What violet foliage will descend?

While government stocks are being sold off in holidays of fraternity, a bell of pink fire rings in the clouds.

Heightening a pleasant taste of India ink, a black powder rains gently down on my wakeful evening.—I lower the chandelier flames, I throw myself on my bed, and, turned toward the darkness, I see you, my girls, my queens!

Workmen

Oh, that warm February morning! The inopportune south wind came and revived our memories of being absurd paupers, the poverty of our young days.

Henrika had on a cotton skirt with white and brown checks, which must have been worn last century, a ribboned bonnet, and a silk neckerchief. It was much sadder than a mourning outfit. We were taking a stroll on the edge of town. The sky was overcast, and that south wind brought out all the ugly smells of the ravaged gardens and the withered meadows.

That probably didn't tire out my woman as much as it did me. In a puddle left over from the flood of a month previously, in a rather high path, she called to my attention some very small fish.

The town, with its smoke and the noise of its artisans and tradesmen, followed us very far along our roads. Oh, the other world, the domicile blessed by heaven and the shade! The south wind was reminding me of the wretched happenings of my childhood, my summertime despair, the horrible quantity of strength and knowledge that fate has always kept distant from me. No! We won't spend the summer in this miserly land where we'll never be anything but engaged orphans. I no longer want this hardened arm to drag along *a beloved image.*

Les ponts

Des ciels gris de cristal. Un bizarre dessin de ponts, ceux-ci droits, ceux-là bombés, d'autres descendant ou obliquant en angles sur les premiers, et ces figures se renouvelant dans les autres circuits éclairés du canal, mais tous tellement longs et légers que les rives chargées de dômes s'abaissent et s'amoindrissent. Quelques-uns de ces ponts sont encore chargés de masures. D'autres soutiennent des mâts, des signaux, de frêles parapets. Des accords mineurs se croisent, et filent, des cordes montent des berges. On distingue une veste rouge, peut-être d'autres costumes et des instruments de musique. Sont-ce des airs populaires, des bouts de concerts seigneuriaux, des restants d'hymnes publics? L'eau est grise et bleue, large comme un bras de mer. — Un rayon blanc, tombant du haut du ciel, anéantit cette comédie.

Ville

Je suis un éphémère et point trop mécontent citoyen d'une métropole crue moderne parce que tout goût connu a été éludé dans les ameublements et l'extérieur des maisons aussi bien que dans le plan de la ville. Ici vous ne signaleriez les traces d'aucun monument de superstition. La morale et la langue sont réduites à leur plus simple expression, enfin! Ces millions de gens qui n'ont pas besoin de se connaître amènent si pareillement l'éducation, le métier et la vieillesse, que ce cours de vie doit être plusieurs fois moins long que ce qu'une statistique folle trouve pour les peuples du continent. Aussi comme, de ma fenêtre, je vois des spectres nouveaux roulant à travers l'épaisse et éternelle fumée de charbon, — notre ombre des bois, notre nuit d'été! — des Érinnyes nouvelles, devant mon cottage qui est ma patrie et tout mon cœur puisque tout ici ressemble à ceci, — la Mort sans pleurs, notre active fille et servante, et un Amour désespéré, et un joli Crime piaulant dans la boue de la rue.

The Bridges

Crystal-gray skies.[31] A bizarre pattern of bridges, some straight, others arched, others descending or jutting out at an angle to the first ones, and these figures repeated in the other illuminated paths around the canal, but all of the bridges so long and light that the dome-laden banks are lowered and diminished. A few of these bridges are still encumbered with shanties. Others support poles, signal posts, weak parapets. Minor chords cross, and pay out, ropes[32] rise from the embankments. One can make out a red jacket, perhaps other costumes, and musical instruments. Are those popular tunes, snippets of noblemen's concerts, remnants of civic hymns? The water is gray and blue, wide as an inlet of the sea.—A white sunbeam, falling from high in the sky, annihilates this comedy.

City

I am an ephemeral and not too discontented citizen of a metropolis considered modern because all known good taste has been evaded in the furnishings and exteriors of the houses, and also in the layout of the city. Here you couldn't find a trace of any monument to superstition. Morality and language are reduced to their simplest terms, at last! These millions of people, who have no need to make one another's acquaintance, conduct their upbringing, occupations, and old age so similarly that the course of their life must be several times shorter than that which mad statistics find to be true of the nations on the Continent. And so, how many new ghosts I see from my window rolling through the thick, eternal coal smoke,—our woodland shade, our summer night!—new Furies, in front of my cottage, which is my homeland and all my heart, since everything here resembles this,—Death without tears, our active daughter and servant, and a desperate Love, and a pretty Crime whimpering in the mud of the street.

---

31. The plural form *ciels* (as opposed to *cieux*) usually refers to skies in paintings, or to sky pieces, painted cloths that conceal the flies in theaters. 32. *Cordes* can also mean "string instruments" or "string music"; the sentence is full of such ambiguities.

Ornières

À droite l'aube d'été éveille les feuilles et les vapeurs et les bruits de ce coin du parc, et les talus de gauche tiennent dans leur ombre violette les mille rapides ornières de la route humide. Défilé de féeries. En effet: des chars chargés d'animaux de bois doré, de mâts et de toiles bariolées, au grand galop de vingt chevaux de cirque tachetés, et les enfants et les hommes sur leurs bêtes les plus étonnantes; — vingt véhicules, bossés, pavoisés et fleuris comme des carrosses anciens ou de contes, pleins d'enfants attifés pour une pastorale suburbaine. Même des cercueils sous leur dais de nuit dressant les panaches d'ébène, filant au trot des grandes juments bleues et noires.

Villes (II)

Ce sont des villes! C'est un peuple pour qui se sont montés ces Alleghanys et ces Libans de rêve! Des chalets de cristal et de bois qui se meuvent sur des rails et des poulies invisibles. Les vieux cratères ceints de colosses et de palmiers de cuivre rugissent mélodieusement dans les feux. Des fêtes amoureuses sonnent sur les canaux pendus derrière les chalets. La chasse des carillons crie dans les gorges. Des corporations de chanteurs géants accourent dans des vêtements et des oriflammes éclatants comme la lumière des cimes. Sur les plates-formes au milieu des gouffres les Rolands sonnent leur bravoure. Sur les passerelles de l'abîme et les toits des auberges l'ardeur du ciel pavoise les mâts. L'écroulement des apothéoses rejoint les champs des hauteurs où les centauresses séraphiques évoluent parmi les avalanches. Audessus du niveau des plus hautes crêtes une mer troublée par la naissance éternelle de Vénus, chargée de flottes orphéoniques et de la rumeur des perles et des conques précieuses, — la mer s'assombrit parfois avec des éclats mortels. Sur les versants des moissons de fleurs grandes comme nos armes et nos coupes, mugissent. Des cortèges de Mabs en robes rousses, opalines, montent des ravines. Là-haut, les pieds dans la cascade et les ronces, les cerfs tettent Diane. Les Bacchantes des banlieues sanglotent et la lune brûle et hurle. Vénus entre dans les cavernes des forgerons et des ermites. Des groupes de beffrois chantent les idées des peuples. Des châteaux bâtis en os sort la

Wagon Tracks

To the right, the summer dawn awakens the leaves, vapors, and sounds of this corner of the park, and the slopes to the left contain in their violet shade the thousand rapid tracks of the damp road. A fairyland parade. Indeed: wagons loaded with animals of gilded wood, poles and multicolored canvas, at the quick gallop of twenty spotted circus horses, and the children and men on their most amazing animals;—twenty vehicles, carved in relief, beflagged and beflowered like coaches of the olden days or those in fairy tales, filled with children all dolled up for some suburban shepherd's play. Even coffins, beneath their canopy of night, lifting ebony plumes, moving past at the trot of the big blue and black mares.

Cities (II)

These are cities! This is a nation for whom these dream Alleghenies and Lebanons were erected! Chalets of glass and wood which move on rails and invisible pulleys. The old craters surrounded by colossi and copper palm trees roar melodiously in the fire. Love feasts are heard on the canals hung behind the chalets. The hunt of the carillons shouts in throats.[33] Guilds of gigantic singers come running in garments and oriflammes as glaring as the light of the summits. On the platforms in the midst of the abysses, Rolands blow the horns of their bravery. On the footbridges over the precipice and the inn roofs, the heat of the sky beflags the poles. The crumbling of the apotheoses rejoins the fields on the heights where the seraphic female centaurs maneuver amid the avalanches. Above the level of the highest crests, a sea churned up by the eternal birth of Venus, laden with choral-society fleets and the sound of pearls and precious seashells,—the sea is darkened at times with mortal bursts. On the slopes, harvests of flowers, as big as our weapons and our goblets, bellow. Corteges of Mabs in russet and opaline gowns, rise from the torrents. Up there, their feet in the cascade and the brambles, the stags suckle Diana's breasts. The Bacchantes of the suburbs sob and the moon burns and howls. Venus enters the caverns of the blacksmiths and the hermits. Groups of belfries sing the ideas of the nations. From the castles built of bones issues the unknown music. All legends perform evolutions, and impulses[24] dash into

---

33. Or: "in ravines."   34. Or: "elks."

musique inconnue. Toutes les légendes évoluent et les élans se ruent dans les bourgs. Le paradis des orages s'effondre. Les sauvages dansent sans cesse la fête de la nuit. Et une heure je suis descendu dans le mouvement d'un boulevard de Bagdad où des compagnies ont chanté la joie du travail nouveau, sous une brise épaisse, circulant sans pouvoir éluder les fabuleux fantômes des monts où l'on a dû se retrouver.

Quels bons bras, quelle belle heure me rendront cette région d'où viennent mes sommeils et mes moindres mouvements?

Vagabonds

Pitoyable frère! Que d'atroces veillées je lui dus! «Je ne me saisissais pas fervemment de cette entreprise. Je m'étais joué de son infirmité. Par ma faute nous retournerions en exil, en esclavage.» Il me supposait un guignon et une innocence très bizarres, et il ajoutait des raisons inquiétantes.

Je répondais en ricanant à ce satanique docteur, et finissais par gagner la fenêtre. Je créais, par delà la campagne traversée par des bandes de musique rare, les fantômes du futur luxe nocturne.

Après cette distraction vaguement hygiénique, je m'étendais sur une paillasse. Et, presque chaque nuit, aussitôt endormi, le pauvre frère se levait, la bouche pourrie, les yeux arrachés, — tel qu'il se rêvait! — et me tirait dans la salle en hurlant son songe de chagrin idiot.

J'avais en effet, en toute sincérité d'esprit, pris l'engagement de le rendre à son état primitif de fils du soleil, — et nous errions, nourris du vin des cavernes et du biscuit de la route, moi pressé de trouver le lieu et la formule.

Villes (I)

L'Acropole officielle outre les conceptions de la barbarie moderne les plus colossales. Impossible d'exprimer le jour mat produit par le ciel immuablement gris, l'éclat impérial des bâtisses, et la neige éternelle du sol. On a reproduit dans un goût d'énormité singulier toutes les merveilles classiques de l'architecture. J'assiste à des expositions de peinture dans des locaux vingt fois plus vastes qu'Hampton-Court. Quelle peinture! Un Nabuchodonosor norwégien a fait construire les escaliers des ministères; les subalternes que j'ai pu voir sont déjà plus

the market towns. The paradise of storms collapses. The wild men ceaselessly dance the celebration of night. And, one hour, I descended into the bustle of a boulevard in Bagdad, where gatherings sang the joy of new labor, in a dense breeze, moving about without being able to avoid the fabulous phantoms of the mountains where they must have met one another.

What good arms, what lovely hour will restore to me that region from which my slumbers and my slightest motions come?

Vagabonds

Pitiable brother! How many awful sleepless nights I owed him! "I wasn't seizing upon our venture fervently. I had made game of his infirmity. On account of me we would return to exile, to slavery." He imagined I was very bizarrely unlucky and innocent, and he used to add troubling reasons.

I would reply to that satanic doctor with a nasty laugh, and I'd end up by reaching the window. Beyond the countryside crossed by bands of rare music I would create the phantoms of future nocturnal luxury.

After that vaguely hygienic distraction, I'd stretch out on a pallet. And, almost every night, as soon as I was asleep, my poor brother would get up, his mouth decayed, his eyes torn out—the way he dreamed himself to be!—and would pull me into the main room, howling his dream of idiotic sorrow.

In fact, in all sincerity of spirit, I had committed myself to restore him to his original state of son of the sun,—and we'd roam about, feeding on the wine of forest fountains and wayfarers' biscuit, I in a hurry to find the place and the formula.

Cities (I)

The official Acropolis carries to excess the most colossal conceptions of modern barbarism. Impossible to describe the dull light produced by the unchangeably gray sky, the imperial glare of the masonry, and the eternal snow on the ground. In a taste of unusual outrageousness, all the classical wonders of architecture have been reproduced. I attend exhibitions of paintings in locales twenty times vaster than Hampton Court. And what paintings! A Norwegian Nebuchadnezzar has had the staircases of the ministries built; the underlings I was able to catch

fiers que des Brahmas et j'ai tremblé à l'aspect de colosses des gardiens et officiers de constructions. Par le groupement des bâtiments en squares, cours et terrasses fermées, on a évincé les cochers. Les parcs représentent la nature primitive travaillée par un art superbe. Le haut quartier a des parties inexplicables: un bras de mer, sans bateaux, roule sa nappe de grésil bleu entre des quais chargés de candélabres géants. Un pont court conduit à une poterne immédiatement sous le dôme de la Sainte-Chapelle. Ce dôme est une armature d'acier artistique de quinze mille pieds de diamètre environ.

Sur quelques points des passerelles de cuivre, des plates-formes, des escaliers qui contournent les halles et les piliers, j'ai cru pouvoir juger la profondeur de la ville! C'est le prodige dont je n'ai pu me rendre compte: quels sont les niveaux des autres quartiers sur ou sous l'acropole? Pour l'étranger de notre temps la reconnaissance est impossible. Le quartier commerçant est un circus d'un seul style, avec galeries à arcades. On ne voit pas de boutiques. Mais la neige de la chaussée est écrasée; quelques nababs aussi rares que les promeneurs d'un matin de dimanche à Londres, se dirigent vers une diligence de diamants. Quelques divans de velours rouge: on sert des boissons polaires dont le prix varie de huit cents à huit mille roupies. À l'idée de chercher des théâtres sur ce circus, je me réponds que les boutiques doivent contenir des drames assez sombres. Je pense qu'il y a une police, mais la loi doit être tellement étrange, que je renonce à me faire une idée des aventuriers d'ici.

Le faubourg aussi élégant qu'une belle rue de Paris est favorisé d'un air de lumière. L'élément démocratique compte quelque cent âmes. Là encore les maisons ne se suivent pas; le faubourg se perd bizarrement dans la campagne, le «Comté» qui remplit l'occident éternel des forêts et des plantations prodigieuses où les gentilshommes sauvages chassent leurs chroniques sous la lumière qu'on a créée.

sight of are already prouder than Brahmas, and I trembled at the gigantic appearance of the watchmen and construction supervisors.[35] By grouping buildings in squares, courts, and closed terraces, they've squeezed out the coachmen. The parks represent pristine nature remodeled by superb skill. The high-lying[36] quarter has inexplicable parts: a boatless inlet of the sea rolls its sheet of blue granular ice between docks laden with gigantic candelabra. A short bridge leads to a postern directly below the dome of the Sainte-Chapelle. This dome is a framework of artistic steel about fifteen thousand feet in diameter.

By a few locales provided with copper footbridges, platforms, and staircases that wind around the covered markets and pillars, I thought I was able to estimate the depth of the city! It's the miracle that I haven't been able to take in mentally: at what level are the other neighborhoods above or below the acropolis? For the foreigner of our day and age, a complete reconnaissance is impossible. The business district is a "circus"[37] in a single style, with arcaded galleries. One sees no shops. But the snow on the roadway is trampled; a few nabobs, as rare as strollers on a Sunday morning in London, make their way toward a diamond coach. A few red-velvet divans: they serve polar drinks the price of which varies from eight hundred to eight thousand rupees. At the thought of looking for theaters along this circus, I reply to myself that the shops must contain dramas that are somber enough. I think that there's a police force, but the law must be so strange that I give up trying to imagine what the sharpers here must be like.

The suburb, as elegant as a fine street in Paris, is favored by an atmosphere of brightness. The democratic element adds up to a few hundred souls. There, too, the houses aren't in a row; the suburb blends bizarrely into the open countryside, the "county" that fills the eternal Occident with the prodigious forests and cultivated properties on which the unsociable country squires hunt for their news reports under artificial light.

---

35. Or, reading *à l'aspect des gardiens de colosses et officiers de constructions:* "at the appearance of the keepers of colossi and construction supervisors."   36. Or: "well-to-do."   37. A round group of buildings, or traffic circle, as in "Piccadilly Circus."

Veillées

I

C'est le repos éclairé, ni fièvre ni langueur, sur le lit ou sur le pré.
C'est l'ami ni ardent ni faible. L'ami.
C'est l'aimée ni tourmentante ni tourmentée. L'aimée.
L'air et le monde point cherchés. La vie.
— Était-ce donc ceci?
— Et le rêve fraîchit.

II

L'éclairage revient à l'arbre de bâtisse. Des deux extrémités de la salle, décors quelconques, des élévations harmoniques se joignent. La muraille en face du veilleur est une succession psychologique de coupes de frises, de bandes atmosphériques et d'accidences géologiques. — Rêve intense et rapide de groupes sentimentaux avec des êtres de tous les caractères parmi toutes les apparences.

III

Les lampes et les tapis de la veillée font le bruit des vagues, la nuit, le long de la coque et autour du steerage.
La mer de la veillée, telle que les seins d'Amélie.
Les tapisseries, jusqu'à mi-hauteur, des taillis de dentelle, teinte d'émeraude, où se jettent les tourterelles de la veillée.

La plaque du foyer noir, de réels soleils des grèves: ah! puits des magies; seule vue d'aurore, cette fois.

Evenings[38]

I

It's enlightened repose, neither fever nor languor, in bed or in the meadow.

It's a friend neither ardent nor weak. A friend.

It's the beloved woman neither tormenting nor tormented. The beloved woman.

The air and the world not sought for. Life.

—So it was this?

—And the dream becomes cooler.

II

Illumination returns to the masonry tree.[39] From the two ends of the room, commonplace decorations and harmonic elevations join together. The high wall facing the wakeful man is a psychological succession of cross-sections of friezes, atmospheric strata, and geological irregularities of terrain.—An intense, rapid dream of sentimental groups with beings of every possible nature amid every possible outward appearance.

III

The lamps and rugs of the wakeful evening make the sound of waves, at night, all along the hull and around the steerage.

The sea of the evening, like Amélie's breasts.

The tapestries, up to midheight, thickets of lace, dyed emerald, into which the turtledoves of the evening plunge.

The fireback of the black hearth, real suns on the shores: ah, wells of magic!—the only view of the dawn, this time.

38. *Veillée* most often refers to a social evening spent with neighbors in rural areas, but here it may mean a sleepless night, or "vigil." 39. One translator renders *arbre de bâtisse* as "king post." (*Bâtisse* can refer to either stone or frame construction.)

Mystique

Sur la pente du talus les anges tournent leurs robes de laine dans les herbages d'acier et d'émeraude.

Des prés de flammes bondissent jusqu'au sommet du mamelon. À gauche le terreau de l'arête est piétiné par tous les homicides et toutes les batailles, et tous les bruits désastreux filent leur courbe. Derrière l'arête de droite la ligne des orients, des progrès.

Et tandis que la bande en haut du tableau est formée de la rumeur tournante et bondissante des conques des mers et des huits humaines,

La douceur fleurie des étoiles et du ciel et du reste descend en face du talus comme un panier, contre notre face, et fait l'abîme fleurant et bleu là-dessous.

Aube

J'ai embrassé l'aube d'été.

Rien ne bougeait encore au front des palais. L'eau était morte. Les camps d'ombres ne quittaient pas la route du bois. J'ai marché, réveillant les haleines vives et tièdes, et les pierreries regardèrent, et les ailes se levèrent sans bruit.

La première entreprise fut, dans le sentier déjà empli de frais et blêmes éclats, une fleur qui me dit son nom.

Je ris au wasserfall blond qui s'échevela à travers les sapins: à la cime argentée je reconnus la déesse.

Alors je levai un à un les voiles. Dans l'allée, en agitant les bras. Par la plaine, où je l'ai dénoncée au coq. À la grand'ville elle fuyait parmi les clochers et les dômes, et courant comme un mendiant sur les quais de marbre, je la chassais.

En haut de la route, près d'un bois de lauriers, je l'ai entourée avec ses voiles amassés, et j'ai senti un peu son immense corps. L'aube et l'enfant tombèrent au bas du bois.

Au réveil il était midi.

Fleurs

D'un gradin d'or, — parmi les cordons de soie, les gazes grises, les velours verts et les disques de cristal qui noircissent comme du bronze

Mystical

On the incline of the embankment the angels turn their woolen robes in the steel and emerald grass.

Meadows of flames spring up to the summit of the rounded hill. At the left the mulch of the ridge is trodden by every murder and every battle, and all disastrous sounds spin out their curved path. Behind the right-hand ridge the line of sunrises, of progress.

And while the strip at the top of the picture is made up of the turning and springing noises of the shells of human seas and nights,

The flowery gentleness of the stars, the sky, and the rest descends opposite the embankment like a basket, against our face, and makes the abyss below fragrant and blue.

Dawn

I have kissed the summer dawn.

Nothing was stirring yet on the face of the palaces. The water was dead. The camps of shadow were not abandoning the forest road. I walked, awakening the vivid, warm exhalations, and the precious stones watched, and the wings arose noiselessly.

The first venture, on the path already filled with cool, pale bursts of light, was a flower that told me its name.

I laughed at the yellow *wasserfall*[40] that became disheveled through the firs: at the silvery peak I recognized the goddess.

Then I lifted the veils one by one. In the tree-lined lane, waving my arms. Across the plain, where I denounced her to the rooster. In the big city she was fleeing amid the steeples and domes, and, running like a beggar on the marble docks, I was pursuing her.

At the top of the road, near a laurel wood, I encircled her with her gathered veils, and I felt to some extent her immense body. The dawn and the child fell to the bottom of the woods.

Upon awakening, it was noon.

Flowers

From a golden tier—amid the silk cords, the gray gauzes, the green velvets, and the crystal disks that grow black like bronze in the sun—

---

40. German for "waterfall."

au soleil, — je vois la digitale s'ouvrir sur un tapis de filigranes d'argent, d'yeux et de chevelures.

Des pièces d'or jaune semées sur l'agate, des piliers d'acajou supportant un dôme d'émeraudes, des bouquets de satin blanc et de fines verges de rubis entourent la rose d'eau.

Tels qu'un dieu aux énormes yeux bleus et aux formes de neige, la mer et le ciel attirent aux terrasses de marbre la foule des jeunes et fortes roses.

Nocturne vulgaire

Un souffle ouvre des brèches opéradiques dans les cloisons, — brouille le pivotement des toits rongés, — disperse les limites des foyers, — éclipse les croisées. — Le long de la vigne, m'étant appuyé du pied à une gargouille, — je suis descendu dans ce carrosse dont l'époque est assez indiquée par les glaces convexes, les panneaux bombés et les sophas contournés. — Corbillard de mon sommeil, isolé, maison de berger de ma niaiserie, le véhicule vire sur le gazon de la grande route effacée; et dans un défaut en haut de la glace de droite tournoient les blêmes figures lunaires, feuilles, seins. — Un vert et un bleu très foncés envahissent l'image. Dételage aux environs d'une tache de gravier.

— Ici, va-t-on siffler pour l'orage, et les Sodomes, — et les Solymes, — et les bêtes féroces et les armées,

— (Postillon et bêtes de songe reprendront-ils sous les plus suffocantes futaies, pour m'enfoncer jusqu'aux yeux dans la source de soie),

— Et nous envoyer, fouettés à travers les eaux clapotantes et les boissons répandues, rouler sur l'aboi des dogues . . .

— Un souffle disperse les limites du foyer.

Marine

Les chars d'argent et de cuivre —
Les proues d'acier et d'argent —
Battent l'écume, —
Soulèvent les souches des ronces —

I see the foxglove opening on a carpet of silver filigree, eyes, and heads of hair.

Coins of yellow gold scattered on the agate, pillars of mahogany supporting a dome of emeralds, bouquets of white satin and slender ruby rods surround the water rose.

Like a god with enormous blue eyes and a shape of snow, the sea and the sky attract the crowd of strong young roses to the marble terraces.

Cheap Nocturne

A gust opens operatic[41] breaches in the partitions—jumbles the pivoting of the decayed roofs—disperses the frontiers of the hearths— eclipses the casements.—All along the vine, having leaned my foot against a waterspout—I descended into this carriage whose era is sufficiently indicated by its convex windows, rounded panels, and warped seats.—Hearse of my slumber, isolated, shepherd's hut of my foolishness, the vehicle veers on the turf of the obliterated highway; and in a blemish at the top of the right-hand window there's a whirling of pale lunar figures, leaves, breasts.—A very deep green and blue invade the image. The horses are unharnessed in the proximity of a blur of gravel.

—Here, will someone whistle for the storm, and the Sodoms—and the Salems—and the ferocious beasts and the armies,

—(Will the postilion and the dream beasts resume beneath the most stifling forests, in order to bury me up to the eyes in the silk fountain?)

—And send us, lashed through the lapping waters and the spilled drinks, rolling onto the barking of the mastiffs? . . .

—A gust disperses the frontiers of the hearth.

Seascape

The silver and copper chariots—
the steel and silver prows—
churn up the foam,—
raise up the bramble stumps—

41. The adjective may refer to the elaborate transformation scenes current in the operatic stagecraft of Rimbaud's day.

Les courants de la lande,
Et les ornières immenses du reflux,
Filent circulairement vers l'est,
Vers les piliers de la forêt, —
Vers les fûts de la jetée,
Dont l'angle est heurté par des
tourbillons de lumière.

Fête d'hiver

La cascade sonne derrière les huttes d'opéra-comique. Des girandoles prolongent, dans les vergers et les allées voisins du Méandre, — les verts et les rouges du couchant. Nymphes d'Horace coiffées au Premier Empire, — Rondes Sibériennes, Chinoises de Boucher.

Angoisse

Se peut-il qu'Elle me fasse pardonner les ambitions continuellement écrasées, — qu'une fin aisée répare les âges d'indigence, — qu'un jour de succès nous endorme sur la honte de notre inhabileté fatale.

(O palmes! diamant! — Amour, force! — plus haut que toutes joies et gloires! — de toutes façons, partout, — Démon, dieu, — Jeunesse de cet être-ci; moi!)

Que des accidents de féerie scientifique et des mouvements de fraternité sociale soient chéris comme restitution progressive de la franchise première? . . .

Mais la Vampire qui nous rend gentils commande que nous nous amusions avec ce qu'elle nous laisse, ou qu'autrement nous soyons plus drôles.

Rouler aux blessures, par l'air lassant et la mer; aux supplices, par le silence des eaux et de l'air meurtriers; aux tortures qui rient, dans leur silence atrocement houleux.

the currents of the moor,
and the immense tracks of the ebbtide,
proceed eastward in a circle,
toward the piles of the forest,—
toward the boles of the pier,
whose corner is jolted by
whirlwinds of light.

Winter Holiday

The waterfall roars behind the comic-opera cabins. Girandoles,[42] in the orchards and the tree-lined lanes near the Meander,—prolong the greens and reds of the sunset. Horatian nymphs with First Empire hairdos,—plump Siberian women, Chinese women right out of a Boucher painting.

Anguish

Is it possible that She will cause me to be forgiven for my constantly crushed ambitions?—That a well-to-do old age will make up for the eras of poverty?—That one day of success will numb our senses to the shame of our fatal incompetence? . . .

(O palms of victory! Diamond!—Love, strength!—higher than all joys and glories!—in every way, everywhere,—demon, god,—youth of this being; me!)

. . . That phenomena of scientific marvels and movements of social fraternity will be cherished as the progressive restitution of our original freedom? . . .

But the Vampire who makes nice people of us orders us to amuse ourselves with whatever she leaves us, or else to be more comical.

To roll in wounds, in the exhausting air and the sea; in tortures, in the silence of the murderous waters and air; in laughing torments, in their atrociously tempestuous silence.

---

42. This word could mean "chandeliers," "spinning fireworks," "clusters [of flowers or jewels]," or "[table] centerpieces."

Métropolitain

Du détroit d'indigo aux mers d'Ossian, sur le sable rose et orange qu'a lavé le ciel vineux viennent de monter et de se croiser des boulevards de cristal habités incontinent par de jeunes familles pauvres qui s'alimentent chez les fruitiers. Rien de riche. — La ville!

Du désert de bitume fuient droit en déroute avec les nappes de brumes échelonnées en bandes affreuses au ciel qui se recourbe, se recule et descend, formé de la plus sinistre fumée noire que puisse faire l'Océan en deuil, les casques, les roues, les barques, les croupes. — La bataille!

Lève la tête: ce pont de bois, arqué; les derniers potagers de Samarie; ces masques enluminés sous la lanterne fouettée par la nuit froide; l'ondine niaise à la robe bruyante, au bas de la rivière; les crânes lumineux dans les plants de pois — et les autres fantas-magories. — La campagne.

Des routes bordées de grilles et de murs, contenant à peine leurs bosquets, et les atroces fleurs qu'on appellerait cœurs et sœurs, Damas damnant de longueur, — possessions de féeriques aristocraties ultra-Rhénanes, Japonaises, Guaranies, propres encore à recevoir la musique des anciens — et il y a des auberges qui pour toujours n'ou-vrent déjà plus — il y a des princesses, et si tu n'es pas trop accablé, l'étude des astres — Le ciel.

Le matin où avec Elle, vous vous débattîtes parmi les éclats de neige, les lèvres vertes, les glaces, les drapeaux noirs et les rayons bleus, et les parfums pourpres du soleil des pôles, — ta force.

Barbare

Bien après les jours et les saisons, et les êtres et les pays,

Le pavillon en viande saignante sur la soie des mers et des fleurs arctiques; (elles n'existent pas.)

Remis des vieilles fanfares d'héroïsme — qui nous attaquent en-core le cœur et la tête — loin des anciens assassins —

Oh! Le pavillon en viande saignante sur la soie des mers et des fleurs arctiques: (elles n'existent pas.)

Metropolitan[43]

From the indigo straits to the seas of Ossian, on the pink and orange sand that has been washed by the wine-colored sky, there have just arisen and crossed one another crystal boulevards immediately peopled by impoverished young families who buy their food at the greengrocer's. Nothing rich.—The city!

From the asphalt desert there flee straight ahead in utter defeat— with the sheets of fog staggered in frightful horizontal bands against the curving, recoiling, and descending sky composed of the most sinister black smoke that the mourning-clad ocean can produce—helmets, wheels, boats, horses' rumps.—The battle!

Raise your head; this arched wooden bridge; the last kitchen gardens of Samaria; these highly colored masks beneath the streetlamp that is lashed by the cold night; the silly undine with a rustling dress, at the bottom of the stream; the luminous skulls in the sweetpea nursery—and the rest of the phantasmagoria.—The countryside.

Roads edged with iron gates and walls, scarcely holding in their clumps of trees, and the hideous flowers that could be called hearts and sisters, Damascus damning at length,—estates of fantastic aristocrats from across the Rhine, Japanese, Guarani, still suitable for receiving the music of the ancients—and there are inns which by now will never, ever open again—there are princesses, and if you're not too overwhelmed, the study of the heavenly bodies—the sky.

The morning on which, with Her, you struggled amid the bright bursts of snow, the green lips, the ice, the black flags and the blue beams, and the purple fragrance of the polar sun—your strength.

Barbarous

Long after the days and the seasons, and the beings and the countries,

The banner of bleeding meat on the silk of the seas and arctic flowers (they don't exist).

Recovered from the old heroic fanfares—which still attack our heart and head—far from the former assassins—

Oh, the banner of bleeding meat on the silk of the seas and arctic flowers (they don't exist)!

---

43. This title is often associated with the London Underground (*métro*; subway), but it probably just means "[pertaining to] the metropolis."

Douceurs!

Les brasiers, pleuvant aux rafales de givre, — Douceurs! — les feux à la pluie du vent de diamants jetée par le cœur terrestre éternellement carbonisé pour nous. — Ô monde! —

(Loin des vieilles retraites et des vieilles flammes, qu'on entend, qu'on sent,)

Les brasiers et les écumes. La musique, virement des gouffres et choc des glaçons aux astres.

Ô Douceurs, ô monde, ô musique! Et là, les formes, les sueurs, les chevelures et les yeux, flottant. Et les larmes blanches, bouillantes, — ô douceurs! — et la voix féminine arrivée au fond des volcans et des grottes arctiques.

Le pavillon . . .

Solde

À vendre ce que les Juifs n'ont pas vendu, ce que noblesse ni crime n'ont goûté, ce qu'ignorent l'amour maudit et la probité infernale des masses: ce que le temps ni la science n'ont pas à reconnaître:

Les Voix reconstituées; l'éveil fraternel de toutes les énergies chorales et orchestrales et leurs applications instantanées; l'occasion, unique, de dégager nos sens!

À vendre les Corps sans prix, hors de toute race, de tout monde, de tout sexe, de toute descendance! Les richesses jaillissant à chaque démarche! Solde de diamants sans contrôle!

À vendre l'anarchie pour les masses; la satisfaction irrépressible pour les amateurs supérieurs; la mort atroce pour les fidèles et les amants!

À vendre les habitations et les migrations, sports, féeries et comforts parfaits, et le bruit, le mouvement et l'avenir qu'ils font!

À vendre les applications de calcul et les sauts d'harmonie inouïs. Les trouvailles et les termes non soupçonnés, possession immédiate,

Élan insensé et infini aux splendeurs invisibles, aux délices insensibles, — et ses secrets affolants pour chaque vice — et sa gaîté effrayante pour la foule —

À vendre les Corps, les voix, l'immense opulence inquestionable, ce qu'on ne vendra jamais. Les vendeurs ne sont pas à bout

Gentleness!

The braziers, raining in the squalls of hoarfrost.—Gentleness!—The fires in the diamond-wind rain emitted by the terrestrial heart eternally burnt to a crisp for us.—O world!—

(Far from the old retreats and the old flames which can be heard, can be felt,)

The braziers and the foam. The music, a veering of abysses and a jolt of ice floes against the heavenly bodies.

O gentleness, O world, O music! And there, forms, sweat, heads of hair, and eyes, floating. And the white, boiling tears,—O gentleness!—and the woman's voice reaching the bottom of the volcanoes and arctic grottos.

The flag . . .

Clearance Sale

On sale: whatever the Jews didn't sell, whatever neither nobility nor crime has tasted, whatever is unknown to accursed love and the infernal honesty of the masses: whatever neither time nor science will acknowledge:

Reconstituted Voices; the fraternal awakening of all choral and orchestral energies and their immediate applications; the unique opportunity to unburden our senses!

On sale: the Bodies without price,[44] outside every notion of race, social milieu, sex, and ancestry! The wealth gushing from each step taken! An unchecked clearance sale of diamonds!

On sale: anarchy for the masses; irrepressible satisfaction for the higher class of dilettantes; a horrible death for faithful ones and lovers!

On sale: residences and migrations, sports, wonderlands and perfect creature comforts, and the noise, action, and future that they create!

On sale: applied calculus and unheard-of leaps of harmony. Discoveries and unsuspected terms—immediate possession!—

An insane, infinite impulse toward invisible splendors, toward impalpable delights,—and maddening secrets for every vice—and frightening jollity for the crowd—

On sale: the Bodies, the voices, immense unquestionable opulence, whatever will never be sold. The vendors haven't run out of clearance

---

44. *Sans prix* can have the two diametrically opposed meanings "priceless" or "worthless."

de solde! Les voyageurs n'ont pas à rendre leur commission de si tôt!

Fairy

Pour Hélène se conjurèrent les sèves ornamentales dans les ombres vierges et les clartés impassibles dans le silence astral. L'ardeur de l'été fut confiée à des oiseaux muets et l'indolence requise à une barque de deuils sans prix par des anses d'amours morts et de parfums affaissés.

— Après le moment de l'air des bûcheronnes à la rumeur du torrent sous la ruine des bois, de la sonnerie des bestiaux à l'écho des vals, et des cris des steppes. —

Pour l'enfance d'Hélène frissonnèrent les fourrures et les ombres — et le sein des pauvres, et les légendes du ciel.

Et ses yeux et sa danse supérieurs encore aux éclats précieux, aux influences froides, au plaisir du décor et de l'heure uniques.

Guerre

Enfant, certains ciels ont affiné mon optique: tous les caractères nuancèrent ma physionomie. Les Phénomènes s'émurent. — À présent, l'inflexion éternelle des moments et l'infini des mathématiques me chassent par ce monde où je subis tous les succès civils, respecté de l'enfance étrange et des affections énormes. — Je songe à une Guerre de droit ou de force, de logique bien imprévue.

C'est aussi simple qu'une phrase musicale.

Jeunesse

I: Dimanche

Les calculs de côté, l'inévitable descente du ciel et la visite des souvenirs et la séance des rythmes occupent la demeure, la tête et le monde de l'esprit.

— Un cheval détale sur le turf suburbain, et le long des cultures et des boisements, percé par la peste carbonique. Une misérable femme

items! The traveling salesmen don't have to hand over their accounts for a good while!

Fairy

For Helen the ornamental plant-saps conspired in the virgin shade and impassive patches of brightness amid astral silence. The summer heat was entrusted to mute birds, and requisite indolence to a mourning-boat without price on coves of dead loves and sagging aromas.

—After the moment of the aria of the woodcutters' wives to the sound of the rushing brook beneath the ruins of the forest; of the carillon of the cattle to the echo from the valleys; and of the shouts from the steppes.—

For Helen's childhood the furs and the shadows shuddered—as did the bosom of the poor, and the legends of the sky.

And her eyes and her dance, even superior to precious bursts of light, to cold influence, to the pleasure of the unique décor and hour.

War

In my childhood, certain skies sharpened my way of seeing: all characters introduced light and shade into my features. The Phenomena were stirred up.—At present, the eternal inflexion of the moments and the infinity of mathematics pursue me through this world, in which I experience every civic success, respected by strange children and enormous affections. —I dream of a War just or agressive, with a quite unforeseen logic.

It's as simple as a musical phrase.

Youth

I: Sunday

Calculations set aside, the inevitable descent of the sky and the visit from memories and the session of rhythms occupy the home, the head, and the world of the mind.

—A horse dashes off on the suburban racetrack, and all along the cultivated fields and the plantings of trees, a horse pierced by car-

de drame, quelque part dans le monde, soupire après des abandons
improbables. Les desperadoes languissent après l'orage, l'ivresse et
les blessures. De petits enfants étouffent des malédictions le long des
rivières. — Reprenons l'étude au bruit de l'œuvre dévorante qui se rassemble
et remonte dans les masses.

II: Sonnet

Homme de constitution ordinaire, la chair
n'était-elle pas un fruit pendu dans le verger; — ô
journées enfantes! — le corps un trésor à prodiguer; – ô
aimer, le péril ou la force de Psyché? La terre
avait des versants fertiles en princes et en artistes
et la descendance et la race vous poussaient aux
crimes et aux deuils: le monde votre fortune et votre
péril. Mais à présent, ce labeur comblé, — toi, tes calculs,
— toi, tes impatiences — ne sont plus que votre danse et
votre voix, non fixées et point forcées, quoique d'un double
événement d'invention et de succès + une raison,
— en l'humanité fraternelle et discrète par l'univers,
sans images; — la force et le droit réfléchissent la
danse et la voix à présent seulement appréciées.

III: Vingt ans

Les voix instructives exilées . . . L'ingénuité physique amèrement ras-
sise . . . — Adagio — Ah! l'égoïsme infini de l'adolescence, l'opti-
misme studieux: que le monde était plein de fleurs cet été! Les airs et
les formes mourant . . . — Un chœur, pour calmer l'impuissance et
l'absence! Un chœur de verres, de mélodies nocturnes . . . En effet les
nerfs vont vite chasser.

IV

Tu en es encore à la tentation d'Antoine. L'ébat du zèle écourté, les
tics d'orgueil puéril, l'affaissement et l'effroi.
Mais tu te mettras à ce travail: toutes les possibilités harmoniques
et architecturales s'émouvront autour de ton siège. Des êtres parfaits,

bonic plague. A wretched woman out of some melodrama, some-
where in the world, sighs for improbable unconstraints. The despera-
dos languish for storm, drunkenness, and wounds. Little children sti-
fle curses all along the streams.—

Let us resume our studies to the sound of the devouring work that
is gathering and rising up among the masses.

II: Sonnet

Man of ordinary constitution, wasn't
flesh a fruit hanging in the orchard?—O
days of childhood!—the body, a treasure to squander?—O
to love, the peril or strength of Psyche? The earth
had slopes fertile in princes and artists,
and your ancestry and race impelled you to
crimes and mourning: the world your fortune and your
peril. But now, that toil gratified,—you, your reckonings,
—you, your impatience—are no longer anything but your dance and
your voice, not fixed and not at all forced, though of a double
outcome of invention and success, as well as[45] a reason,
—in the fraternal and discreet humanity all over the universe,
without images;—strength and justice reflect the
dance and voice that are only now appreciated.

III: At Twenty

The instructive voices in exile . . . Physical artlessness bitterly sobered
. . .—Adagio—Ah, the infinite selfishness of adolescence, the studious
optimism: how full of flowers the world was that summer! The atmos-
phere and the shapes dying away . . .—A chorus, to calm impotence
and absence! A chorus of glasses, of nocturnal melodies . . . Indeed,
my nerves will soon become unstable.

IV

You're still at the stage of the temptation of St. Anthony. The curtailed
revel of zeal, the tics of childish pride, the sagging and the fright.

But you will apply yourself to this work: every harmonic and archi-
tectural possibility will be set in motion around your seat. Perfect, un-

---

45. Taking the "+" to stand for *et* or *plus*.

imprévus, s'offriront à tes expériences. Dans tes environs affluera rêveusement la curiosité d'anciennes foules et de luxes oisifs. Ta mémoire et tes sens ne seront que la nourriture de ton impulsion créatrice. Quant au monde, quand tu sortiras, que sera-t-il devenu? En tout cas, rien des apparences actuelles.

Promontoire

L'aube d'or et la soirée frissonnante trouvent notre brick en large en face de cette villa et de ses dépendances, qui forment un promontoire aussi étendu que l'Épire et le Péloponnèse, ou que la grande île du Japon, ou que l'Arabie! Des fanums qu'éclaire la rentrée des théories, d'immenses vues de la défense des côtes modernes; des dunes illustrées de chaudes fleurs et de bacchanales; de grands canaux de Carthage et des Embankments d'une Venise louche; de molles éruptions d'Etnas et des crevasses de fleurs et d'eaux des glaciers; des lavoirs entourés de peupliers d'Allemagne; des talus de parcs singuliers penchant des têtes d'Arbre du Japon; les façades circulaires des «Royal» ou des «Grand» de Scarbro' ou de Brooklyn; et leurs railways flanquent, creusent, surplombent les dispositions de cet Hôtel, choisies dans l'histoire des plus élégantes et des plus colossales constructions de l'Italie, de l'Amérique et de l'Asie, dont les fenêtres et les terrasses à présent pleines d'éclairages, de boissons et de brises riches, sont ouvertes à l'esprit des voyageurs et des nobles — qui permettent, aux heures du jour, à toutes les tarentelles des côtes, — et même aux ritournelles des vallées illustres de l'art, de décorer merveilleusement les façades du Palais-Promontoire.

Scènes

L'ancienne Comédie poursuit ses accords et divise ses Idylles:
Des boulevards de tréteaux.
Un long pier en bois d'un bout à l'autre d'un champ rocailleux où la foule barbare évolue sous les arbres dépouillés.
Dans des corridors de gaze noire suivant le pas des promeneurs aux lanternes et aux feuilles.

foreseen beings will offer themselves for your experiments. In your vicinity the curiosity of ancient crowds and of idle luxuries will throng. Your memory and your senses will be only the sustenance of your creative drive. As for the world, once you're out of it, what will become of it? In any case, nothing that is apparent at present.

Promontory

The golden dawn and the shivering evening find our brig on the open sea opposite that villa and its outbuildings, which form a promontory as extensive as Epirus and the Peloponnese, or as the main island of Japan, or as Arabia! Temples lit by the return of the religious processions, immense views of the defense of modern coasts; dunes illustrated by hot flowers and bacchanales; large canals of Carthage and embankments of some disreputable Venice; soft eruptions of Etnas and crevasses of flowers and runoff from glaciers; washhouses surrounded by German poplars; slopes of singular parks bending heads of the Japan tree; the circular facades of Royal or Grand Hotels of Scarborough or Brooklyn; and their railways flank, dig through, and overhang the design of that hotel, a design selected from the history of the most elegant and colossal edifices of Italy, America, and Asia, its windows and terraces, now full of light fixtures, beverages, and rich breezes, open to the spirit of travelers and noblemen—who permit the hours of the day, all the tarantellas of the coasts—and even the ritornellos of the famous valleys of art, to decorate wondrously the facades of the Promontory Palace.[46]

Theatrical Scenes

The Old Comedy pursues its harmonies and divides up its idylls:
    Boulevards of makeshift stages.
    A long wooden pier from one end to another of a stony field in which the barbarous crowd maneuvers beneath the bare trees.
    In corridors of black gauze following the footsteps of strollers with lanterns and leaves.

---

46. In some French editions, the punctuation at the end is: . . . *du Palais. Promontoire*. Thus, the translation would have to be: ". . . of the Palace. Promontory."

Des oiseaux des mystères s'abattent sur un ponton de maçonnerie mû par l'archipel couvert des embarcations des spectateurs.

Des scènes lyriques accompagnées de flûte et de tambour s'inclinent dans des réduits ménagés sous les plafonds, autour des salons de clubs modernes ou des salles de l'Orient ancien.

La féerie manœuvre au sommet d'un amphithéâtre couronné par les taillis, — ou s'agite et module pour les Béotiens, dans l'ombre des futaies mouvantes sur l'arête des cultures.

L'opéra-comique se divise sur une scène à l'arête d'intersection de dix cloisons dressées de la galerie aux feux.

Soir historique

En quelque soir, par exemple, que se trouve le touriste naïf, retiré de nos horreurs économiques, la main d'un maître anime le clavecin des prés; on joue aux cartes au fond de l'étang, miroir évocateur des reines et des mignonnes, on a les saintes, les voiles, et les fils d'harmonie, et les chromatismes légendaires, sur le couchant.

Il frissonne au passage des chasses et des hordes. La comédie goûte sur les tréteaux de gazon. Et l'embarras des pauvres et des faibles sur ces plans stupides!

À sa vision esclave, — l'Allemagne s'échafaude vers des lunes; les déserts tartares s'éclairent — les révoltes anciennes grouillent dans le centre du Céleste Empire; par les escaliers et les fauteuils de rois, un petit monde blême et plat, Afrique et Occidents, va s'édifier. Puis un ballet de mers et de nuits connues, une chimie sans valeur, et des mélodies impossibles.

La même magie bourgeoise à tous les points où la malle nous déposera! Le plus élémentaire physicien sent qu'il n'est plus possible de se soumettre à cette atmosphère personnelle, brume de remords physiques, dont la constatation est déjà une affliction.

Non! — Le moment de l'étuve, des mers enlevées, des embrasements souterrains, de la planète emportée, et des exterminations conséquentes, certitudes si peu malignement indiquées dans la Bible et par les Nornes et qu'il sera donné à l'être sérieux de surveiller. — Cependant ce ne sera point un effet de légende!

Birds from mystery plays[47] swoop down onto a masonry pontoon moved by the archipelago covered with the boats of the spectators.

Lyric scenes accompanied by flute and drum are set at an angle into nooks hollowed out below the ceilings, around parlors of modern clubs or rooms from the ancient Orient.

The fairy play maneuvers at the summit of an amphitheater wreathed by thickets,—or fidgets and modulates for the Boeotians, in the shade of forests moving on the ridge of cultivated fields.

The comic opera is divided up on a stage at the angle of intersection of ten partitions mounted from the balcony to the footlights.

Historic Evening

On whatever evening, for example, that you'll find the naïve tourist, withdrawn from our economic horrors, the hand of a master enlivens the harpsichord of the meadows; there's a card game at the bottom of the pond, a mirror evoking queens and female favorites; you have the female saints, the veils,[48] and the sons[49] of harmony, and the legendary color schemes, against the sunset.

He shivers as the hunts and the hordes pass by. The comedy picnics[50] on the makeshift stage of turf. And the difficulties[51] of the poor and weak on these stupid planes!

To his enslaved sight,—Germany piles up toward moons; Tartar deserts are illuminated—ancient rebellions teem in the center of the Celestial Empire; on the staircases and armchairs of kings, a little world, pale and insipid, Africa and Occidents, will be constructed. Then a ballet of known seas and nights, a valueless chemistry, and impossible melodies.

The same middle-class magic at every spot where the mail coach sets us down! The most rudimentary natural philosopher feels that it's no longer possible to submit to this personal atmosphere, a fog of physical remorse, to acknowledge which is already an affliction.

No! The moment of the sweat bath, of unleashed seas, of underground conflagrations, of the frenzied planet, and of the subsequent exterminations, certitudes indicated with so little cleverness in the Bible and by the Norns, and which it will fall to the lot of the serious creature to observe.—And yet the result won't be a matter of legend!

---

47. Some texts read *comédiens* ("[who are] actors") instead of *des mystères.*   48. Or: "sails."   49. Or: "threads."   50. Or, reading *goutte* instead of *goûte*: "drips."   51. Or: "plethora."

Bottom

La réalité étant trop épineuse pour mon grand caractère, — je me trouvai néanmoins chez ma dame, en gros oiseau gris bleu s'essorant vers les moulures du plafond et traînant l'aile dans les ombres de la soirée.

Je fus, au pied du baldaquin supportant ses bijoux adorés et ses chefs-d'œuvre physiques, un gros ours aux gencives violettes et au poil chenu de chagrin, les yeux aux cristaux et aux argents des consoles.

Tout se fit ombre et aquarium ardent.

Au matin, — aube de juin batailleuse, — je courus aux champs, âne, claironnant et brandissant mon grief, jusqu'à ce que les Sabines de la banlieue vinrent se jeter à mon poitrail.

H

Toutes les monstruosités violent les gestes atroces d'Hortense. Sa solitude est la mécanique érotique, sa lassitude, la dynamique amoureuse. Sous la surveillance d'une enfance elle a été, à des époques nombreuses, l'ardente hygiène des races. Sa porte est ouverte à la misère. Là, la moralité des êtres actuels se décorpore en sa passion ou en son action. — O terrible frisson des amours novices, sur le sol sanglant et par l'hydrogène clarteux! trouvez Hortense.

Mouvement

Le mouvement de lacet sur la berge des chutes du fleuve,
Le gouffre à l'étambot,
La célérité de la rampe,
L'énorme passade du courant
Mènent par les lumières inouïes
Et la nouveauté chimique
Les voyageurs entourés des trombes du val
Et du strom.

❀   ❀   ❀

Bottom[52]

Reality being too thorny for my lofty character,—I nonetheless found myself at my lady's house, in the shape of a large blue-gray bird taking flight toward the moldings on the ceiling and dragging my wing in the evening shadows.

At the foot of the baldachin that supported her beloved jewels and her physical masterpieces, I was a big bear with violet gums and fur hoary with chagrin, my eyes upon the glass and silver of the pier tables.

Everything became darkness and a burning aquarium.

In the morning,—a belligerent June dawn—I ran to the fields, as a donkey, trumpeting and brandishing my grievance, until the Sabine women of the suburb came and threw themselves on my chest.

H[53]

All monstrosities violate Hortense's hideous gestures. Her solitude is erotic mechanics; her weariness is amorous dynamics. Under the watchful gaze of children she has been, in numerous eras, the ardent hygiene of the races. Her door is open to paupers. There, the code of morals of present-day beings loses its substance in her passive or active stance.—O terrible shudder of inexperienced love, on the bleeding earth and lit by hydrogen![54] Find Hortense.

Movement

The side-to-side rocking on the bank of the river-falls,
the abyss at the sternpost,
the speed of the gradient,
the enormous to-and-fro movement of the current
lead, through unheard-of light
and chemical novelties,
the travelers surrounded by the waterspouts of the valley
and of the strom.[55]

✾   ✾   ✾

---

52. The reference is to the character in *A Midsummer Night's Dream.*   53. Most commentators agree that H stands for *habitude*, the habit of masturbation. 54. Gaslight.   55. German for "current."

Ce sont les conquérants du monde
cherchant la fortune chimique personnelle;
Le sport et le comfort voyagent avec eux;
Ils emmènent l'éducation
Des races, des classes et des bêtes, sur ce Vaisseau.
Repos et vertige
À la lumière diluvienne,
Aux terribles soirs d'étude.

Car de la causerie parmi les appareils, — le sang, les fleurs, le feu, les
    bijoux —
Des comptes agités à ce bord fuyard,
— On voit, roulant comme une digue au-delà de la route hydraulique
    motrice,
Monstrueux, s'éclairant sans fin, — leur stock d'études; —
Eux chassés dans l'extase harmonique,
Et l'héroïsme de la découverte.

Aux accidents atmosphériques les plus surprenants
Un couple de jeunesse s'isole sur l'arche,
— Est-ce ancienne sauvagerie qu'on pardonne? —
Et chante et se poste.

Dévotion

À ma sœur Louise Vanaen de Voringhem: — Sa cornette bleue
tournée à la mer du Nord. — Pour les naufragés.

À ma sœur Léonie Aubois d'Ashby. Baou. — l'herbe d'été bour-
donnante et puante. — Pour la fièvre des mères et des enfants.

À Lulu, — démon — qui a conservé un goût pour les oratoires du
temps des Amies et de son éducation incomplète. Pour les hommes!
À madame°°°.

À l'adolescent que je fus. À ce saint vieillard, ermitage ou
mission.

À l'esprit des pauvres. Et à un très haut clergé.

Aussi bien à tout culte en telle place de culte mémoriale et parmi
tels événements qu'il faille se rendre, suivant les aspirations du mo-
ment ou bien notre propre vice sérieux.

They are the conquerors of the world
seeking personal chemical fortune;
sport and material comfort travel with them;
they are taking along the upbringing
of races, classes, and animals on this vessel.
Repose and dizziness
in the light of the flood,
in the terrible evenings of study.

For, from the conversation amid the apparatus—the blood, the flow-
ers, the fire, the jewels—
agitated accounts on this fugitive vessel,
—one can see, rolling like a dike beyond the propulsive hydraulic
route,
their stock of studies—monstrous, lighting itself endlessly;—
themselves driven out into harmonic ecstasy,
and the heroism of discovery.

Amid the most surprising atmospheric phenomena
a youthful pair isolate themselves on the ark,
—is it forgivable instinctive timidity?—
and sing and take their stand.

Devout Prayer

To my sister Louise Vanaen of Voringhem:—Her blue nun's coif
turned toward the sea of the North.—For the shipwrecked.

To my sister Léonie Aubois of Ashby. Baou.[56]—the humming and
stinking summer grass.—for the fever of mothers and children.

To Lulu—a demon—who has retained a taste for the oratories of
the days of the girl friends[57] and of her incomplete upbringing. For
the men! To Madame°°°.

To the adolescent I once was. To that holy old man, hermitage or
mission.

To the spirit of the poor. And to a very high clergy.

Also, to every form of worship, in whatever memorial place of worship
and amid whatever events, which it is necessary to yield to, in accordance
with the aspirations of the moment or else our own serious vice.

---

56. Essentially meaningless? A dog's bark? A Malay word for "stink"? These are only
some of the conjectures.   57. Probably alludes to lesbians.

Ce soir à Circeto des hautes glaces, grasse comme le poisson, et enluminée comme les dix mois de la nuit rouge, — (son cœur ambre et spunk), — pour ma seule prière muette comme ces régions de nuit et précédant des bravoures plus violentes que ce chaos polaire.

À tout prix et avec tous les airs, même dans des voyages métaphysiques. — Mais plus *alors*.

Démocratie

«Le drapeau va au paysage immonde, et notre patois étouffe le tambour.

«Aux centres nous alimenterons la plus cynique prostitution. Nous massacrerons les révoltes logiques.

«Aux pays poivrés et détrempés! — au service des plus monstrueuses exploitations industrielles ou militaires.

«Au revoir ici, n'importe où. Conscrits du bon vouloir, nous aurons la philosophie féroce; ignorants pour la science, roués pour le confort; la crevaison pour le monde qui va. C'est la vraie marche. En avant, route!»

Génie

Il est l'affection et le présent puisqu'il a fait la maison ouverte à l'hiver écumeux et à la rumeur de l'été, lui qui a purifié les boissons et les aliments, lui qui est le charme des lieux fuyants et le délice surhumain des stations. Il est l'affection et l'avenir, la force et l'amour que nous, debout dans les rages et les ennuis, nous voyons passer dans le ciel de tempête et les drapeaux d'extase.

Il est l'amour, mesure parfaite et réinventée, raison merveilleuse et imprévue, et l'éternité: machine aimée des qualités fatales. Nous avons tous eu l'épouvante de sa concession et de la nôtre: ô jouissance de notre santé, élan de nos facultés, affection égoïste et passion pour lui, lui qui nous aime pour sa vie infinie . . .

Et nous nous le rappelons et il voyage . . . Et si l'Adoration s'en va, sonne, sa promesse sonne: «Arrière ces superstitions, ces an-

This evening, to Circeto of the tall mirrors, Circeto as fat as a fish and bedaubed like the ten months of the red night,—(her heart amber and spunk),[58]—for my sole prayer, as mute as those regions of night, and preceding bravuras more violent than this polar chaos.

At any price and with all airs, even in metaphysical journeys.—But more[59] *then.*

Democracy

"The flag travels to the unclean landscape, and our dialect drowns out the native drum.

"In the urban centers we shall foster the most cynical prostitution. We shall massacre logical rebellions.

"To the spice-growing, rain-sodden countries!—in the service of the most monstrous industrial or military exploitations.

"Good-bye here, no matter where we're bound. Conscripts of good will, we shall have a ferocious philosophy; ignorant when it comes to science, profligates when it comes to comfort; let the world as it is go and croak! That's true progress. Forward march!"

Guardian Spirit

He is affection and the present, because he opened the house to frothy winter and to the sounds of summer, he who purified the drink and food, he who is the charm of the fleeting locales and the super-human delight of the resting-places. He is affection and the future, the strength and love that we, erect amid the rage and the boredom, see passing by us in the stormy sky and the ecstatic flags.

He is love, a perfect, reinvented measure, a wonderful, unforeseen rationality, and eternity: a mechanism beloved by fated capacities. We have all felt the fright of his yielding and ours: O the enjoyment of our health, the energy of our faculties, selfish affection and passion for him, for him who loves us for the sake of his infinite life. . . .

And we remember him and he travels. . . . And if adoration departs, ring, his promise rings: "Away with these superstitions, these obsolete

---

58. Besides "tinder" and "mettle," *spunk* may also mean "sperm."   59. Or: "But no longer. . . ."

ciens corps, ces ménages et ces âges. C'est cette époque-ci qui a sombré!»

Il ne s'en ira pas, il ne redescendra pas d'un ciel, il n'accomplira pas la rédemption des colères de femmes et des gaîtés des hommes et de tout ce péché: car c'est fait, lui étant, et étant aimé.

O ses souffles, ses têtes, ses courses; la terrible célérité de la perfection des formes et de l'action.

O fécondité de l'esprit et immensité de l'univers!

Son corps! le dégagement rêvé, le brisement de la grâce croisée de violence nouvelle!

Sa vue, sa vue! tous les agenouillages anciens et les peines *relevés* à sa suite.

Son jour! l'abolition de toutes souffrances sonores et mouvantes dans la musique plus intense.

Son pas! les migrations plus énormes que les anciennes invasions.

O lui et nous! l'orgueil plus bienveillant que les charités perdues.

O monde! et le chant clair des malheurs nouveaux!

Il nous a connus tous et nous a tous aimés. Sachons, cette nuit d'hiver, de cap en cap, du pôle tumultueux au château, de la foule à la plage, de regards en regards, forces et sentiments las, le héler et le voir, et le renvoyer, et sous les marées et au haut des déserts de neige, suivre ses vues, ses souffles, son corps, son jour.

bodies, these couples, and these eras. It's the present epoch that has foundered!"

He won't depart, he won't descend again from some heaven, he won't bring about the redemption of women's anger and men's merriment and all of that sin: for it's already accomplished, since he exists and is loved.

Oh, his promptings, his facial expressions, his errands; the terrible swiftness of the perfection of forms and action!

O fecundity of mind and immensity of the universe!

His body! The dreamed-off disencumberment, the shattering of the grace that is interbred with new violence!

The sight of him, the sight of him! All ancient genuflections and sorrows relieved in his train.

His daylight! The abolition of all sounding and moving agonies in the most intense music.

His footstep! Migrations more enormous than the ancient invasions.

O he and we! Pride more benevolent than wasted charities.

O world! And the clear song of the new misfortunes!

He has known us all and loved us all. This winter night, from cape to cape, from the tumultuous pole to the castle, from the crowd to the beach, from gaze to gaze, our strength and feelings weary, let us strive to hail him and see him, and to send him back, and, beneath the tides and at the top of the snowy wildernesses, to follow his views, his promptings, his body, his daylight.

POÉSIES CHOISIES

Lés étrennes des orphelins

I

La chambre est pleine d'ombre; on entend vaguement
De deux enfants le triste et doux chuchotement.
Leur front se penche, encore alourdi par le rêve,
Sous le long rideau blanc qui tremble et se soulève . . .
— Au dehors les oiseaux se rapprochent frileux;
Leur aile s'engourdit sous le ton gris des cieux;
Et la nouvelle Année, à la suite brumeuse,
Laissant traîner les plis de sa robe neigeuse,
Sourit avec des pleurs, et chante en grelottant . . .

II

Or les petits enfants, sous le rideau flottant,
Parlent bas comme on fait dans une nuit obscure.
Ils écoutent, pensifs, comme un lointain murmure . . .
Ils tressaillent souvent à la claire voix d'or
Du timbre matinal, qui frappe et frappe encor
Son refrain métallique et son globe de verre . . .
— Puis, la chambre est glacée . . . on voit traîner à terre,
Épars autour des lits, des vêtements de deuil:
L'âpre bise d'hiver qui se lamente au seuil
Souffle dans le logis son haleine morose!
On sent, dans tout cela, qu'il manque quelque chose . . .
— Il n'est donc point de mère à ces petits enfants,
De mère au frais sourire, aux regards triomphants?
Elle a donc oublié, le soir, seule et penchée,
D'exciter une flamme à la cendre arrachée,

SELECTED POEMS IN VERSE

The Orphans' New Year Gifts

I

The room is filled with shadow; there is vaguely heard
the sad, soft whispering of two children.
Their heads are bowed, still made heavy by dreams,
under the long white bed curtain that trembles and rises. . . .
—Outdoors the chilly birds huddle together;
their wings are numb beneath the gray tone of the skies;
and the new year, with its misty retinue,
letting the folds of its snowy gown trail behind,
smiles amid tears, and sings while shivering. . . .

II

Now, the little children, beneath the waving curtain,
speak quietly as people do on a dark night.
They pensively listen to what seems to be a distant murmur. . . .
They often start at the clear golden voice
of the morning clock, which strikes and strikes again
its metallic refrain in its glass globe. . . .
—Besides, the room is cold . . . one sees lying on the floor,
scattered around the beds, mourning garments:
the harsh winter wind lamenting on the threshold
blows its gloomy gust into the dwelling!
In all this, one senses that something is missing. . . .
—Do these little children have no mother, then,
no mother with a bright smile and a triumphant gaze?
So then, she forgot, on the previous evening, alone and stooped,
to ignite a flame snatched from the ashes,

D'amonceler sur eux la laine et l'édredon
Avant de les quitter en leur criant: pardon.
Elle n'a point prévu la froideur matinale,
Ni bien fermé le seuil à la bise hivernale? . . .
— Le rêve maternel, c'est le tiède tapis,
C'est le nid cotonneux où les enfants tapis,
Comme de beaux oiseaux que balancent les branches,
Dorment leur doux sommeil plein de visions blanches! . . .
— Et là, — c'est comme un nid sans plumes, sans chaleur,
Où les petits ont froid, ne dorment pas, ont peur;
Un nid que doit avoir glacé la bise amère . . .

III

Votre cœur l'a compris: — ces enfants sont sans mère.
Plus de mère au logis! — et le père est bien loin! . . .
— Une vieille servante, alors, en a pris soin.
Les petits sont tout seuls en la maison glacée;
Orphelins de quatre ans, voilà qu'en leur pensée
S'éveille, par degrés, un souvenir riant . . .
C'est comme un chapelet qu'on égrène en priant:
— Ah! quel beau matin, que ce matin des étrennes!
Chacun, pendant la nuit, avait rêvé des siennes
Dans quelque songe étrange où l'on voyait joujoux,
Bonbons habillés d'or, étincelants bijoux,
Tourbillonner, danser une danse sonore,
Puis fuir sous les rideaux, puis reparaître encore!
On s'éveillait matin, on se levait joyeux,
La lèvre affriandée, en se frottant les yeux . . .
On allait, les cheveux emmêlés sur la tête,
Les yeux tout rayonnants, comme aux grands jours de fête,
Et les petits pieds nus effleurant le plancher,
Aux portes des parents tout doucement toucher . . .
On entrait! . . . Puis alors les souhaits . . . en chemise,
Les baisers répétés, et la gaîté permise!

IV

Ah! c'était si charmant, ces mots dits tant de fois!
— Mais comme il est changé, le logis d'autrefois:

to heap over them the wool and the eiderdown
before leaving them while calling to them: "Forgive!"
She failed to foresee the morning chill,
and didn't tightly shut the threshold against the winter wind? . . .
—The maternal dream is the warm cover,
the downy nest in which the snuggled children,
like beautiful birds rocked by the boughs,
sleep their sweet slumber filled with white visions! . . .
—And there—it's like a nest without feathers or warmth,
in which the little ones are cold, sleepless, afraid;
a nest which the bitter wind must have frozen. . . .

III

Your heart has understood:—these children are motherless.
No more mother at home!—and their father far, far away! . . .
—An old servant woman took care of them then.
The little ones are all alone in the frozen house;
four-year-old orphans, see how in their mind
a happy memory awakens little by little. . . .
It's like a rosary of beads told while praying:
—Ah, what a lovely morning, this morn of New Year's gifts!
Each one, during the night, had dreamt of his own
in some strange dream in which could be seen toys,
candies wrapped in gold, sparkling jewels,
whirling about, dancing a sonorous dance,
then fleeing beneath the curtains, only to reappear!
They used to wake up in the morning, get out of bed gleefully,
their lips allured, rubbing their eyes . . .
they would walk, their hair tousled on their heads,
their eyes brightly beaming, as on high holidays,
and their little bare feet grazing the floor,
to touch their parents' doors very gently . . .
they would go in! . . . After that, the holiday good wishes . . . in
        nightshirts,
the repeated kisses, and the freedom to make merry!

IV

Ah, they were so charming, those words so often spoken!
—But how their home has changed from what it used to be:

Un grand feu pétillait, clair, dans la cheminée,
Toute la vieille chambre était illuminée;
Et les reflets vermeils, sortis du grand foyer,
Sur les meubles vernis aimaient à tournoyer . . .
— L'armoire était sans clefs! . . . sans clefs, la grande armoire!
On regardait souvent sa porte brune et noire . . .
Sans clefs! . . . c'était étrange! . . . on rêvait bien des fois
Aux mystères dormant entre ses flancs de bois,
Et l'on croyait ouïr, au fond de la serrure
Béante, un bruit lointain, vague et joyeux murmure . . .
— La chambre des parents est bien vide, aujourd'hui:
Aucun reflet vermeil sous la porte n'a lui;
Il n'est point de parents, de foyer, de clefs prises:
Partant, point de baisers, point de douces surprises!
Oh! que le jour de l'an sera triste pour eux!
— Et, tout pensifs, tandis que de leurs grands yeux bleus,
Silencieusement tombe une larme amère,
Ils murmurent: «Quand donc reviendra notre mère?»

V

Maintenant, les petits sommeillent tristement:
Vous diriez, à les voir, qu'ils pleurent en dormant,
Tant leurs yeux sont gonflés et leur souffle pénible!
Les tout petits enfants ont le cœur si sensible!
— Mais l'ange des berceaux vient essuyer leurs yeux,
Et dans ce lourd sommeil met un rêve joyeux,
Un rêve si joyeux, que leur lèvre mi-close,
Souriante, semblait murmurer quelque chose . . .
— Ils rêvent que, penchés sur leur petit bras rond,
Doux geste du réveil, ils avancent le front,
Et leur vague regard tout autour d'eux se pose . . .
Ils se croient endormis dans un paradis rose . . .
Au foyer plein d'éclairs chante gaîment le feu . . .
Par la fenêtre on voit là-bas un beau ciel bleu;
La nature s'éveille et de rayons s'enivre . . .
La terre, demi-nue, heureuse de revivre,
A des frissons de joie aux baisers du soleil . . .
Et dans le vieux logis tout est tiède et vermeil:
Les sombres vêtements ne jonchent plus la terre,
La bise sous le seuil a fini par se taire . . .

a big, bright fire would crackle in the fireplace,
the old room was entirely illuminated;
and the vermilion reflections cast by the large hearth
liked to skip about on the polished furniture. . . .
—The armoire had no keys in it . . . no keys, the big armoire!
They often looked at its brown and black door. . . .
No keys! . . . How odd! . . . Many a time they dreamed
of the mysteries sleeping between its wooden sides,
and they thought they heard, behind the gaping
keyhole, a distant sound, a vague, joyous murmur. . . .
—Their parents' room is quite empty today:
no vermilion reflection has gleamed beneath the door;
there are no parents, no hearth, no taken keys:
therefore, no kisses, no sweet surprises!
Oh, how sad New Year's Day will be for them!
—And, quite pensive, while from their big blue eyes
a bitter tear silently falls,
they murmur: "But when will Mother come back?"

V

Now the little ones are sleeping sadly:
to see them, you'd say they were weeping as they slept,
their eyes are so swollen and their breathing so heavy!
Very young children have such a sensitive heart!
—But the angel of cradles comes to wipe their eyes,
and in that heavy sleep gives them a happy dream,
a dream so happy that their parted lips
smile and seem to murmur something. . . .
—They dream that, leaning on their little plump arms,
a sweet gesture of awakening, they thrust their heads forward,
and their confused eyes rest on everything around them. . . .
They think they're asleep in a pink paradise. . . .
In the hearth full of flashes the fire sings gaily. . . .
Out the window they see a bright blue sky yonder;
nature awakens and grows drunk on sunbeams . . .
the earth, seminude, glad to be revived,
shudders with joy at the sun's kisses . . .
and in the old house all is warm and vermilion:
the dark clothes are no longer scattered on the floor,
the wind under the threshold has finally fallen silent. . . .

On dirait qu'une fée a passé dans cela!...
— Les enfants, tout joyeux, ont jeté deux cris ... Là,
Près du lit maternel, sous un beau rayon rose,
Là, sur le grand tapis, resplendit quelque chose ...
Ce sont des médaillons argentés, noirs et blancs,
De la nacre et du jais aux reflets scintillants;
Des petits cadres noirs, des couronnes de verre,
Ayant trois mots gravés en or: «À NOTRE MÈRE!»

Sensation

Par les soirs bleus d'été, j'irai dans les sentiers,
Picoté par les blés, fouler l'herbe menue:
Rêveur, j'en sentirai la fraîcheur à mes pieds.
Je laisserai le vent baigner ma tête nue.

Je ne parlerai pas, je ne penserai rien:
Mais l'amour infini me montera dans l'âme,
Et j'irai loin, bien loin, comme un bohémien,
Par la Nature, — heureux comme avec une femme.

Soleil et chair

I

Le Soleil, le foyer de tendresse et de vie,
Verse l'amour brûlant à la terre ravie,
Et, quand on est couché sur la vallée, on sent
Que la terre est nubile et déborde de sang;
Que son immense sein, soulevé par un âme,
Est d'amour comme Dieu, de chair comme la femme,
Et qu'il renferme, gros de sève et de rayons,
Le grand fourmillement de tous les embryons!

Et tout croît, et tout monte!

                — O Vénus, ô Déesse!
Je regrette les temps de l'antique jeunesse,
Des satyres lascifs, des faunes animaux,

You'd say that a fairy had had a hand in it! . . .
—The children, very happy, have uttered two cries. . . . There,
near their mother's bed, in a beautiful pink sunbeam,
there, on the big carpet, something is shining . . .
it's silvery medallions, black and white,
with sparkling reflections of mother-of-pearl and jet;
little black frames, glass wreaths,[60]
with three words engraved in gold: "TO OUR MOTHER!"

Sensation

On the blue summer evenings, I shall walk down the paths,
pricked by the standing grain, treading the fine grass:
dreamily, I shall feel its coolness on my feet.
I shall let the wind bathe my bare head.

I won't speak, I shall have no thoughts:
but infinite love will well up in my soul,
and I shall go far, very far, like a Gypsy,
through Nature,—as happy as if I were with a woman.

Sun and Flesh

I

The sun, hearth of affections and life,
pours ardent love upon the ecstatic earth,
and, when you're lying in the valley, you sense
that the earth is nubile and is overflowing with blood;
that its vast bosom, heaving with soul,
is made of love, like God; of flesh, like woman;
and that, pregnant with sap and sunbeams, it contains
the mighty teeming of all embryos!

And everything grows, and everything rises!

                                        —O Venus, O goddess!
I long for the days of the youth of antiquity,
lascivious satyrs, beastlike Fauns,

___
60. Funeral wreaths made up of glass beads.

Dieux qui mordaient d'amour l'écorce des rameaux
Et dans les nénufars baisaient la Nymphe blonde!
Je regrette les temps où la sève du monde,
L'eau du fleuve, le sang rose des arbres verts
Dans les veines de Pan mettaient un univers!
Où le sol palpitait, vert, sous ses pieds de chèvre;
Où, baisant mollement le clair syrinx, sa lèvre
Modulait sous le ciel le grand hymne d'amour;
Où, debout sur la plaine, il entendait autour
Répondre à son appel la Nature vivante;
Où les arbres muets, berçant l'oiseau qui chante,
La terre berçant l'homme, et tout l'Océan bleu
Et tous les animaux aimaient, aimaient en Dieu!
Je regrette les temps de la grande Cybèle
Qu'on disait parcourir, gigantesquement belle,
Sur un grand char d'airain, les splendides cités;
Son double sein versait dans les immensités
Le pur ruissellement de la vie infinie.
L'Homme suçait, heureux, sa mamelle bénie,
Comme un petit enfant, jouant sur ses genoux.
— Parce qu'il était fort, l'Homme était chaste et doux.

Misère! Maintenant il dit: Je sais les choses,
Et va, les yeux fermés et les oreilles closes.
— Et pourtant, plus de dieux! plus de dieux! l'Homme est Roi,
L'Homme est Dieu! Mais l'Amour, voilà la grande Foi!
Oh! si l'homme puisait encore à ta mamelle,
Grande mère des dieux et des hommes, Cybèle;
S'il n'avait pas laissé l'immortelle Astarté
Qui jadis, émergeant dans l'immense clarté
Des flots bleus, fleur de chair que la vague parfume,
Montra son nombril rose où vint neiger l'écume,
Et fit chanter, Déesse aux grands yeux noirs vainqueurs,
Le rossignol aux bois et l'amour dans les cœurs!

II

Je crois en toi! Je crois en toi! Divine mère,

gods who, in love, bit the bark of boughs
and in the water lilies kissed the blonde nymph!
I long for the days when the world's sap,
the river waters, the pink blood of the green trees
put a universe in Pan's veins!
When the ground palpitated, green, beneath his goat's-feet;
when, softly kissing the clear reed flute, his lips
modulated the great hymn of love beneath the sky;
when, standing on the plain, he heard, all around,
living Nature answering his call;
when the mute trees, cradling the singing bird,
the earth cradling man, and all the blue ocean
and all the animals loved, loved in the name of God!
I long for the days of mighty Cybele,
who, titanically beautiful, was said to travel through
the resplendent cities on a great bronze chariot;
her two breasts poured into the vast spaces
the pure streaming of infinite life.
Man, happy, suckled at her blessed teat,
like a little child playing on her lap.
—Because he was strong, man was chaste and gentle.

Woe! Now he says: "I understand the world,"
and he goes about with closed eyes and deaf ears.
—And so,[61] no more gods! No more gods! Man is king,
man is God! But love, that's the great religion!
Oh, if man were only still nursing at your breast,
great mother of the gods and men, Cybele;
if he hadn't abandoned immortal Astarte,[62]
who once, emerging from the vast brightness
of the blue waters, a flower of flesh perfumed by the waves,
displayed her pink navel on which the foam snowed,
and, a goddess with great, dark, conquering eyes, made
the nightingale sing in the woods and love sing in our hearts!

II

I believe in you! I believe in you! Divine mother,

---

61. The sense seems to require a "therefore" rather than a "however." Perhaps *pourtant* should read *partant*.   62. This ancient Syrian goddess of love here stands in for the Greek Aphrodite and the Roman Venus, whose birth is described.

Aphrodité marine! — Oh! la route est amère
Depuis que l'autre Dieu nous attelle à sa croix;
Chair, Marbre, Fleur, Vénus, c'est en toi que je crois!
— Oui, l'Homme est triste et laid, triste sous le ciel vaste.
Il a des vêtements, parce qu'il n'est plus chaste,
Parce qu'il a sali son fier buste de dieu,
Et qu'il a rabougri, comme une idole au feu,
Son corps Olympien aux servitudes sales!
Oui, même après la mort, dans les squelettes pâles
Il veut vivre, insultant la première beauté!
— Et l'Idole où tu mis tant de virginité,
Où tu divinisas notre argile, la Femme,
Afin que l'Homme pût éclairer sa pauvre âme
Et monter lentement, dans un immense amour,
De la prison terrestre à la beauté du jour,
La Femme ne sait plus même être Courtisane!
— C'est une bonne farce! et le monde ricane
Au nom doux et sacré de la grande Vénus!

III

Si les temps revenaient, les temps qui sont venus!
— Car l'Homme a fini! l'Homme a joué tous les rôles!
Au grand jour, fatigué de briser des idoles
Il ressuscitera, libre de tous ses Dieux,
Et, comme il est du ciel, il scrutera les cieux!
L'idéal, la pensée invincible, éternelle,
Tout; le dieu qui vit, sous son argile charnelle,
Montera, montera, brûlera sous son front!
Et quand tu le verras sonder tout l'horizon,
Contempteur des vieux jougs, libre de toute crainte,
Tu viendras lui donner la Rédemption sainte!
— Splendide, radieuse, au sein des grandes mers
Tu surgiras, jetant sur le vaste Univers
L'Amour infini dans un infini sourire!
Le Monde vibrera comme une immense lyre
Dans le frémissement d'un immense baiser!

— Le Monde a soif d'amour: tu viendras l'apaiser.

sea-born Aphrodite!—Oh, our path has been bitter
ever since that other God harnessed us to his Cross;
Flesh, marble, flower, Venus, it's you I believe in!
—Yes, man is sad and ugly, sad beneath the immense sky.
He wears clothes because he is no longer chaste,
because he has sullied his proud godly portrait,
and because, like an idol in the fire, he has stunted
his Olympian body with filthy acts of servility!
Yes, even after death, he wishes to live
as a pale skeleton, insulting his primal beauty!
—And the idol in which you placed so much virginity,
in which you deified our clay—woman—
so that man could enlighten his poor soul
and slowly rise, in a vast love,
from his earthly prison into the beauty of daylight,
woman is no longer even capable of being a courtesan!
—What a rich joke! And the world snickers
at the sweet, sacred name of great Venus!

III

If only those bygone days could return!
For man is finished! Man has played every part!
On the great day, weary of breaking idols,
he shall come back to life, free of all his gods,
and, since he is from heaven, he shall scan the skies!
The ideal, the invincible, eternal thought,
everything; the living god, beneath his fleshly clay,
will rise, rise, will burn beneath his brow!
And when you see him fathom the whole horizon,
scornful of former yokes, free of all fear,
you will come and give him holy redemption!
—Resplendent, radiant, in the bosom of the great seas
you will arise, casting upon the immense universe
infinite love in an infinite smile!
The world will vibrate like a huge lyre
in the trembling of a vast kiss!

The world is thirsting for love: you will come and sate it.

O! L'Homme a relevé sa tête libre et fière!
Et le rayon soudain de la beauté première
Fait palpiter le dieu dans l'autel de la chair!
Heureux du bien présent, pâle du mal souffert,
L'Homme veut tout sonder, — et savoir! La Pensée,
La cavale longtemps, si longtemps oppressée
S'élance de son front! Elle saura Pourquoi! . . .
Qu'elle bondisse libre, et l'Homme aura la Foi!
— Pourquoi l'azur muet et l'espace insondable?
Pourquoi les astres d'or fourmillant comme un sable?
Si l'on montait toujours, que verrait-on là-haut?
Un Pasteur mène-t-il cet immense troupeau
De mondes cheminant dans l'horreur de l'espace?
Et tous ces mondes-là, que l'éther vaste embrasse,
Vibrent-ils aux accents d'une éternelle voix?
— Et l'Homme, peut-il voir? peut-il dire: Je crois?
La voix de la pensée est-elle plus qu'un rêve?
Si l'homme naît si tôt, si la vie est si brève,
D'où vient-il? Sombre-t-il dans l'Océan profond
Des Germes, des Fœtus, des Embryons, au fond
De l'immense Creuset d'où la Mère-Nature
Le ressuscitera, vivante créature,
Pour aimer dans la rose, et croître dans les blés? . . .

Nous ne pouvons savoir! — Nous sommes accablés
D'un manteau d'ignorance et d'étroites chimères!
Singes d'hommes tombés de la vulve des mères,
Notre pâle raison nous cache l'infini!
Nous voulons regarder: — le Doute nous punit!
Le doute, morne oiseau, nous frappe de son aile . . .
— Et l'horizon s'enfuit d'une fuite éternelle! . . .

Le grand ciel est ouvert! les mystères sont morts
Devant l'Homme, debout, qui croise ses bras forts
Dans l'immense splendeur de la riche nature!
Il chante . . . et le bois chante, et le fleuve murmure
Un chant plein de bonheur qui monte vers le jour! . . .
— C'est la Rédemption! c'est l'amour! c'est l'amour! . . .

Oh! Man has lifted his free, proud head![63]
And the sudden beam of primal beauty
makes the god quiver in the altar of the flesh!
Happy in his present good state, pale with the evil he suffered,
man wishes to fathom—and know—everything! Thought,
that mare long, so long oppressed,
darts forth from his brow! She shall find out Why! . . .
Let her bound freely, and man will have his faith!
—Why the mute azure and unfathomable space?
Why the golden heavenly bodies teeming like sand?
If you kept on ascending, what would you see up there?
Does some Shepherd conduct that huge flock
Of worlds moving through the awesome expanse of space?
And all those worlds, which the vast ether embraces,
do they vibrate to the tones of some eternal voice?
—And can man see? Can he say: "I believe"?
Is the voice of thought anything more than a dream?
If man is born so soon, if life is so short,
where does he come from? Does he sink in the deep ocean
of seeds, fetuses, embryos, to the bottom
of the vast crucible from which Mother Nature
will recall him to life, a living creature,
so he can love amid roses and grow in the wheatfield? . . .

We can't know this!—We are overwhelmed
by a mantle of ignorance and narrow chimeras!
Apes of men issuing from our mother's wombs,
our pallid power of reasoning hides infinity from us!
We wish to behold:—doubt punishes us!
Doubt, that dreary bird, strikes us with its wing . . .
—and the horizon flees in an eternal flight! . . .

The great sky is open! The mysteries are dead
in front of man, standing erect, who crosses his strong arms
in the immense splendor of rich Nature!
He sings . . . and the forest sings, and the river murmurs
a song filled with happiness that rises toward the daylight! . . .
—It is redemption! It is love! It is love! . . .

---

63. The last 36 lines of section III are not included in some editions.

IV

O splendeur de la chair! ô splendeur idéale!
O renouveau d'amour, aurore triomphale
Où, courbant à leurs pieds les Dieux et les Héros,
Kallipyge la blanche et le petit Éros
Effleureront, couverts de la neige des roses,
Les femmes et les fleurs sous leurs beaux pieds écloses!
— O grande Ariadné, qui jettes tes sanglots
Sur la rive, en voyant fuir là-bas sur les flots,
Blanche sous le soleil, la voile de Thésée,
O douce vierge enfant qu'une nuit a brisée,
Tais-toi! Sur son char d'or brodé de noirs raisins,
Lysios, promené dans les champs Phrygiens
Par les tigres lascifs et les panthères rousses,
Le long des fleuves bleus rougit les sombres mousses.
— Zeus, Taureau, sur son cou berce comme une enfant
Le corps nu d'Europé, qui jette son bras blanc
Au cou nerveux du Dieu frissonnant dans la vague.
Il tourne lentement vers elle son œil vague;
Elle, laisse traîner sa pâle joue en fleur
Au front de Zeus; ses yeux sont fermés; elle meurt
Dans un divin baiser, et le flot qui murmure
De son écume d'or fleurit sa chevelure.
— Entre le laurier-rose et le lotus jaseur
Glisse amoureusement le grand Cygne rêveur
Embrassant la Léda des blancheurs de son aile;
— Et tandis que Cypris passe, étrangement belle,
Et, cambrant les rondeurs splendides de ses reins,
Étale fièrement l'or de ses larges seins
Et son ventre neigeux brodé de mousse noire,
— Héraclès, le Dompteur, qui, comme d'une gloire
Fort, ceint son vaste corps de la peau du lion,
S'avance, front terrible et doux, à l'horizon!
Par la lune d'été vaguement éclairée,
Debout, nue, et rêvant dans sa pâleur dorée
Que tache le flot lourd de ses longs cheveux bleus,
Dans la clairière sombre, où la mousse s'étoile,

IV

O splendor of the flesh! O ideal of splendor!
O rebirth of love, triumphal dawn
on which, subjugating gods and heroes at their feet,
white Callipyge[64] and little Eros,
covered with a snow of roses, will graze
women and flowers with their beautiful blossoming feet!
—O great Ariadne, you who utter your sobs
on the shore, seeing Theseus' sail,
white in the sun, fleeing on the waters yonder,
O sweet virginal child whom one night shattered,
be still! On his golden chariot adorned with dark grapes
Lysios,[65] driven through the Phrygian fields
by lustful tigers and russet panthers,
is reddening the dark moss along the blue rivers.
—Zeus, as a bull, is cradling on his neck like a child
the nude body of Europa, who throws her white arm
around the sinewy neck of the god shivering in the waves.
He slowly turns toward her his hazy eyes;
she lets her pale, flowery cheek linger
on Zeus's brow; her eyes are shut; she is dying
in a divine kiss, and the murmuring waters
flower her hair with their golden foam.
—Between the rose laurel and the chattering lotus
the great dreaming swan glides amorously,
embracing Leda with the whiteness of his wing;
—And while Cypris[66] passes, strangely beautiful,
and, arching the splendid curves of her haunches,
proudly displays the gold of her broad breasts
and her snowy belly edged with black moss,
—Heracles, the Tamer, who, strong as if with glory,
girds his huge body with the lion's skin,
advances with terrifying and gentle brow to the horizon!
Hazily lit by the summer moon,
erect, nude, and dreaming in her gilded pallor
that is stained by the heavy flood of her long blue hair,
in the dark glade where the moss is starry,

---

64. An epithet of Aphrodite: "with beautiful buttocks."   65. An epithet of Dionysus (ostensibly "liberating").   66. Another epithet of Aphrodite, who was particularly worshipped in Cyprus.

La Dryade regarde au ciel silencieux . . .
— La blanche Séléné laisse flotter son voile,
Craintive, sur les pieds du bel Endymion,
Et lui jette un baiser dans un pâle rayon . . .
— La Source pleure au loin dans une longue extase . . .
C'est la nymphe qui rêve, un coude sur son vase,
Au beau jeune homme blanc que son onde a pressé.
— Une brise d'amour dans la nuit a passé,
Et, dans les bois sacrés, dans l'horreur des grands arbres,
Majestueusement debout, les sombres Marbres,
Les Dieux, au front desquels le Bouvreuil fait son nid,
— Les Dieux écoutent l'Homme et le Monde infini!

Ophélie

I

Sur l'onde calme et noire où dorment les étoiles
La blanche Ophélia flotte comme un grand lys,
Flotte très lentement, couchée en ses longs voiles . . .
— On entend dans les bois lointains des hallalis.

Voici plus de mille ans que la triste Ophélie
Passe, fantôme blanc, sur le long fleuve noir,
Voici plus de mille ans que sa douce folie
Murmure sa romance à la brise du soir.

Le vent baise ses seins et déploie en corolle
Ses grands voiles bercés mollement par les eaux;
Les saules frissonnants pleurent sur son épaule,
Sur son grand front rêveur s'inclinent les roseaux.

Les nénuphars froissés soupirent autour d'elle;
Elle éveille parfois, dans un aune qui dort,
Quelque nid, d'où s'échappe un petit frisson d'aile:
— Un chant mystérieux tombe des astres d'or.

II

O pâle Ophélia! belle comme la neige!
Oui tu mourus, enfant, par un fleuve emporté!

the dryad looks at the silent sky. . . .
—White Selene lets her veil float,
timid, over the feet of handsome Endymion,
and throws him a kiss in a pale moonbeam. . . .
—The fountain weeps in the distance in prolonged rapture . . .
it's the nymph dreaming, one elbow on her urn,
of the handsome, fair young man whom her waters pressed upon.
—A breeze of love has passed by in the night,
and, in the sacred woods, in the awful shade of the tall trees,
majestically erect, the dark marble figures,
the gods, on whose brow the bullfinch builds its nest,
—the gods listen to man and the infinite world!

Ophelia

I

On the calm dark waters where the stars sleep
white Ophelia floats like a great lily,
floats very slowly, recombent in her long veils. . . .
—You can hear huntsmen blowing the mort in distant forests.

It's over a thousand years now that sad Ophelia
has been passing like a white ghost on the long black river,
over a thousand years that her gentle madness
has been murmuring its ballad in the evening breeze.

The wind kisses her breasts and spreads in a corolla
her great veils softly rocked by the waters;
the trembling willows weep above her shoulder;
on her wide, dreaming brow the reeds bend down.

The water lilies she brushes against sigh around her;
she awakens at moments, in a sleeping alder,
some nest from which escapes a slight shudder of wings:
—a mysterious chant descends from the golden stars.

II

O pale Ophelia, beautiful as snow!
Yes, child, you died, swept away by a river!

C'est que les vents tombant des grand monts de Norwège
T'avaient parlé tout bas de l'âpre liberté;

C'est qu'un souffle, tordant ta grande chevelure,
À ton esprit rêveur portait d'étranges bruits;
Que ton cœur écoutait le chant de la Nature
Dans les plaintes de l'arbre et les soupirs des nuits;

C'est que la voix des mers folles, immense râle,
Brisait ton sein d'enfant, trop humain et trop doux;
C'est qu'un matin d'avril, un beau cavalier pâle,
Un pauvre fou, s'assit muet à tes genoux!

Ciel! Amour! Liberté! Quel rêve, ô pauvre Folle!
Tu te fondais à lui comme une neige au feu:
Tes grandes visions étranglaient ta parole
— Et l'Infini terrible effara ton œil bleu!

III

— Et le Poète dit qu'aux rayons des étoiles
Tu viens chercher, la nuit, les fleurs que tu cueillis;
Et qu'il a vu sur l'eau, couchée en ses longs voiles,
La blanche Ophélia flotter, comme un grand lys.

À la musique

Place de la Gare, à Charleville.

Sur la place taillée en mesquines pelouses,
Square où tout est correct, les arbres et les fleurs,
Tous les bourgeois poussifs qu'étranglent les chaleurs
Portent, les jeudis soirs, leurs bêtises jalouses.

— L'orchestre militaire, au milieu du jardin,
Balance ses schakos dans la Valse des fifres:
— Autour, aux premiers rangs, parade le gandin;
Le notaire pend à ses breloques à chiffres.

Des rentiers à lorgnons soulignent tous les couacs:
Les gros bureaux bouffis traînent leurs grosses dames

It's because the winds descending from the great mountains of Norway
had spoken to you very quietly of stern freedom;

it's because a gust, twisting your long hair,
brought strange sounds to your dreaming mind;
because your heart listened to the song of nature
in the tree's laments and the sighs of the nights;

it's because the voice of the mad seas, a huge death-rattle,
shattered your childlike bosom, too human and too gentle;
it's because, one April morning, a handsome, pale horseman,
a poor madman, sat down mutely at your feet!

Heaven! Love! Freedom! What a dream, O poor madwoman!
You melted in it like snow in fire:
Your lofty visions stifled your speech
—and awesome infinity frightened your blue eyes!

III

—And the poet tells that, in the beams from the stars,
you come at night to seek the flowers you gathered;
and that, on the waters he has seen, recumbent in her long veils,
white Ophelia floating, like a great lily.

To Music[67]

> *Railroad Station Square, Charleville.*

Onto the square that's divided into paltry lawns,
a square where everything's correct, trees and flowers,
all the short-winded bourgeois suffocated by the heat
bring their cherished follies on Thursday evenings.

—The military band, in the center of the garden,
moves its shakos to and fro in the "Pipers' Waltz":
—Around them, in the first rows, the dandies show off;
The notary hangs from his monogrammed watch charms.

The lorgnetted well-to-do dwell on each sour note:
the big, puffy bureaucrats drag along their large ladies,

---

67. Or: "To the Band."

Auprès desquelles vont, officieux cornacs,
Celles dont les volants ont des airs de réclames;

Sur les bancs verts, des clubs d'épiciers retraités
qui tisonnent le sable avec leur canne à pomme,
Fort sérieusement discutent les traités,
Puis prisent en argent, et reprennent: «En somme! . . .»

Épatant sur son banc les rondeurs de ses reins,
Un bourgeois à boutons clairs, bedaine flamande,
Savoure son onnaing d'où le tabac par brins
Déborde — vous savez, c'est de la contrebande; —

Le long des gazons verts ricanent les voyous;
Et, rendus amoureux par le chant des trombones,
Très naïfs, et fumant des roses, les pioupious
Caressent les bébés pour enjôler les bonnes . . .

— Moi, je suis, débraillé comme un étudiant,
Sous les marronniers verts les alertes fillettes:
Elles le savent bien; et tournent en riant,
Vers moi, leurs yeux tout pleins de choses indiscrètes.

Je ne dis pas un mot: je regarde toujours
La chair de leurs cous blancs brodés de mèches folles:
Je suis, sous le corsage et les frêles atours,
Le dos divin après la courbe des épaules.

J'ai bientôt déniché la bottine, le bas . . .
— Je reconstruis les corps, brûlé de belles fièvres.
Elles me trouvent drôle et se parlent tout bas . . .
— Et mes désirs brutaux s'accrochent à leurs lèvres . . .

Vénus anadyomène

Comme d'un cercueil vert en fer-blanc, une tête
De femme à cheveux bruns fortement pommadés
D'une vieille baignoire émerge, lente et bête,
Avec des déficits assez mal ravaudés;

beside whom, like officious elephant keepers, walk
the women whose flounces look like advertisements;[68]

on the green benches, clubs of retired grocers,
poking up the sand with their knobbed walking sticks,
discuss the trade agreements very earnestly,
then take snuff from silver boxes, and continue: "In short . . . !"

Flattening the roundness of his haunches on a bench,
a bourgeois with bright buttons and a Flemish paunch
enjoys his costly pipe from Onnaing,[69] from which the tobacco
shavings protrude—you know, it's contraband;—

All along the green grass plots, the young hoodlums snicker;
and, made amorous by the music of the trombones,
very naïve, and smoking cheap cigarettes,[70] the soldier boys
caress the babies to wheedle their nursemaids. . . .

—As for me, as slovenly as a student, I follow
the brisk little girls beneath the green chestnut trees:
they're well aware of it, and laughingly turn
toward me their eyes chockfull of indiscretions.

I don't say a word: I keep looking at
the flesh of their white necks, edged by escaping tresses:
beneath their bodice and their fragile finery, I follow
their divine backs below the curve of the shoulders.

Before long, I've detected their half-boots and stockings . . .
—I reconstruct their bodies, as I burn with lovely fevers.
They find me comical and whisper to one another . . .
—and my brutal desires get caught on their lips.[71] . . .

Venus Anadyomene[72]

As from a green tin coffin, the head
of a woman with heavily pomaded brown hair
emerges from an old bathtub, slowly and foolishly,
with defects quite poorly patched up;

---

68. The wives' female "companions."   69. Near Valenciennes in northern France.
70. Called *roses* because they were packaged in pink paper.   71. Another, sanitized,
version of the last line is: *Et je sens les baisers qui me viennent aux lèvres* ("and I feel
the kisses coming to my lips").   72. "Emerging [from the sea]" (Greek).

Puis le col gras et gris, les larges omoplates
Qui saillent; le dos court qui rentre et qui ressort;
Puis les rondeurs des reins semblent prendre l'essor;
La graisse sous la peau paraît en feuilles plates;

L'échine est un peu rouge, et le tout sent un goût
Horrible étrangement; on remarque surtout
Des singularités qu'il faut voir à la loupe . . .

Les reins portent deux mots gravés: Clara Venus;
— Et tout ce corps remue et tend sa large croupe
Belle hideusement d'un ulcère à l'anus.

Les effarés

Noirs dans la neige et dans la brume,
Au grand soupirail qui s'allume,
    Leurs culs en rond,

À genoux, cinq petits, — misère! —
Regardent le boulanger faire
    Le lourd pain blond . . .

Ils voient le fort bras blanc qui tourne
La pâte grise, et qui l'enfourne
    Dans un trou clair.

Ils écoutent le bon pain cuire.
Le boulanger au gras sourire
    Chante un vieil air.

Ils sont blottis, pas un ne bouge,
Au souffle du soupirail rouge,
    Chaud comme un sein.

Et quand pendant que minuit sonne,
Façonné, pétillant et jaune,
    On sort le pain;

Quand, sous les poutres enfumées,
Chantent les croûtes parfumées,
    Et les grillons;

then the fat gray neck, the wide shoulder blades
that protrude; the short back sinking in and out again;
then the curves of the haunches seem to take flight;
the fat below the skin shows up in flat layers;

the spine is a little red, and the ensemble has a taste
that's strangely horrifying; especially noticeable are
special features that must be studied with a magnifying glass. . . .

Her haunches bear two engraved words: "Clara[73] Venus";
—and the whole body quivers, extending its broad rump
hideously adorned by a sore on the anus.

The Awestruck Children

Dark in the snow and fog,
by the large, illuminated air vent,
    their behinds in a circle,

on their knees, five little ones—oh, misery!—
watch the baker making
    the heavy yellow bread. . . .

They see the strong white arm turning
the gray dough and thrusting it
    into a bright opening.

They listen to the good bread baking.
The baker with his broad smile
    sings an old song.

They're cowering (not one moves)
by the exhalation from the red vent,
    warm as a breast.

And when, at the stroke of midnight,
the bread is taken out,
    formed, crackling, and yellow;

when, beneath the smoke-darkened beams,
the aromatic crusts sing,
    and the crickets;

---

73. "Bright," or "illustrious" (Latin).

Quand ce trou chaud souffle la vie;
Ils ont leur âme si ravie
    Sous leurs haillons,

Ils se ressentent si bien vivre,
Les pauvres petits plein de givre,
    — Qu'ils sont là, tous,

Collant leurs petits museaux roses
Au grillage, chantant des choses
    Entre les trous,

Mais bien bas, — comme une prière . . .
Repliés vers cette lumière
    Du ciel rouvert,

— Si fort, qu'ils crèvent leur culotte,
  Et que leur lange blanc tremblote
    Au vent d'hiver . . .

Roman

I

On n'est pas sérieux, quand on a dix-sept ans.
— Un beau soir, foin des bocks et de la limonade,
Des cafés tapageurs aux lustres éclatants!
— On va sous les tilleuls verts de la promenade.

Les tilleuls sentent bon dans les bons soirs de juin!
L'air est parfois si doux, qu'on ferme la paupière;
Le vent chargé de bruits, — la ville n'est pas loin, —
A des parfums de vigne et des parfums de bière . . .

II

— Voilà qu'on aperçoit un tout petit chiffon
D'azur sombre, encadré d'une petite branche,
Piqué d'une mauvaise étoile, qui se fond
Avec de doux frissons, petite et toute blanche . . .

Nuit de juin! Dix-sept ans! — On se laisse griser.
La sève est du champagne et vous monte à la tête . . .

when that hot hole breathes life,
their soul is so enraptured
    beneath their rags,

they feel so much alive,
those poor little ones full of hoarfrost,
    that they all remain there

gluing their little pink snouts
to the grating, singing things
    between the holes,

but very quietly—like a prayer—
as they bend toward that light
    from reopened heaven

—so forcefully that they burst their trousers
—and their white underwear trembles
    in the winter wind. . . .

Romantic Novel

I

A boy isn't solemn at the age of seventeen.
—One fine evening, to hell with beer and lemonade,
and the noisy cafés with glaring chandeliers!
—He goes to the promenade, beneath the green lindens.

The lindens smell good on fine June evenings!
At times the air is so sweet, you close your eyes;
the breeze laden with sounds—the town isn't far—
carries aromas of vineyards and aromas of beer. . . .

II

—And there! You make out a tiny tatter
of dark azure, framed by a little branch,
studded by an evil star which melts
with sweet shudders, small and all white. . . .

June night! Seventeen!—You let yourself get tipsy.
The sap is champagne and goes to your head . . .

On divague; on se sent aux lèvres un baiser
Qui palpite là, comme une petite bête . . .

III

Le cœur fou Robinsonne à travers les romans,
— Lorsque, dans la clarté d'un pâle réverbère,
Passe une demoiselle aux petits airs charmants,
Sous l'ombre du faux-col effrayant de son père . . .

Et, comme elle vous trouve immensément naïf,
Tout en faisant trotter ses petites bottines,
Elle se tourne, alerte et d'un mouvement vif . . .
— Sur vos lèvres alors meurent les cavatines . . .

IV

Vous êtes amoureux. Loué jusqu'au mois d'août.
Vous êtes amoureux. — Vos sonnets La font rire.
Tous vos amis s'en vont, vous êtes mauvais goût.
— Puis l'adorée, un soir, a daigné vous écrire . . .!

— Ce soir-là, . . . — vous rentrez aux cafés éclatants,
Vos demandez des bocks ou de la limonade . . .
— On n'est pas sérieux, quand on a dix-sept ans
Et qu'on a des tilleuls verts sur la promenade.

Rêvé pour l'hiver

À °°° Elle.

L'hiver, nous irons dans un petit wagon rose
     Avec des coussins bleus.
Nous serons bien. Un nid de baisers fous repose
     Dans chaque coin moelleux.

Tu fermeras l'œil, pour ne point voir, par la glace,
     Grimacer les ombres des soirs,
Ces monstruosités hargneuses, populace
     De démons noirs et de loups noirs.

your mind wanders; on your lips you feel a kiss
which throbs there, like a little animal. . . .

III

Like Robinson Crusoe, your crazy heart explores romantic novels
—when, in the glow of a pale lamppost,
a young lady goes by, with charming little ways,
in the shadow of her father's frightening detachable collar . . .

and, since she finds you enormously naïve,
while making her little half-boots trot
she turns briskly, with an agile motion . . .
—then the romantic tunes die away on your lips. . . .

IV

You're in love. Rented until the month of August.
You're in love.—Your sonnets make *her* laugh.
All your friends shun you, you're out of fashion.
—Then, one evening, your beloved has deigned to write to you! . . .

—That evening . . . you return to the glaring cafés,
you order beers or lemonade . . .
—A boy isn't solemn at the age of seventeen,
when he has green lindens on the promenade.

Dreamed-of for the Winter

To °°° Her.

In the winter, we'll ride in a little pink railroad car
        with blue cushions.
We'll feel cozy. A nest of wild kisses reposes
        in every soft corner.

You'll close your eyes, so you can't look out the window and see
        the evening shadows grimacing,
those ill-tempered monstrosities, a populace
        of black demons and black wolves.

Puis tu te sentiras la joue égratignée . . .
Un petit baiser, comme une folle araignée,
    Te courra par le cou . . .

Et tu me diras: «Cherche!» en inclinant la tête,
— Et nous prendrons du temps à trouver cette bête
    — Qui voyage beaucoup . . .

Le dormeur du val

C'est un trou de verdure où chante une rivière
Accrochant follement aux herbes des haillons
D'argent; où le soleil, de la montagne fière,
Luit: c'est un petit val qui mousse de rayons.

Un soldat jeune, bouche ouverte, tête nue,
Et la nuque baignant dans le frais cresson bleu,
Dort; il est étendu dans l'herbe, sous la nue,
Pâle dans son lit vert où la lumière pleut.

Les pieds dans les glaïeuls, il dort. Souriant comme
Sourirait un enfant malade, il fait un somme:
Nature, berce-le chaudement: il a froid.

Les parfums ne font pas frissonner sa narine;
Il dort dans le soleil, la main sur sa poitrine
Tranquille. Il a deux trous rouges au côté droit.

Au Cabaret-Vert [cinq heures du soir]

Depuis huit jours, j'avais déchiré mes bottines
Aux cailloux des chemins. J'entrais à Charleroi.
— Au Cabaret-Vert: je demandai des tartines
De beurre et du jambon qui fût à moitié froid.

Bienheureux, j'allongeai les jambes sous la table
Verte: je contemplai les sujets très naïfs
De la tapisserie. — Et ce fut adorable,
Quand la fille aux tétons énormes, aux yeux vifs,

Then you'll feel your cheek scratched . . .
a little kiss, like a madcap spider,
　　　will run down your neck . . .

and, bending your head, you'll say to me: "Look for it!"
—And we'll take our time finding that creature
　　　—which is covering a lot of ground. . . .

The Sleeper in the Vale

There's a gap in the greenery, where a stream sings
as it madly leaves behind silvery tatters caught
on the grass; where the sun, from the proud mountain,
shines: it's a little vale frothing with sunbeams.

A young soldier, his mouth open, his head bare,
and his nape bathing in the cool blue cress,
is sleeping; he's stretched out in the grass, under the clouds,
pale in his green bed where light rains down.

His feat in the irises, he sleeps. Smiling as
a sick child would smile, he's taking a nap:
Nature, cradle him warmly: he's cold.

The fragrances don't make his nostrils quiver;
he sleeps in the sun, his hand on his tranquil
chest. He has two red holes in his right side.

At the "Green Tavern"[74] [five P.M.]

For a week I'd been ripping up my half-boots
on the pebbles of the roads. I was now entering Charleroi.
—At the Green Tavern: I ordered slices of bread
and butter, and ham that should be half cold.

Happily I stretched out my legs under the green
table: I studied the very naïve depictions
in the wallpaper.[75]—And it was delightful
when the barmaid with huge breasts and lively eyes—

---

74. There was a real Maison Verte in Charleroi (Belgium), the town to which
Rimbaud hiked in October 1870, looking for work.   75. Or" "tapestry."

— Celle-là, ce n'est pas un baiser qui l'épeure! —
Rieuse, m'apporta des tartines de beurre,
Du jambon tiède, dans un plat colorié,

Du jambon rose et blanc parfumé d'une gousse
D'ail, — et m'emplit la chope immense, avec sa mousse
Que dorait un rayon de soleil arriéré.

La maline

Dans la salle à manger brune, que parfumait
Une odeur de vernis et de fruits, à mon aise
Je ramassais un plat de je ne sais quel met
Belge, et je m'épatais dans mon immense chaise.

En mangeant, j'écoutais l'horloge, — heureux et coi.
La cuisine s'ouvrit avec une bouffée,
— Et la servante vint, je ne sais pas pourquoi,
Fichu moitié défait, malinement coiffée

Et, tout en promenant son petit doigt tremblant
Sur sa joue, un velours de pêche rose et blanc,
En faisant, de sa lèvre enfantine, une moue,

Elle arrangeait les plats, près de moi, pour m'aiser;
— Puis, comme ça, — bien sûr, pour avoir un baiser, —
Tout bas: «Sens donc, j'ai pris une froid sur la joue . . .»

Le buffet

C'est un large buffet sculpté; le chêne sombre,
Très vieux, a pris cet air si bon des vieilles gens;
Le buffet est ouvert, et verse dans son ombre
Comme un flot de vin vieux, des parfums engageants;

Tout plein, c'est un fouillis de vieilles vieilleries,
De linges odorants et jaunes, de chiffons
De femmes ou d'enfants, de dentelles flétries,
De fichus de grand-mère où sont peints des griffons;

— C'est là qu'on trouverait les médaillons, les mèches
De cheveux blancs ou blonds, les portraits, les fleurs sèches

a kiss wouldn't frighten *her*!—
laughingly brought me my bread and butter
and lukewarm ham on a brightly painted plate,

pink and white ham scened with a clove
of garlic,—and filled my enormous tankard, with its foam
gilded by a belated ray of sunshine.

The Sly Minx

In the brown dining room, which was scented
with the smell of furniture polish and fruit, at an easy pace
I was assembling a platter of some Belgian food
or other, sprawling in my enormous chair.

While eating—happy and calm—I listened to the clock.
The kitchen door opened with a smell of cooking
—and the maid arrived, I don't know why,
with her neckerchief half undone, with a cunning headdress,

and, while running her little trembling finger
over her cheek, a pink and white peach down,
and pouting with her childlike lip,

she cleared away the dishes near me to make things easier for me,
—then, out of nowhere—to get a kiss, I'm sure—she said
very low: "Listen, I've caught me a chill on the cheek." . . .

The Sideboard

It's a big carved sideboard; the dark oak,
very old, has taken on that very kind look old folks have;
the sideboard is open, and pours into its shadow,
like a stream of old wine, attractive aromas;

chockful, it's a rummage of old outworn things,
fragrant yellow linens, scraps of cloth
for women or children, faded lace,
Grandma's neckerchiefs with griffins painted on them;

—in it you could find lockets, locks
of white or blonde hair, portraits, dried flowers

Dont le parfum se mêle à des parfums de fruits.

— O buffet du vieux temps, tu sais bien des histoires,
Et tu voudrais conter tes contes, et tu bruis
Quand s'ouvrent lentement tes grandes portes noires.

Ma Bohème

(Fantaisie)

Je m'en allais, les poings dans mes poches crevées;
Mon paletot aussi devenait idéal:
J'allais sous le ciel, Muse! et j'étais ton féal;
Oh! là là! que d'amours splendides j'ai rêvées!

Mon unique culotte avait un large trou.
— Petit-Poucet rêveur, j'égrenais dans ma course
Des rimes. Mon auberge était à la Grande-Ourse.
— Mes étoiles au ciel avaient un doux frou-frou

Et je les écoutais, assis au bord des routes,
Ces bons soirs de septembre où je sentais des gouttes
De rosée à mon front, comme un vin de vigueur;

Où, rimant au milieu des ombres fantastiques,
Comme des lyres, je tirais les élastiques
De mes souliers blessés, un pied près de mon cœur!

Les corbeaux

Seigneur, quand froide est la prairie,
Quand dans les hameaux abattus,
Les longs angelus se sont tus . . .
Sur la nature défleurie
Faites s'abattre des grands cieux
Les chers corbeaux délicieux.

Armée étrange aux cris sévères,
Les vents froids attaquent vos nids!

whose aroma is mingled with aromas of fruit.

—O sideboard of bygone days, you know many a story,
and you'd like to tell your tales, and you creak
when your big black doors are slowly opened.

My Bohemia

(Fantasy)

I was departing, my fists in my ripped pockets;
my overcoat, too, was becoming merely a Platonic idea:
I was walking outdoors, Muse, and I was your liege man!
Oh, my, what marvelous love affairs I dreamed of!

My one and only pair of pants had a wide hole in them.
—A dreaming Tom Thumb, as I went I scattered
rhymes.[76] My inn was at the Sign of the Big Dipper.
—My stars in the sky rustled softly like satin

and I listened to them as I sat on the roadsides,
those fine September evenings, on which I felt drops
of dew on my forehead, like a bracing wine;

on which, rhyming amid the fantastic shadows,
I plucked, like lyres, the elastic sides
of my wounded shoes, one foot next to my heart!

The Crows

Lord, when the meadow is cold,
when in the downcast hamlets
the long Angeluses have fallen silent . . .
onto Nature, which has lost its blossom,
make the dear, delightful crows
swoop down from the broad heavens.

Strange army with harsh cries,
the cold winds attack your nests!

---

76. Perrault's Tom Thumb figure shares some traits with the Grimm Brothers'
Hänsel, and drops pebbles and crumbs to find his way home from the forest.

Vous, le long des fleuves jaunis,
Sur les routes aux vieux calvaires,
Sur les fossés et sur les trous
Dispersez-vous, ralliez-vous!

Par milliers, sur les champs de France,
Où dorment des morts d'avant-hier,
Tournoyez, n'est-ce pas, l'hiver,
Pour que chaque passant repense!
Sois donc le crieur du devoir,
O notre funèbre oiseau noir!

Mais, saints du ciel, en haut du chêne,
Mât perdu dans le soir charmé,
Laissez les fauvettes de mai
Pour ceux qu'au fond du bois enchaîne,
Dans l'herbe d'où l'on ne peut fuir,
La défaite sans avenir.

Les assis

Noirs de loupes, grêlés, les yeux cerclés de bagues
Vertes, leurs doigts boulus crispés à leurs fémurs,
Le sinciput plaqué de hargnosités vagues
Comme les floraisons lépreuses des vieux murs;

Ils ont greffé dans des amours épileptiques
Leur fantasque ossature aux grands squelettes noirs
De leurs chaises; leurs pieds aux barreaux rachitiques
S'entrelacent pour les matins et pour les soirs!

Ces vieillards ont toujours fait tresse avec leurs sièges,
Sentant les soleils vifs percaliser leur peau
Ou, les yeux à la vitre où se fanent les neiges,
Tremblant du tremblement douloureux du crapaud.

Et les Sièges leur ont des bontés: culottée
De brun, la paille cède aux angles de leurs reins;
L'âme des vieux soleils s'allume, emmaillotée
Dans ces tresses d'épis où fermentaient les grains.

Et les Assis, genoux aux dents, verts pianistes,
Les dix doigts sous leur siège aux rumeurs de tambour,

You, along the yellowed rivers,
on the roads with old Stations of the Cross,
on the ditches and on the hollows,
disperse and rally!

By the thousands, on the fields of France,
where those who died the other day sleep,
whirl about, won't you, in the winter,
to make each passerby stop and think!
Be thus the public crier of duty,
O our funereal black bird!

But, saints of the sky, at the top of the oak,
a mast lost in the spellbound evening,
leave the warblers of May
to those enchained in the depths of the forest,
in the grass from which they cannot flee,
by the defeat without a promise for the future.

The Sedentary

Dark with wens, pockmarked, their eyes circled with green
rings, their knobby fingers tightly clutching their femurs,
the top of their heads coated with an indefinable nastiness
like the branching leprous stains on old walls,

in epileptic romances they have grafted
their whimsical bones to the big black skeletons
of their chairs; their feet and the rickety crossbars
are intertwined morning and evening!

These old men have always been braided with their seats,
feeling the bright sunshine make binding cloth of their skin
or, their eyes on the pane where the snow fades,
atremble with the painful trembling of a toad.

And the seats show them kindnesses; mellowed to a shade
of brown, the straw yields to the angles of their haunches;
the soul of bygone sunshine grows bright, swaddled
in those braided stalks in which the grains fermented.

and the seated ones, knees pulled up to their teeth, green pianists,
their ten fingers making drumlike noises under their chairs,

S'écoutent clapoter des barcarolles tristes,
Et leurs caboches vont dans des roulis d'amour.

— Oh! ne les faites pas lever! C'est le naufrage . . .
Ils surgissent, grondant comme des chats giflés,
Ouvrant lentement leurs omoplates, ô rage!
Tout leur pantalon bouffe à leurs reins boursouflés.

Et vous les écoutez, cognant leurs têtes chauves
Aux murs sombres, plaquant et plaquant leurs pieds tors,
Et leurs boutons d'habit sont des prunelles fauves
Qui vous accrochent l'œil du fond des corridors!

Puis ils ont une main invisible qui tue:
Au retour, leur regard filtre ce venin noir
Qui charge l'œil souffrant de la chienne battue,
Et vous suez, pris dans un atroce entonnoir.

Rassis, les poings noyés dans des manchettes sales,
Ils songent à ceux-là qui les ont fait lever
Et, de l'aurore au soir, des grappes d'amygdales
Sous leurs mentons chétifs s'agitent à crever.

Quand l'austère sommeil a baissé leurs visières,
Ils rêvent sur leur bras de sièges fécondés,
De vrais petits amours de chaises en lisière
Par lesquelles de fiers bureaux seront bordés;

Des fleurs d'encre crachant des pollens en virgule
Les bercent, le long des calices accroupis
Tels qu'au fil des glaïeuls le vol des libellules
— Et leur membre s'agace à des barbes d'épis.

Tête de faune

Dans la feuillée, écrin vert taché d'or,
Dans la feuillée incertaine et fleurie
De fleurs splendides où le baiser dort,
Vif et crevant l'exquise broderie,

Un faune effaré montre ses deux yeux
Et mord les fleurs rouges de ses dents blanches.

listen to one another performing sad barcaroles like water lapping,
and their noggins shake to rolling waves of love.

Oh, don't make them get up! That's their shipwreck. . . .
They arise, growling like cats that have been slapped,
slowly separating their shoulder blades, O fury!
Their trousers bag out entirely over their bloated haunches.

And you can hear them banging their bald heads
on the dark walls, pressing, pressing down their warped feet,
and their jacket buttons are tawny pupils
that catch your eye from the far end of the corridors!

Then they have an invisible hand that kills:
when they return, their gaze distills that black venom
which fills the suffering eyes of whipped bitches,
and you sweat, caught in an atrocious funnel.

Seated once more, their fists drowned in their dirty cuffs,
they dream of those who have made them get up
and, from dawn to eve, clusters of tonsils
quiver to the bursting point below their puny chins.

When austere slumber has lowered their eyeshades,
head on arm, they dream of impregnated chairs,
real little darlings of chairs on leading strings
which will be arranged around proud offices;

flowers of ink spitting out comma-shaped pollen
rock them to sleep, alongside squatting calyxes
resembling the flight of dragonflies down a row of irises
—and their members are excited by the beards of wheat.[77]

Faun's Head

In the foliage, a green casket flecked with gold,
in the foliage dappled and flowered
with resplendent flowers in which kisses sleep,
vitally bursting that exquisite embroidery

an awestruck faun shows his two eyes
and bites the red flowers with his white teeth.

---

77. The straw of their chair bottoms.

Brunie et sanglante ainsi qu'un vin vieux
Sa lèvre éclate en rires sous les branches.

Et quand il a fui — tel qu'un écureuil —
Son rire tremble encore à chaque feuille
Et l'on voit épeuré par un bouvreuil
Le Baiser d'or du Bois, qui se recueille.

Oraison du soir

Je vis assis, tel qu'un ange aux mains d'un barbier,
Empoignant une chope à fortes cannelures,
L'hypogastre et le col cambrés, une Gambier
Aux dents, sous l'air gonflé d'impalpables voilures.

Tels que les excréments chauds d'un vieux colombier,
Mille Rêves en moi font de douces brûlures:
Puis par instants mon cœur triste est comme un aubier
Qu'ensanglante l'or jeune et sombre des coulures.

Puis, quand j'ai ravalé mes rêves avec soin,
Je me tourne, ayant bu trente ou quarante chopes,
Et me recueille, pour lâcher l'âcre besoin:

Doux comme le Seigneur du cèdre et des hysopes,
Je pisse vers les cieux bruns, très haut et très loin,
Avec l'assentiment des grands héliotropes.

Mes petites amoureuses

Un hydrolat lacrymal lave
        Les cieux vert-chou:
Sous l'arbre tendronnier qui bave,
        Vos caoutchoucs

Blancs de lunes particulières
        Aux pialats ronds,

Burnished and bloody as an old wine,
his lips explode in laughter under the branches.

And after he has fled—like a squirrel—
his laughter still trembles on every leaf
and you can see frightened by a bullfinch
the golden Kiss of the Woods, in meditation.

Evening Prayer

I live sitting down, like an angel in a barber's hands,
grasping a deeply grooved beer mug,
my lower belly and neck arched, a cheap Gambier pipe[78]
in my teeth, in the air swollen by impalpable sets of sails.

Like the warm droppings in an old dovecote,
a thousand dreams cause sweet burnings in me:
then at moments my sad heart is like a tree's vascular tissue
bloodied by the young, dark gold of the leaking sap.

Then, after I've carefully choked back my dreams,
I turn, having drunk thirty or forty mugs,
and I collect myself, in order to answer my acrid needs:

As gentle as the Lord of the cedar and the hyssop,
I piss toward the brown skies, very high and very far,
to the approbation of the tall heliotropes.

My Little Sweethearts

A lachrymal hydrate[79] bathes
          the cabbage-green skies:
under the budding[80] tree which dribbles,
          your rubber overshoes,

white with moons peculiar
          to the round raindrops,[81]

---

78. Named for its Parisian manufacturer.   79. This probably means "the rain.'"
80. The French *tendronnier* would remind a French reader of *tendron* ("young girl").
81. No one really knows what these lines mean, especially the otherwise unknown
word *pialats;* this translation is based on editors' conjectures.

Entrechoquez vos genouillères,
 Mes laiderons!

Nous nous aimions à cette époque,
 Bleu laideron!
On mangeait des œufs à la coque
 Et du mouron!

Un soir, tu me sacras poète,
 Blond laideron:
Descends ici, que je te fouette
 En mon giron;

J'ai dégueulé ta bandoline,
 Noir laideron;
Tu couperais ma mandoline
 Au fil du front.

Pouah! mes salives desséchées,
 Roux laideron,
Infectent encor les tranchées
 De ton sein rond!

O mes petites amoureuses,
 Que je vous hais!
Plaquez de fouffes douloureuses
 Vos tétons laids!

Piétinez mes vieilles terrines
 De sentiment;
— Hop donc! soyez-moi ballerines
 Pour un moment!...

Vos omoplates se déboîtent,
 O mes amours!
Une étoile à vos reins qui boitent
 Tournez vos tours!

Et c'est pourtant pour ces éclanches
 Que j'ai rimé!
Je voudrais vous casser les hanches
 D'avoir aimé!

Fade amas d'étoiles ratées,
 Comblez les coins!

knock your kneecaps together,
       my little uglies!

We loved each other in those days,
       little blue ugly!
We used to eat soft-boiled eggs
       and chickweed!

One evening, you ordained me poet,
       little blonde ugly:
come down here, so I can whip you
       on my lap;

I vomited your brilliantine,
       little dark-haired ugly:
you'd cut my mandolin
       on your sharp forehead.

Bah! My dried-up saliva,
       little redheaded ugly,
still pollutes the trenches
       of your round bosom!

O my little sweethearts,
       how I hate you!
Pad your ugly tits
       with sorrowful rags!

Trample on my old sentimental
       earthenware pots;
—hop to it! Be ballerinas
       for a minute! . . .

Your shoulder blades get dislocated,
       O my darlings!
With a star on your limping haunches
       perform your pirouettes!

And yet it was for those shoulders of mutton
       that I wrote my poems!
I'd like to break your hips
       for having loved you!

Insipid heap of failed stars,
       fill up the nooks and crannies!

— Vous crèverez en Dieu, bâtées
    D'ignobles soins!

Sous les lunes particulières
    Aux pialats ronds,
Entrechoquez vos genouillères,
    Mes laiderons!

Accroupissements

Bien tard, quand il se sent l'estomac écœuré,
Le frère Milotus, un œil à la lucarne
D'où le soleil, clair comme un chaudron récuré,
Lui darde une migraine et fait son regard darne,
Déplace dans les draps son ventre de curé.

Il se démène sous sa couverture grise
Et descend, ses genoux à son ventre tremblant,
Effaré comme un vieux qui mangerait sa prise;
Car il lui faut, le poing à l'anse d'un pot blanc,
À ses reins largement retrousser sa chemise!

Or, il s'est accroupi, frileux, les doigts de pied
Repliés, grelottant au clair soleil qui plaque
Des jaunes de brioche aux vitres de papier;
Et le nez du bonhomme où s'allume la laque
Renifle aux rayons, tel qu'un charnel polypier.

Le bonhomme mijote au feu, bras tordus, lippe
Au ventre: il sent glisser ses cuisses dans le feu,
Et ses chausses roussir, et s'éteindre sa pipe;
Quelque chose comme un oiseau remue un peu
À son ventre serein comme un monceau de tripe!

Autour, dort un fouillis de meubles abrutis
Dans des haillons de crasse et sur de sales ventres;
Des escabeaux, crapauds étranges, sont blottis
Aux coins noirs: des buffets ont des gueules de chantres
Qu'entr'ouvre un sommeil plein d'horribles appétits.

L'écœurante chaleur gorge la chambre étroite;
Le cerveau du bonhomme est bourré de chiffons.
Il écoute les poils pousser dans sa peau moite,

—You'll croak in God's name, burdened
    with ignoble worries!

Under the moons peculiar
    to the round raindrops,
knock your kneecaps together,
    my little uglies!

Squattings

Very late, when he feels his stomach upset,
Friar Milotus, one eye on the dormer window
from which the sun, bright as a scoured cauldron,
shoots a migraine at him and dazzles his vision,
shifts his priestly belly around in the bedclothes.

He tosses and turns under his gray blanket
and gets out of bed, his knees against his trembling belly,
frightened like an old man who's swallowed his snuff;
because, his fist on the handle of a white pot, he must
roll up his nightshirt all the way to his haunches!

Now, he's squatting, feeling chilly, his toes
curled up, shivering in the bright sunshine that plasters
spots as yellow as a brioche on the paper windowpanes;
and the fellow's nose, glowing red as lacquer,
sniffs in the sunbeams like a polypary of human flesh.

The fellow is simmering on the fire, arms twisted, thick lips
on his belly: he feels his thighs slipping into the fire
and his breeches starting to burn, and his pipe going out;
something like a bird quivers a little
in his belly serene as a pile of tripe!

Round about, there sleeps a mishmosh of mindless furniture
draped in greasy scraps of cloth, on dirty bellies;
stools, like odd toads, crouch
in the dark corners: sideboards have maws like church cantors,
partly opened by a slumber full of horrible appetites.

The nauseating heat gorges the narrow room;
the fellow's brain is stuffed with rags.
He listens to his body hair growing in his damp skin,

Et, parfois, en hoquets fort gravement bouffons
S'échappe, secouant son escabeau qui boite . . .

Et le soir, aux rayons de lune, qui lui font
Aux contours du cul des bavures de lumière,
Une ombre avec détails s'accroupit, sur un fond
De neige rose ainsi qu'une rose trémière . . .
Fantasque, un nez poursuit Vénus au ciel profond.

Les poètes de sept ans

À M. P. Demeny.

Et la Mère, fermant le livre du devoir,
S'en allait satisfaite et très fière, sans voir,
Dans les yeux bleus et sous le front plein d'éminences,
L'âme de son enfant livrée aux répugnances.

Tout le jour il suait d'obéissance; très
Intelligent; pourtant des tics noirs, quelques traits,
Semblaient prouver en lui d'âcres hypocrisies.
Dans l'ombre des couloirs aux tentures moisies,
En passant il tirait la langue, les deux poings
À l'aine, et dans ses yeux fermés voyait des points.
Une porte s'ouvrait sur le soir: à la lampe
On le voyait, là-haut, qui râlait sur la rampe,
Sous un golfe de jour pendant du toit. L'été
Surtout, vaincu, stupide, il était entêté
À se renfermer dans la fraîcheur des latrines:
Il pensait là, tranquille et livrant ses narines.

Quand, lavé des odeurs du jour, le jardinet
Derrière la maison, en hiver, s'illunait,
Gisant au pied d'un mur, enterré dans la marne
Et pour des visions écrasant son œil darne,
Il écoutait grouiller les galeux espaliers.
Pitié! Ces enfants seuls étaient ses familiers
Qui, chétifs, fronts nus, œil déteignant sur la joue,
Cachant de maigres doigts jaunes et noirs de boue
Sous des habits puant la foire et tout vieillots,

and, at moments, he finds vent in most solemnly funny
hiccups, which shake his limping stool. . . .

And in the evening, in the moonbeams, which create
smudges of light around the edges of his behind,
a detailed shadow squats, against a background
of snow as pink as a hollyhock. . . .
A whimsical nose pursues Venus in the depths of the sky.

The Seven-Year-Old Poets

To Mr. P[aul] Demeny.[82]

And the mother, shutting the school exercise book,
went away contented and very proud, without seeing,
in his blue eyes below his forehead full of protuberances,
her child's soul a prey to repugnance.

All day long, he sweated with obedience; very
intelligent; yet, certain unhealthy tics, certain habits
seemed to prove he was sourly hypocritical.
In the shadow of the hallways with their moldy wallpaper,
he would stick out his tongue as he walked, his two fists
against his groin, and in his closed eyes he'd see spots.
A door opened onto the evening; in the lamplight
he could be seen up there emitting a death rattle on the stairs,
beneath a gulf of daylight suspended from the roof. In summer
especially, overcome, in a stupor, he would stubbornly
lock himself away in the coolness of the latrine:
there he'd think calmly, indulging his nostrils.

When, cleansed of the day's odors, the little garden
behind the house was filled with moonlight in wintertime,
he'd lie at the foot of a wall, buried in the marl,
and squeezing shut his dazzled eyes, to receive visions,
he'd listen to the life teeming in the scurfy espaliers.
A pity! Only those children were his playfellows
who—puny, bare-browed, with eyes fading onto their cheeks,
hiding thin fingers yellow and black with mud
under clothes stinking of excrement and quite old-fashioned—

82. A mentor and correspondent of Rimbaud's.

Conversaient avec la douceur des idiots!
Et si, l'ayant surpris à des pitiés immondes,
Sa mère s'effrayait; les tendresses, profondes,
De l'enfant se jetaient sur cet étonnement.
C'était bon. Elle avait le bleu regard, — qui ment!

À sept ans, il faisait des romans, sur la vie
Du grand désert, où luit la Liberté ravie,
Forêts, soleils, rives, savanes! — Il s'aidait
De journaux illustrés où, rouge, il regardait
Des Espagnoles rire et des Italiennes.
Quant venait, l'œil brun, folle, en robes d'indiennes,
— Huit ans, — la fille des ouvriers d'à côté,
La petite brutale, et qu'elle avait sauté,
Dans un coin, sur son dos, en secouant ses tresses,
Et qu'il était sous elle, il lui mordait les fesses,
Car elle ne portait jamais de pantalons;
— Et, par elle meurtri des poings et des talons,
Remportait les saveurs de sa peau dans sa chambre.

Il craignait les blafards dimanches de décembre,
Où, pommadé, sur un guéridon d'acajou,
Il lisait une Bible à la tranche vert-chou;
Des rêves l'oppressaient chaque nuit dans l'alcôve.
Il n'aimait pas Dieu; mais les hommes, qu'au soir fauve,
Noirs, en blouse, il voyait rentrer dans le faubourg
Où les crieurs, en trois roulements de tambour,
Font autour des édits rire et gronder les foules.
— Il rêvait la prairie amoureuse, où des houles
Lumineuses, parfums sains, pubescences d'or,
Font leur remuement calme et prennent leur essor!

Et comme il savourait surtout les sombres choses,
Quand, dans la chambre nue aux persiennes closes,
Haute et bleue, âcrement prise d'humidité,
Il lisait son roman sans cesse médité,
Plein de lourds ciels ocreux et de forêts noyées,
De fleurs de chair aux bois sidérals déployées,
Vertige, écroulements, déroutes et pitié!
— Tandis que se faisait la rumeur du quartier,
En bas, — Seul, et couché sur des pièces de toile
Écrue, et pressentant violemment la voile!

conversed with the gentleness of idiots!
And if, having caught him expressing unclean compassion,
his mother got scared, the profound affectionateness
of the child pounced on that astonishment.
It was all right. She had seen those blue eyes—which lie!

At the age of seven, he made up novels about life
in the great desert, where stolen Liberty shines,
forests, suns, shores, savannas!—He used as an aid
picture magazines in which, blushing, he'd look at
Spanish and Italian women laughing.
When, her eyes brown, a madcap in calico dresses,
eight years old, the daughter of the laborers next door would visit,
that wild little thing, and she'd jump
on his back in a corner, shaking her tresses,
and he was under her, he'd bite her buttocks,
because she never wore any drawers;
—and, bruised by her fists and her heels,
he'd carry the taste of her skin back to his room.

He feared the wan December Sundays
when, his hair pomaded, on a mahogany pedestal table,
he'd read a Bible with cabbage-green edges;
dreams oppressed him nightly in his bedroom.
He didn't love God, but loved the men whom, in the tawny dusk,
he saw returning, grimy, in smocks, to their outlying neighborhood
where the town criers, to three drumrolls,
make the crowds laugh and grumble at their proclamations.
—He would dream of the meadow in love, where surges
of light, healthful aromas, golden downinesses,
stir calmly and take flight!

And how he especially enjoyed somber things,
when, in his bare room with closed shutters,
a lofty, blue room always acridly damp,
he'd read his novel, which he thought about ceaselessly,
full of heavy ochre skies and drowned forests,
flowers of flesh unfurled in the sidereal woods,
giddiness, landslides, defeats, and compassion!
—while the noises of the neighborhood could be heard
below—solitary, he lay on pieces of unbleached
canvas, which violently prefigured a ship's sail!

Les pauvres à l'église

Parqués entre des bancs de chêne, aux coins d'église
Qu'attiédit puamment leur souffle, tous leurs yeux
Vers le chœur ruisselant d'orrie et la maîtrise
Aux vingt gueules gueulant les cantiques pieux;

Comme un parfum de pain humant l'odeur de cire,
Heureux, humiliés comme des chiens battus,
Les Pauvres au bon Dieu, le patron et le sire,
Tendent leurs oremus risibles et têtus.

Aux femmes, c'est bien bon de faire des bancs lisses,
Après les six jours noirs où Dieu les fait souffrir!
Elles bercent, tordus dans d'étranges pelisses,
Des espèces d'enfants qui pleurent à mourir.

Leurs seins crasseux dehors, ces mangeuses de soupe,
Une prière aux yeux et ne priant jamais,
Regardent parader mauvaisement un groupe
De gamines avec leurs chapeaux déformés.

Dehors, le froid, la faim, l'homme en ribote:
C'est bon. Encore une heure; après, les maux sans noms!
— Cependant, alentour, geint, nasille, chuchote
Une collection de vieilles à fanons:

Ces effarés y sont et ces épileptiques
Dont on se détournait hier aux carrefours;
Et, fringalant du nez dans des missels antiques,
Ces aveugles qu'un chien introduit dans les cours.

Et tous, bavant la foi mendiante et stupide,
Récitent la complainte infinie à Jésus
Qui rêve en haut, jauni par le vitrail livide,
Loin des maigres mauvais et des méchants pansus,

Loin des senteurs de viande et d'étoffes moisies,
Farce prostrée et sombre aux gestes repoussants;
— Et l'oraison fleurit d'expressions choisies,
Et les mysticités prennent des tons pressants,

The Poor in Church

Penned in between oaken pews, in the corners of the church
that their stinking breath warms, the eyes of all of them
directed at the chancel dripping with gold ornaments and the choir
with its twenty yaps yapping pious hymns;

inhaling the smell of wax as if the aroma of bread,
happy, humiliated like beaten dogs,
to God, their protector and their master, the poor
dispatch their laughable, obstinate "let us pray."

For the women, it feels good to smooth down the pews
after the six black days on which God makes them suffer!
They rock children of a sort, wrapped in odd, twisted pelisses
and crying to beat the band.

Their greasy breasts hanging out, those soup-eaters,
a prayer in their eyes but never praying,
watch a group of little girls strutting around
maliciously with their shapeless hats.

Outdoors, the cold, hunger, their husbands on a drunken spree:[83]
It's all right. One more hour; then the nameless woes!
—Meanwhile, round about, the groans, nasal talk, and whispers
of a collection of old women with dewlaps:

those dazedly frightened people are there, and those epileptics
whom you shunned yesterday at crossings;
and, "hungering" with their nose in ancient missals,
those blind men whom their dogs lead into your courtyard.

And all of them, drooling their beggarly, stupid faith,
recite their infinite ballad to Jesus,
who's dreaming up there, yellowed by the livid stained glass,
far from the evilminded skinny and the spiteful fat-bellied,

far from the odors of moldy meat and cloth,
that prostrate, somber farce with repulsive gestures;
—and the prayer blossoms out into refined phrases,
and the mystic utterances take on urgent tones,

---

83. This verse is two syllables short, and some editors supply a word of their own
choice.

Quand, des nefs où périt le soleil, plis de soie
Banals, sourires verts, les Dames des quartiers
Distingués, — ô Jésus! — les malades du foie
Font baiser leurs longs doigts jaunes aux bénitiers.

Le cœur volé

Mon triste cœur bave à la poupe,
Mon cœur couvert de caporal:
Ils y lancent des jets de soupe,
Mon triste cœur bave à la poupe:
Sous les quolibets de la troupe
Qui pousse un rire général,
Mon triste cœur bave à la poupe,
Mon cœur couvert de caporal!

Ithyphalliques et pioupiesques
Leurs quolibets l'ont dépravé!
Au gouvernail on voit des fresques
Ithyphalliques et pioupiesques.
O flots abracadabrantesques,
Prenez mon cœur, qu'il soit lavé!
Ithyphalliques et pioupiesques
Leurs quolibets l'ont dépravé!

Quand ils auront tari leurs chiques,
Comment agir, ô cœur volé?
Ce seront des hoquets bachiques
Quand ils auront tari leurs chiques:
J'aurai des sursauts stomachiques,
Moi, si mon cœur est ravalé:
Quand ils auront tari leurs chiques
Comment agir, ô cœur volé?

Les mains de Jeanne-Marie

Jeanne-Marie a des mains fortes,
Mains sombres que l'été tanna,

when, from the side aisles where the sunlight dies, banal
silk pleats, green smiles, the ladies from the well-to-do
neighborhoods,—O Jesus!—those with liver ailments,
make the holy-water stoups kiss their long yellow fingers.

The Stolen Heart

My sad heart is dribbling at the stern,[84]
my heart covered with cheap tobacco:[85]
they're shooting streams of soup at it;
my sad heart is dribbling at the stern:
to the gibes and jeers of the troop,
which utters a general laugh,
my sad heart is dribbling at the stern,
my heart covered with cheap tobacco.

Ithyphallic and like soldier boys,
their gibes and jeers have depraved it!
at the rudder you can see frescoes that are
ithyphallic and like soldier boys.
O abracadabra waves,
take my heart, let it be cleansed!
Ithyphallic and like soldier boys,
their gibes and jeers have depraved it!

After they've dried up their quids,
how am I to behave, O stolen heart?
There will be bacchic hiccups
after they've dried up their quids:
I'll suffer from gripes in the stomach,
that I will, if my heart is degraded:
after they've dried up their quids,
how am I to behave, O stolen heart?

The Hands of Jeanne-Marie

Jeanne-Marie has strong hands,
dark hands which the summer tanned,

---

84. The mention of "stern" indicates which part of the body is to be understood by
the euphemistic "heart."   85. Or: "covered with a corporal."

Mains pâles comme des mains mortes.
— Sont-ce des mains de Juana?

Ont-elles pris les crèmes brunes
Sur les mares des voluptés?
Ont-elles trempé dans les lunes
Aux étangs de sérénités?

Ont-elles bu des cieux barbares,
Calmes sur les genoux charmants?
Ont-elles roulé des cigares
Ou trafiqué des diamants?

Sur les pieds ardents des Madones
Ont-elles fané des fleurs d'or?
C'est le sang noir des belladones
Qui dans leur paume éclate et dort.

Mains chasseresses des diptères
Dont bombinent les bleuisons
Aurorales, vers les nectaires?
Mains décanteuses de poisons?

Oh! quel Rêve les a saisies
Dans les pandiculations?
Un rêve inouï des Asies,
Des Khenghavars ou des Sions?

— Ces mains n'ont pas vendu d'oranges,
Ni bruni sur les pieds des dieux:
Ces mains n'ont pas lavé les langes
Des lourds petits enfants sans yeux.

Ce ne sont pas mains de cousine
Ni d'ouvrières aux gros fronts
Que brûle, aux bois puant l'usine,
Un soleil ivre de goudrons.

Ce sont des ployeuses d'échines,
Des mains qui ne font jamais mal,
Plus fatales que des machines,
Plus fortes que tout un cheval!

hands as pale as dead hands.
—Are they the hands of a Juana?[86]

Have they obtained their brown creaminess
from the pools of sensuous love?
Have they dipped into the moonlight
on the ponds of serenity?

Have they imbibed barbarous skies,
resting calmly on her charming knees?
Have they rolled cigars
or trafficked in diamonds?

Have they made golden flowers fade
at the ardent feet of Madonnas?
It's the black blood of belladonnas
that flares up and sleeps in their palms.

Hands that chase the flies
whose dawn-blue bodies
buzz around nectaries?
Hands that decant poisons?

Oh, what dream has seized them
while she stretched upon awakening?
An unheard-of dream of Asia,
of Khenghaver[87] or of Zion?

—These hands haven't sold oranges,
nor have they turned brown at the feet of gods:
these hands haven't washed the diapers
of heavy, eyeless infants.

They aren't the hands of a seamstress[88]
or of a broad-browed laboring woman
who is burned, in forests stinking like factories,
by a sun drunk on tar and pitch.

They are benders of backbones,
hands that never do harm,
more doom-bearing than machines,
stronger than an entire horse!

---

86. Probably just means "a Spanish woman" (this stanza is heavily indebted to
Théophile Gautier's poem "Carmen"), but other theories have been put forward.
87. Apparently an imaginary place.   88. Or perhaps: "a loose woman."

Remuant comme des fournaises,
Et secouant tous ses frissons,
Leur chair chante des Marseillaises
Et jamais les Eleisons!

Ça serrerait vos cous, ô femmes
Mauvaises, ça broierait vos mains,
Femmes nobles, vos mains infâmes
Pleines de blancs et de carmins.

L'éclat de ces mains amoureuses
Tourne le crâne des brebis!
Dans leurs phalanges savoureuses
Le grand soleil met un rubis!

Une tache de populace
Les brunit comme un sein d'hier;
Le dos de ces Mains est la place
Qu'en baisa tout Révolté fier!

Elles ont pâli, merveilleuses,
Au grand soleil d'amour chargé,
Sur le bronze des mitrailleuses
À travers Paris insurgé!

Ah! quelquefois, ô Mains sacrées,
À vos poings, Mains où tremblent nos
Lèvres jamais désenivrées,
Crie une chaîne aux clairs anneaux!

Et c'est un soubresaut étrange
Dans nos êtres, quand, quelquefois,
On veut vous déhâler, Mains d'ange,
En vous faisant saigner les doigts!

Voyelles

A noir, E blanc, I rouge, U vert, O bleu: voyelles,
Je dirai quelque jour vos naissances latentes:

In motion like furnaces,
and shaking away all her shudders,
their flesh sings the "Marseillaise"
and never a "Kyrie eleison"![89]

They could squeeze your necks, O evil
women, they could crush your hands,
noblewomen, you vile hands
full of white and red colorings.

The glare of those amorous hands
turns the skull of sheep!
Into their savory finger joints
the midday sun sets a ruby!

A stain of common blood
tans them like a breast of yesteryear;
the back of those hands is the place
where every proud revolutionary kissed them!

Wondrous, they have turned pale
in the midday sun laden with love,
on the bronze of the mitrailleuses[90]
across insurgent Paris!

Ah! at times, O hallowed hands,
on your wrists, O hands on which our
lips, never becoming sober, tremble,
a chain with bright links[91] creaks!

And it gives a queer start
to our whole being when, at times,
people want to make you paler, angel's hands,
by making your fingers bleed!

Vowels

Black A, white E, red I, green U, blue O—vowels—
some day I shall speak of your latent births:

---

89. "Lord have mercy!" (Greek), the words that begin the mass.   90. A multibar-
reled gun used in the Franco-Prussian War and the Commune fighting.
91. Handcuffs.

A, noir corset velu des mouches éclatantes
Qui bombinent autour des puanteurs cruelles,

Golfes d'ombre; E, candeurs des vapeurs et des tentes,
Lances des glaciers fiers, rois blancs, frissons d'ombelles;
I, pourpres, sang craché, rire des lèvres belles
Dans la colère ou les ivresses pénitentes;

U, cycles, vibrement divins des mers virides,
Paix des pâtis semés d'animaux, paix des rides
Que l'alchimie imprime aux grands fronts studieux;

O, suprême Clairon plein des strideurs étranges,
Silences traversés des Mondes et des Anges:
— O l'Oméga, rayon violet de Ses Yeux!

Les premières Communions

I

Vraiment, c'est bête, ces églises des villages
Où quinze laids marmots encrassant les piliers
Écoutent, grasseyant les divins babillages,
Un noir grotesque dont fermentent les souliers:
Mais le soleil éveille, à travers les feuillages,
Les vieilles couleurs des vitraux irréguliers.

La pierre sent toujours la terre maternelle,
Vous verrez des monceaux de ces cailloux terreux
Dans la campagne en rut qui frémit solennelle,
Portant près des blés lourds, dans les sentiers ocreux,
Ces arbrisseaux brûlés où bleuit la prunelle,
Des nœuds de mûriers noirs et de rosiers fuireux.

Tous les cent ans on rend ces granges respectables
Par un badigeon d'eau bleue et de lait caillé:
Si des mysticités grotesques sont notables
Près de la Notre Dame ou du Saint empaillé,
Des mouches sentant bon l'auberge et les étables
Se gorgent de cire au plancher ensoleillé.

A, the hairy black jacket of the gleaming flies
that buzz around the stench of blood,

gulfs of shadow; E, the whiteness of steam and tents,
lances of the proud glaciers, white kings, trembling of umbels;
I, royal purple, spat-up blood, laughter of lovely lips
in anger or the intoxication of penitence;

U, cycles, divine vibration of verdant seas,
the peace of animal-strewn pastures, the peace of wrinkles
imprinted by alchemy on high, studious brows;

O, the Last Trumpet full of strange stridency,
silences traversed by worlds and angels:
—O the Omega, violet beam from His[92] eyes!

First Communion

I

They're really stupid, those village churches
in which fifteen ugly brats, smearing up the pillars,
listen, as they lisp[93] the divine twaddle,
to a grotesque man in black whose shoes are putrid:
but, passing through the leaves, the sun awakens
the old colors of the uneven stained-glass windows.

The stone always smells of its mother earth,
you'll see heaps of those earth-colored rocks
in the countryside in heat which solemnly shudders
as it bears, near the heavy grain, on the ochre paths,
those scorched shrubs on which the blue sloe grows,
knots of black mulberry trees and dogroses.[94]

Every hundred years those barns are made respectable
by a whitewashing with bluing and curdled milk:
if there's some appreciable mysticism
in the images of the Virgin or the saint who's been stuffed,
flies that have the good smell of inns and stables
gorge themselves on wax on the sunlit floor.

92. Or: "*her.*"   93. Literally: "pronounce the letter *r* in an odd way."   94. Or: "ex-
cremental roses."

L'enfant se doit surtout à la maison, famille
Des soins naïfs, des bons travaux abrutissants;
Ils sortent, oubliant que la peau leur fourmille
Où le Prêtre du Christ plaqua sets doigts puissants.
On paie au Prêtre un toit ombré d'une charmille
Pour qu'il laisse au soleil tous ces fronts brunissants.

Le premier habit noir, le plus beau jour de tartes,
Sous le Napoléon ou le Petit Tambour
Quelque enluminure où les Josephs et les Marthes
Tirent la langue avec un excessif amour
Et que joindront, au jour de science, deux cartes,
Ces seuls doux souvenirs lui restent du grand jour.

Les filles vont toujours à l'église, contentes
De s'entendre appeler garces par les garçons
Qui font du genre après Messe ou vêpres chantantes.
Eux qui sont destinés au chic des garnisons,
Ils narguent au café les maisons importantes,
Blousés neuf, et gueulant d'effroyables chansons.

Cependant le Curé choisit pour les enfances
Des dessins; dans son clos, les vêpres dites, quand
L'air s'emplit du lointain nasillement des danses,
Ils se sent, en dépit des célestes défenses,
Les doigts de pied ravis et le mollet marquant;
— La nuit vient, noir pirate aux cieux d'or débarquant.

II

Le Prêtre a distingué parmi les catéchistes,
Congrégés des Faubourgs ou des Riches Quartiers,
Cette petite fille inconnue, aux yeux tristes,
Front jaune. Les parents semblent de doux portiers.
«Au grand Jour, le marquant parmi les Catéchistes,
Dieu fera sur ce front neiger ses bénitiers.»

III

La veille du grand Jour, l'enfant se fait malade.
Mieux qu'à l'Église haute aux funèbres rumeurs,

The children are, above all, servants of their families, doing
a number of simple chores, hard tasks that numb their minds;
they go out, forgetting that their skin is tingling
where the priest of Christ impressed his powerful fingers.
the priest gets a house shaded by an arbor in recompense
for releasing all those tanning brows into the sunshine.

The first black suit, the loveliest day of cakes,
below the picture of Napoleon or the little drummer boy,[95]
some colored print in which St. Joseph or Martha
stick out their tongue in an excess of love,
a print that will be joined, on that day of knowledge, by two cards;
these sole sweet mementos are left over from the great day.

The girls keep attending church, pleased
to hear themselves called bitches by the boys
who put on airs after mass or sung vespers.
They, destined for the stylishness of army life,
thumb their noses in the café at the leading families;
wear brand-new smocks, and howl horrible songs.

Meanwhile the parish priest is selecting drawings
for the children; in his close, after saying vespers, when
the air is filled with the distant droning of dances,
in spite of celestial prohibitions he feels
his toes enraptured and his calves marking time;
—Night comes, a black pirate landing on the golden skies.

II

The priest has singled out among the catechism pupils,
assembled from the laborers' quarters or the wealthy parts of town,
this unknown little girl with sad eyes
and a yellow forehead. Her parents seem to be mild caretakers.
"On the great day, marking it among the pupils,
God will make his holy-water stoups snow down on that brow."

III

On the eve of the great day, the girl gets sick.
More than in the lofty church with its funereal sounds,

95. Joseph Bara, killed in 1793 in the service of the Revolution.

D'abord le frisson vient, — le lit n'étant pas fade —
Un frisson surhumain qui retourne: «Je meurs . . .»

Et, comme un vol d'amour fait à ses sœurs stupides,
Elle compte, abattue et les mains sur son cœur,
Les Anges, les Jésus et ses Vierges nitides
Et, calmement, son âme a bu tout son vainqueur.

Adonaï! . . . — Dans les terminaisons latines,
Des cieux moirés de vert baignent les Fronts vermeils
Et tachés du sang pur des célestes poitrines
De grands linges neigeux tombent sur les soleils!

— Pour ses virginités présentes et futures
Elle mord aux fraîcheurs de ta Rémission,
Mais plus que les lys d'eau, plus que les confitures,
Tes pardons sont glacés, ô Reine de Sion!

IV

Puis la Vierge n'est plus que la vierge du livre.
Les mystiques élans se cassent quelquefois . . .
Et vient la pauvreté des images, que cuivre
L'ennui, l'enluminure atroce et les vieux bois;

Des curiosités vaguement impudiques
Épouvantent le rêve aux chastes bleuités
Qui s'est surpris autour des célestes tuniques,
Du linge dont Jésus voile ses nudités.

Elle veut, elle veut, pourtant, l'âme en détresse,
Le front dans l'oreiller creusé par les cris sourds,
Prolonger les éclairs suprêmes de tendresse,
Et bave . . . — L'ombre emplit les maisons et les cours.

Et l'enfant ne peut plus. Elle s'agite, cambre
Les reins et d'une main ouvre le rideau bleu
Pour amener un peu la fraîcheur de la chambre
Sous le drap, vers son ventre et sa poitrine en feu . . .

V

À son réveil, — minuit, — la fenêtre était blanche.
Devant le sommeil bleu des rideaux illunés,

at first a shuddering comes—the bed not being tiresome—
a superhuman shuddering which returns: "I'm dying. . . ."

And, like a loving theft committed on her stupid sisters,
dejected and her hands on her heart, she counts
the angels, the Jesuses, and her gleaming-white Virgins
and calmly her soul has entirely imbibed its conqueror.

Adonai! . . .—In the Latin suffixes,
skies with green moirés bathe the vermilion brows
and, stained with the pure blood of heavenly breasts,
large snowy linens fall onto the suns!

—For her virginity present and future
she bites into the coolness of Your remission of sins,
but colder than water lilies, colder than preserves
is your icy forgiveness, O Queen of Zion!

IV

Then the Virgin is no longer anything but the virgin in the book.
Mystical impulses get worn out sometimes . . .
and there ensues the poverty of images, which get coated
with boredom, the hideousness of colored prints and old woodcuts;

a vaguely immodest curiosity
frightens away the dream of blue chastity
which was taken by surprise lingering about the godly tunics,
the drapery with which Jesus veils his nakedness.

Nevertheless, her soul in distress, her forehead in the pillow
hollowed out by her muffled cries, she wishes, how she wishes
to prolong those supreme flashes of affection,
and she drools. . . .—Shadow fills houses and courtyards.

And the girl has no more strength. She tosses, she arches
her back and with one hand opens the blue bed curtain
to bring some of the coolness of the room
under her sheet, onto her burning belly and bosom. . . .

V

When she awoke—midnight—the window was white.
In front of the blue slumber of the moonlit curtains

La vision la prit des candeurs du dimanche;
Elle avait rêvé rouge. Elle saigna du nez,

Et se sentant bien chaste et pleine de faiblesse
Pour savourer en Dieu son amour revenant,
Elle eut soif de la nuit où s'exalte et s'abaisse
Le cœur, sous l'œil des cieux doux, en les devinant;

De la nuit, Vierge-Mère impalpable, qui baigne
Tous les jeunes émois de ses silences gris,
Elle eut soif de la nuit forte où le cœur qui saigne
Écoule sans témoin sa révolte sans cris.

Et faisant la victime et la petite épouse,
Son étoile la vit, une chandelle aux doigts,
Descendre dans la cour où séchait une blouse,
Spectre blanc, et lever les spectres noirs des toits.

VI

Elle passa sa nuit sainte dans des latrines.
Vers la chandelle, aux trous du toit coulait l'air blanc,
Et quelque vigne folle aux noirceurs purpurines,
En deçà d'une cour voisine s'écroulant.

La lucarne faisait un cœur de lueur vive
Dans la cour où les cieux bas plaquaient d'ors vermeils
Les vitres; les pavés puant l'eau de lessive
Soufraient l'ombre des murs bondés de noirs sommeils.

VII

Qui dira ces langueurs et ces pitiés immondes,
Et ce qu'il lui viendra de haine, ô sales fous,
Dont le travail divin déforme encor les mondes,
Quand la lèpre à la fin mangera ce corps doux?

VIII

Et quand, ayant rentré tous ses nœuds d'hystéries,
Elle verra, sous les tristesses du bonheur,
L'amant rêver au blanc million des Maries,
Au matin de la nuit d'amour, avec douleur:

she was seized by the vision of the whiteness of Sundays;
her dream had been red. Her nose bled,

and feeling quite chaste and full of weakness
to savor in God her returning love,
she thirsted for the night when the heart grows excited
and calm again, under the eyes of the sweet skies, divining them;

for the night, that impalpable Virgin Mother, which bathes
all youthful emotions in its gray silences,
she thirsted for the strong night when the bleeding heart
pours out, free of witnesses, its revolt free of clamor.

And, as she played the victim and the little bride,
her star saw her, a candle in her hand,
walking down to the yard, where a smock was hung out to dry,
a white ghost, and raising the black ghosts of the roofs.

VI

She spent her holy evening in the outhouse.
The white air flowed through the holes in the roof, toward the candle,
as some straying grapevine with its purplish black clusters
collapsed on the near side of a neighboring courtyard.

The skylight cast a heart of glowing light
into the yard, where the low skies coated the windows
with red gold; the paving stones, stinking of lye water,
sulphured the shadow of the walls crammed with black sleep.

VII

Who can recount those languors and those unclean compassions,
and all the hate that will come to her, O you filthy madmen
whose divine efforts still deform the universe,
when the leprosy will at last consume that sweet body?

VIII

And when, having suppressed all her knots of hysteria,
she will see, in the sadness of happiness,
her lover dreaming of the million white Marys
on the morning after their night of love, sorrowfully she'll say:

«Sais-tu que je t'ai fait mourir? J'ai pris ta bouche,
Ton cœur, tout ce qu'on a, tout ce que vous avez;
Et moi, je suis malade: Oh! je veux qu'on me couche
Parmi les Morts des eaux nocturnes abreuvés!

«J'étais bien jeune, et Christ a souillé mes haleines,
Il me bonda jusqu'à la gorge de dégoûts!
Tu baisais mes cheveux profonds comme les laines,
Et je me laissais faire . . . ah! va, c'est bon pour vous,

«Hommes! qui songez peu que la plus amoureuse
Est, sous sa conscience aux ignobles terreurs,
La plus prostituée et la plus douloureuse,
Et que tous nos élans vers vous sont des erreurs!

«Car ma Communion première est bien passée.
Tes baisers, je ne puis jamais les avoir sus:
Et mon cœur et ma chair par ta chair embrassée
Fourmillent du baiser putride de Jésus!»

IX

Alors l'âme pourrie et l'âme désolée
Sentiront ruisseler tes malédictions.
— Ils auront couché sur ta Haine inviolée,
Échappés, pour la mort, des justes passions,

Christ! ô Christ, éternel voleur des énergies,
Dieu qui pour deux mille ans vouas à ta pâleur,
Cloués au sol, de honte et de céphalalgies,
Ou renversés, les fronts des femmes de douleur.

Les chercheuses de poux

Quand le front de l'enfant, plein de rouges tourmentes,
Implore l'essaim blanc des rêves indistincts,
Il vient près de son lit deux grandes sœurs charmantes
Avec de frêles doigts aux ongles argentins.

Elles assoient l'enfant devant une croisée
Grande ouverte où l'air bleu baigne un fouillis de fleurs,
Et dans ses lourds cheveux où tombe la rosée
Promènent leurs doigts fins, terribles et charmeurs.

"Do you know that I've killed you? I've taken your lips,
your heart, all anyone has, all that you men have;
and I, I am ill: oh, I'd like to be laid down
among the dead who drink of the waters of the night!

"I was very young, and Christ polluted my breath,
he crammed me up to the throat with disgust!
You were kissing my hair deep as wool,
and I allowed it . . . ah, you see, it's good for you,

"men! you who have little idea that the most loving woman,
beneath her conscience with its base terrors,
is the one most prostituted and most sorrowful,
and that all our urges for you are mistakes!

"Because my first Communion is far in the past.
I can never have known your kisses:
and my heart and my flesh embraced by your flesh
are tingling with the stinking kiss of Jesus!"

IX

Then the decayed soul and the desolate soul
will hear Your curses raining down.
—They will have lain on Your inviolate hatred,
having escaped from just passions by dying,

Christ! O Christ, eternal thief of energy,
a god who for two thousand years consecrated to your pallor—
nailed to the ground with shame and headaches,
or else overturned—the brows of suffering womanhood.

Women Searching for Lice

When the child's forehead, full of red tempests,
implores the white swarm of indistinct dreams,
there approach his bed two charming big sisters
with delicate fingers that have silvery nails.

They sit the child down in front of a casement
opened wide, where the blue air bathes a tangle of flowers,
and through his heavy hair, on which the dew falls,
they run their slender, awesome, and spellbinding fingers.

Il écoute chanter leurs haleines craintives
Qui fleurent de longs miels végétaux et rosés,
Et qu'interrompt parfois un sifflement, salives
Reprises sur la lèvre ou désirs de baisers.

Il entend leurs cils noirs battant sous les silences
Parfumés; et leurs doigts électriques et doux
Font crépiter parmi ses grises indolences
Sous leurs ongles royaux la mort des petits poux.

Voilà que monte en lui le vin de la Paresse,
Soupir d'harmonica qui pourrait délirer;
L'enfant se sent, selon la lenteur des caresses,
Sourdre et mourir sans cesse un désir de pleurer.

Le bateau ivre

Comme je descendais des Fleuves impassibles,
Je ne me sentis plus guidé par les haleurs:
Des Peaux-Rouges criards les avaient pris pour cibles,
Les ayant cloués nus aux poteaux de couleurs.

J'étais insoucieux de tous les équipages,
Porteur de blés flamands ou de cotons anglais.
Quand avec mes haleurs ont fini ces tapages,
Les Fleuves m'ont laissé descendre où je voulais.

Dans les clapotements furieux des marées,
Moi, l'autre hiver, plus sourd que les cerveaux d'enfants,
Je courus! Et les Péninsules démarrées
N'ont pas subi tohu-bohus plus triomphants.

La tempête a béni mes éveils maritimes.
Plus léger qu'un bouchon j'ai dansé sur les flots
Qu'on appelle rouleurs éternels de victimes,
Dix nuits, sans regretter l'œil niais des falots!

Plus douce qu'aux enfants la chair des pommes sures,
L'eau verte pénétra ma coque de sapin
Et des taches de vins bleus et des vomissures
Me lava, dispersant gouvernail et grappin.

He listens to the song of their timid breath
fragrant with long strands of plant-fed, rose-pink honey
and interrupted at moments by a hissing sound, saliva
retained on the lips, or the yearning for a kiss.

He hears their black lashes beating in the perfumed
silences; and their gentle, electric fingers
make the death of the little lice snap
under their royal nails amid his gray indolence.

Then there rises within him the wine of laziness,
the sigh of a harmonica[96] which might grow delirious;
within him the child feels, according to the slowness of the caresses,
a desire to weep constantly surging and dying away.

The Drunken Boat

As I was proceeding down impassive rivers,
I felt I was no longer guided by the men towing me;
squalling redskins had used them as targets,
having nailed them naked to brightly painted stakes.

I was unconcerned about any crews,
with my cargo of Flemish wheat or English cotton.
When that hubbub had departed along with those towing me,
the rivers let me sail down wherever I wished.

In the furious lapping of the tides,
last winter, duller than children's brains,
I ran! And the unmoored peninsulas
have never experienced more triumphant confusion.

The storm blessed my awakening at sea.
Lighter than a cork, I danced on the waves
that are called eternal rollers of victims,
for ten nights, never missing the silly eye of the lighthouses!

Sweeter than children find the flesh of tart apples,
the green water penetrated my fir hull
and from the stains of blue wines and vomit
washed me clean, scattering the rudder and grappling anchor.

---

96. Or: "musical glasses."

Et dès lors, je me suis baigné dans le Poème
De la Mer, infusé d'astres, et lactescent,
Dévorant les azurs verts; où, flottaison blême
Et ravie, un noyé pensif parfois descend;

Où, teignant tout à coup les bleuités, délires
Et rythmes lents sous les rutilements du jour,
Plus fortes que l'alcool, plus vastes que nos lyres,
Fermentent les rousseurs amères de l'amour!

Je sais les cieux crevant en éclairs, et les trombes
Et les ressacs et les courants: je sais le soir,
L'Aube exaltée ainsi qu'un peuple de colombes,
Et j'ai vu quelquefois ce que l'homme a cru voir!

J'ai vu le soleil bas, taché d'horreurs mystiques,
Illuminant de longs figements violets,
Pareils à des acteurs de drames très antiques
Les flots roulant au loin leurs frissons de volets!

J'ai rêvé la nuit verte aux neiges éblouies,
Baiser montant aux yeux des mers avec lenteurs,
La circulation des sèves inouïes,
Et l'éveil jaune et bleu des phosphores chanteurs!

J'ai suivi, des mois pleins, pareille aux vacheries
Hystériques, la houle à l'assaut des récifs,
Sans songer que les pieds lumineux des Maries
Pussent forcer le mufle aux Océans poussifs!

J'ai heurté, savez-vous, d'incroyables Florides
Mêlant aux fleurs des yeux de panthères à peaux
D'hommes! Des arcs-en-ciel tendus comme des brides
Sous l'horizon des mers, à de glauques troupeaux!

J'ai vu fermenter les marais énormes, nasses
Où pourrit dans les joncs tout un Léviathan!
Des écroulements d'eaux au milieu des bonaces,
Et les lointains vers les gouffres cataractant!

Glaciers, soleils d'argent, flots nacreux, cieux de braises!
Échouages hideux au fond des golfes bruns
Où les serpents géants dévorés des punaises
Choient, des arbres tordus, avec de noirs parfums!

And from then on, I have bathed in the poem
of the sea, infused with stars, and milky,
devouring the green azures; the poem into which, a pale, ravished
floating thing, a pensive drowned man sometimes sinks;

in which (suddenly tinging the blue expanse, the deliriums
and slow rhythms below the glistening of the daylight)
stronger than alcohol, vaster than our lyres,
the bitter russets of love ferment!

I know the skies that burst into lightning, and the waterspouts
and the undertows and the currents: I know the evening,
the dawn as excited as a flock of doves,
and at times I have seen what man has thought he saw!

I've seen the low sun, stained with mystic horrors,
illuminating long violet coagulations,
like actors in very ancient dramas
the waves rolling into the distance their paddle-wheel shudders!

I have dreamt of the green night with dazzled snows,
a kiss rising in slow degrees to the eyes of the seas,
the circulation of unknown saps,
and the yellow-and-blue awakening of singing phosphorescence!

For months on end, I have followed the attack on the reefs
by the surf, similar to hysterical herds of cattle,
without imagining that the luminous feet of the Saint Marys of the Sea
could restrain the muzzle of the short-winded oceans!

I'll have you know that I've jostled incredible Floridas
which mingle with their flowers eyes of panthers that have skins
like men! Rainbows stretched taut like reins,
below the sea's horizon, with blue-green herds!

I've seen fermenting the enormous marshes, nets
in which an entire Leviathan decays in the bulrushes!
Waterslides in the midst of dead calms,
and the distances cataracting toward the abyss!

Glaciers, silver suns, mother-of-pearl waves, skies of hot coals!
Hideous wrecks at the bottom of the brown gulfs
where giant serpents eaten up by bugs
fall, like twisted trees, with black fragrances!

J'aurais voulu montrer aux enfants ces dorades
Du flot bleu, ces poissons d'or, ces poissons chantants.
— Des écumes de fleurs ont bercé mes dérades
Et d'ineffables vents m'ont ailé par instants.

Parfois, martyr lassé des pôles et des zones,
La mer dont le sanglot faisait mon roulis doux
Montait vers moi ses fleurs d'ombre aux ventouses jaunes
Et je restais, ainsi qu'une femme à genoux . . .

Presque île, ballottant sur mes bords les querelles
Et les fientes d'oiseaux clabaudeurs aux yeux blonds.
Et je voguais, lorsqu'à travers mes liens frêles
Des noyés descendaient dormir, à reculons!

Or moi, bateau perdu sous les cheveux des anses,
Jeté par l'ouragan dans l'éther sans oiseau,
Moi dont les Monitors et les voiliers des Hanses
N'auraient pas repêché la carcasse ivre d'eau;

Libre, fumant, monté de brumes violettes,
Moi qui trouais le ciel rougeoyant comme un mur
Qui porte, confiture exquise aux bons poètes,
Des lichens de soleil et des morves d'azur;

Qui courais, taché de lunules électriques,
Planche folle, escorté des hippocampes noirs,
Quand les juillets faisaient crouler à coups de triques
Les cieux ultramarins aux ardents entonnoirs;

Moi qui tremblais, sentant geindre à cinquante lieues
Le rut des Béhémots et les Maelstroms épais,
Fileur éternel des immobilités bleues,
Je regrette l'Europe aux anciens parapets!

J'ai vu des archipels sidéraux! et des îles
Dont les cieux délirants sont ouverts au vogueur:
— Est-ce en ces nuits sans fonds que tu dors et t'exiles,
Million d'oiseaux d'or, ô future Vigueur?

Mais, vrai, j'ai trop pleuré! Les Aubes sont navrantes.
Toute lune est atroce et tout soleil amer:
L'âcre amour m'a gonflé de torpeurs enivrantes.
O que ma quille éclate! O que j'aille à la mer!

I would have liked to show the children those dorados
of the blue waters, those golden fish, those singing fish.
—Foams of flowers have rocked my departures from the roadstead
and ineffable winds have lent me wings at times.

Sometimes, a martyr weary of the poles and the zones,
the sea whose sobbing made my rolling gentle
lifted toward me its flowers of darkness with their yellow suckers
and I'd remain there, like a kneeling woman . . .

a peninsula, tossing around my decks the quarrels
and the droppings of screeching birds with yellow eyes.
And, when drowned men came down to sleep across
my weak cables, I'd sail backwards!

Now, I, a boat lost in the hair of the inlets,
thrown by the hurricane into the birdless ether,
I, whose framework drunken with water couldn't have been
retrieved by a Monitor or by Hanseatic sailing-ships;

free, smoking, equipped with violet fogs,
I, who was piercing the sky that was as red as a wall
bearing that jam beloved of good poets,
lichens of sunshine and mucus of azure;

I, who was running, stained with electric half-moons,
a madcap plank, escorted by the black sea horses,
when Julys made totter with bludgeon blows
the ultramarine skies with burning funnels;

I, who was trembling, hearing fifty leagues off the moaning
of the Behemoths in rut and the dense maelstroms,
an eternal spinner of immobile blue expanses,
I miss Europe with its ancient parapets!

I've seen sidereal archipelagos and islands
whose delirious skies are open to the one sailing by:
—is it on these bottomless nights that you sleep and go into exile,
like a million golden birds, O future vigor?

But, it's true, I've wept too much! The dawns are heartbreaking.
Every moon is atrocious, and every sun bitter:
acrid love has bloated me with intoxicating torpor.
Oh, may my keel burst! Oh, may I sink in the sea!

Si je désire une eau d'Europe, c'est la flache
Noire et froide où vers le crépuscule embaumé
Un enfant accroupi plein de tristesse, lâche
Un bateau frêle comme un papillon de mai.

Je ne puis plus, baigné de vos langueurs, ô lames,
Enlever leur sillage aux porteurs de cotons,
Ni traverser l'orgueil des drapeaux et des flammes,
Ni nager sous les yeux horribles des pontons.

Larme

Loin des oiseaux, des troupeaux, des villageoises,
Je buvais, accroupi dans quelque bruyère
Entourée de tendres bois de noisetiers,
Par un brouillard d'après-midi tiède et vert.

Que pouvais-je boire dans cette jeune Oise,
Ormeaux sans voix, gazon sans fleurs, ciel ouvert.
Que tirais-je à la gourde de colocase?
Quelque liqueur d'or, fade et qui fait suer.

Tel, j'eusse été mauvaise enseigne d'auberge.
Puis l'orage changea le ciel, jusqu'au soir.
Ce furent des pays noirs, des lacs, des perches,
Des colonnades sous la nuit bleue, des gares.

L'eau des bois se perdait sur des sables vierges,
Le vent, du ciel, jetait des glaçons aux mares . . .
Or! tel qu'un pêcheur d'or ou de coquillages,
Dire que je n'ai pas eu souci de boire!

La Rivière de Cassis

La Rivière de Cassis roule ignorée
        En des vaux étranges:
La voix de cent corbeaux l'accompagne, vraie
        Et bonne voix d'anges:

If I long for one body of water in Europe, it's the pool,
black and cold, where, along about the balmy twilight,
a cowering child full of sadness releases
a boat as fragile as a butterfly in May.

Bathed in your languor, O waves, I can no longer
closely follow in the wake of the ships bearing cotton,
or traverse the pride of flags and banners,
or sail beneath the terrifying eyes of the prison hulks.

A Tear

Far from birds, flocks, village women,
I was drinking, on my haunches on some heath
that was surrounded by young hazel thickets,
in a warm, green afternoon mist.

What could I be drinking from this young Oise?[97]
—mute young elms, flowerless turf, clear sky.
What was I drawing from the taro-plant gourd?
Some golden potion, insipid, that brings out a sweat.

In that state, I would have been a bad inn sign.
Then the storm changed the sky, until evening.
There were black lands, lakes, poles,
colonnades in the blue night, railroad stations.

The forest waters were losing themselves in the virgin sand;
the wind, from the sky, was casting blocks of ice into the ponds. . . .
Gold! Like a man fishing for gold or shellfish,
to think that I didn't care about drinking!

The Stream of Cassis[98]

The stream of Cassis flows unknown to man
        in strange vales:
the voice of a hundred crows accompanies it, truly
        a good angelic voice:

---

97. Not the well-known river of that name, but probably a local Ardennes stream.
98. An imaginary proper name? "Currant-colored"?

Avec les grands mouvements des sapinaies
    Quand plusieurs vents plongent.

Tout roule avec des mystères révoltants
    De campagnes d'anciens temps,
De donjons visités, de parcs importants:
    C'est en ces bords qu'on entend
Les passions mortes des chevaliers errants:
    Mais que salubre est le vent!

Que le piéton regarde à ces claires-voies:
    Il ira plus courageux.
Soldats des forêts que le Seigneur envoie,
    Chers corbeaux délicieux!
Faites fuir d'ici le paysan matois
    Qui trinque d'un moignon vieux.

Comédie de la soif

1. Les parents

> Nous sommes tes Grands-Parents,
>   Les Grands!
> Couverts des froides sueurs
> De la lune et des verdures.
> Nos vins secs avaient du cœur!
> Au soleil sans imposture
> Que faut-il à l'homme? boire.

MOI — Mourir aux fleuves barbares.

> Nous sommes tes Grands-Parents
>   Des champs.
> L'eau est au fond des osiers:
> Vois le courant du fossé
> Autour du Château mouillé.
> Descendons en nos celliers;
> Après, le cidre et le lait.

with the large movements of the fir groves
    when several winds dive.

Everything flows with revolting mysteries
    of campaigns[99] of olden days,
of visited castle keeps, of extensive parks:
    it's on these banks that one hears
the dead passions of the knights errant:
    but how healthful the wind is!

Let the foot-traveler look out of these lattices:
    he'll proceed with greater courage.
Forest soldiers sent by the Lord,
    dear, delightful crows!
Drive away from here the crafty peasant
    who clinks glasses with an old stump of an arm.

Comedy of Thirst

1. The Parents

We are your grandparents,
      the great ones!
Covered by the cold sweat
of the moon and the greenery.
Our dry wines were full-bodied!
In the sun without deception
what does man need? To drink.

I: To die in barbarian rivers.

We are your grandparents
      from the country.
The water is at the bottom of the osiers:
see the current of the moat
around the wet castle.
Let's go down to our pantries;
afterwards, cider and milk.[100]

---

99. Or: "countrysides."   100. Another reading (which this editor prefers) omits the semicolon and the comma, making the meaning: "Let's go down to our pantries / to fetch cider and milk."

MOI — Aller où boivent les vaches.

> Nous sommes tes Grands-Parents;
>   Tiens, prends
> Les liqueurs dans nos armoires;
> Le Thé, le Café, si rares,
> Frémissent dans les bouilloires.
> — Vois les images, les fleurs.
> Nous rentrons du cimetière.

MOI — Ah! tarir toutes les urnes!

2. L'esprit

> Éternelles Ondines,
>   Divisez l'eau fine.
> Vénus, sœur de l'azur,
>   Émeus le flot pur.
> Juifs errants de Norwège,
>   Dites-moi la neige.
> Anciens exilés chers,
>   Dites-moi la mer.

MOI — Non, plus ces boissons pures,
>   Ces fleurs d'eau pour verres;
> Légendes ni figures
>   Ne me désaltèrent;
> Chansonnier, ta filleule
>   C'est ma soif si folle
> Hydre intime sans gueules
>   Qui mine et désole.

3. Les amis

> Viens, les Vins vont aux plages,
> Et les flots par millions!
> Vois le Bitter sauvage
> Rouler du haut des monts!
>
> Gagnons, pèlerins, sages,
> L'Absinthe aux verts piliers . . .

MOI — Plus ces paysages.
>   Qu'est l'ivresse, Amis?

✿   ✿   ✿

I: To go where the cows drink.

> We are your grandparents;
>   here, take
> the liquors from our armoires;
> the tea, the coffee, so rare,
> are vibrating in the kettles.
> —See the pictures, the flowers.
> We're coming back from the cemetery.

I: Ah! To dry up all the urns!

2. The Spirit

> Eternal undines,
>   distribute the clear water.
> Venus, sister of the azure,
>   stir up the pure wave.
> Wandering Jews of Norway,
>   tell me about the snow.
> Dear former exiles,
>   tell me about the sea.

I: No, no more of these pure beverages,
>   these aquatic flowers for glasses;
> neither legends nor figures
>   quench my thirst;
> songwriter, your goddaughter
>   is my thirst, so mad,
> an internal hydra without maws
>   which saps the strength and makes one desolate.

3. The Friends

> Come, the wines are going to the beaches,
> and the waves in millions!
> See the wild bitters
> flowing from the mountaintops!

> Like wise pilgrims, let us reach
> absinthe with its green pillars. . . .

I: No more of these landscapes!
> What is drunkenness, friends?

✿   ✿   ✿

J'aime autant, mieux, même,
Pourrir dans l'étang,
Sous l'affreuse crème,
Près des bois flottants.

4. Le pauvre songe

Peut-être un Soir m'attend
Où je boirai tranquille
En quelque vieille Ville,
Et mourrai plus content:
Puisque je suis patient!

Si mon mal se résigne,
Si j'ai jamais quelque or,
Choisirai-je le Nord
Ou le Pays des Vignes? . . .
— Ah songer est indigne

Puisque c'est pure perte!
Et si je redeviens
Le voyageur ancien
Jamais l'auberge verte
Ne peut bien m'être ouverte.

5. Conclusion

Les pigeons qui tremblent dans la prairie,
Le gibier, qui court et qui voit la nuit,
Les bêtes des eaux, la bête asservie,
Les derniers papillons! . . . ont soif aussi.

Mais fondre où fond ce nuage sans guide,
— Oh! favorisé de ce qui est frais!
Expirer en ces violettes humides
Dont les aurores chargent ces forêts?

Bonne pensée du matin

À quatre heures du matin, l'été,
Le Sommeil d'amour dure encore.

I'd just as soon—no, I'd *prefer* to—
rot in the pond,
beneath the frightful cream,
near the floating woods.

4. The Poor Dream

Perhaps an evening awaits me
on which I shall drink calmly
in some old city,
and I shall die more contentedly:
because I'm patient!

If my malaise resigns itself,
if I ever possess any gold,
will I choose the north
or the land of vineyards? . . .
—Ah, dreaming is unworthy

because it's a sheer loss!
And if I become once more
the traveler I used to be,
the green inn may never
be open to me again.

5. Conclusion

The pigeons that tremble in the meadow,
the game animals that run and see at night,
the aquatic animals, the subjugated animal,
the last butterflies! . . . they're thirsty, too.

But to melt where that unguided cloud melts,
—oh, favored by what's fresh and cool!
To expire amid these moist violets
with which the dawns load down these forests?

Kind Thought for the Morning

At four in the morning, in summertime,
love-slumber still lasts.

Sous les bosquets l'aube évapore
   L'odeur du soir fêté.

Mais là-bas dans l'immense chantier
Vers le soleil des Hespérides,
En bras de chemise, les charpentiers
   Déjà s'agitent.

Dans leur désert de mousse, tranquilles,
Ils préparent les lambris précieux
Où la richesse de la ville
   Rira sous de faux cieux.

Ah! pour ces Ouvriers charmants
Sujets d'un roi de Babylone,
Vénus! laisse un peu les Amants,
   Dont l'âme est en couronne.

      O Reine des Bergers!
Porte aux travailleurs l'eau-de-vie,
Pour que leurs forces soient en paix
En attendant le bain dans la mer, à midi.

Bannières de mai

Aux branches claires des tilleuls
Meurt un maladif hallalli.
Mais des chansons spirituelles
Voltigent parmi les groseilles.
Que notre sang rie en nos veines,
Voici s'enchevêtrer les vignes.
Le ciel est joli comme un ange,
L'azur et l'onde communient.
Je sors. Si un rayon me blesse
Je succomberai sur la mousse.

Qu'on patiente et qu'on s'ennuie
C'est trop simple. Fi de mes peines.
Je veux que l'été dramatique
Me lie à son char de fortune.

Beneath the copses the dawn dispels
    the smell of the festive evening.

But over yonder in the vast lumberyard
toward the sun of the Hesperides,
in shirtsleeves the carpenters
    are already bustling about.

In their mossy wilderness, tranquilly,
they are preparing the costly wainscoting
within which the wealth of the city
    will laugh under imitation skies.

Oh, for those charming workmen,
subjects of a king of Babylon,
Venus, for a moment leave those lovers
    whose soul is in the form of a wreath.[101]

    O queen of shepherds,[102]
take the brandy to the laborers,
so that their strength may be in peace
while awaiting a swim in the sea at noon.

Banners of May

In the bright branches of the lindens
a sickly hunting-mort dies away.
But religious songs
flit among the currant bushes.
So that our blood may laugh in our veins,
see how the grapevines tangle together.
The sky is as pretty as an angel,
the azure and the wave are in communion.
I'm going out. If a sunbeam wounds me
I'll succumb on the moss.

To be patient and be bored—
that's too simple. A fig for my troubles!
I want the dramatic summer
to bind me to its chariot of fortune.

---

101. One scholar has suggested that this line alludes to simultaneous multiple sodomy.   102. Here, and in the next poem, "shepherd" surely stands for "lover."

Que par toi beaucoup, ô Nature,
— Ah moins seul et moins nul! — je meure.
Au lieu que les Bergers, c'est drôle,
Meurent à peu près par le monde.

Je veux bien que les saisons m'usent.
À toi, Nature, je me rends;
Et ma faim et toute ma soif.
Et, s'il te plaît, nourris, abreuve.
Rien de rien ne m'illusionne;
C'est rire aux parents, qu'au soleil,
Mais moi je ne veux rire à rien;
Et libre soit cette infortune.

Chanson de la plus haute tour

Oisive jeunesse
À tout asservie,
Par délicatesse
J'ai perdu ma vie.
Ah! Que le temps vienne
Où les cœurs s'éprennent.

Je me suis dit: laisse,
Et qu'on ne te voie:
Et sans la promesse
De plus hautes joies.
Que rien ne t'arrête,
Auguste retraite.

J'ai tant fait patience
Qu'à jamais j'oublie;
Craintes et souffrances
Aux cieux sont parties.
Et la soif malsaine
Obscurcit mes veines.

Ainsi la Prairie
À l'oubli livrée,
Grandie, et fleurie
D'encens et d'ivraies
Au bourdon farouche
De cent sales mouches.

O Nature, greatly at your hands
may I die—ah, less lonely and less of a cipher!
Whereas the shepherds (how comical!)
die more or less at the hands of society.

I'm willing to have the seasons wear me out.
To you, Nature, I surrender,
along with my hunger and all my thirst.
If you wish, give me food and drink.
Nothing whatsoever deludes me;
to laugh at the sun is like laughing at one's parents,
but I don't want to laugh at anything;
and may this ill luck be free.

Song of the Highest Tower

Idle youth,
a slave to everything,
through delicacy of feelings
I've wasted my life.
Ah, let that time come
when hearts fall in love!

I've told myself: drop it,
let no one see you:
and without the promise
of higher joys.
Let nothing stop you,
august retreat.

I've been patient so long
that I'm forever forgetting;
fear and suffering
have departed for the skies.
And an unwholesome thirst
darkens my veins.

Like the meadow
consigned to oblivion,
grown and blossoming
with incense and darnels,
amid the fierce buzzing
of a hundred filthy flies.

Ah! Mille veuvages
De la si pauvre âme
Qui n'a que l'image
De la Notre-Dame!
Est-ce que l'on prie
La Vierge Marie?

Oisive jeunesse
À tout asservie,
Par délicatesse
J'ai perdu ma vie.
Ah! Que le temps vienne
Où les cœurs s'éprennent!

L'éternité

Elle est retrouvée.
Quoi? — L'Éternité.
C'est la mer allée
Avec le soleil.

Âme sentinelle,
Murmurons l'aveu
De la nuit si nulle
Et du jour en feu.

Des humains suffrages,
Des communs élans
Là tu te dégages
Et voles selon.

Puisque de vous seules,
Braises de satin,
Le Devoir s'exhale
Sans qu'on dise: enfin.

Là pas d'espérance,
Nul orietur,
Science avec patience,
Le supplice est sûr.

Ah! A thousand widowhoods
of that soul so impoverished
which possesses nothing but the image
of Our Lady!
Does anyone pray to
the Virgin Mary?

Idle youth,
a slave to everything,
through delicacy of feelings
I've wasted my life.
Ah, let that time come
when hearts fall in love!

Eternity

It has been found again!
What? Eternity.
It's the sea that has departed
with the sun.

Sentinel soul,
let us murmur the confession
of the night so worthless
and the fiery day.

Then you detach yourself
from human approbation,
from everyday impulses,
and you fly wherever you wish.

Because from you alone,
embers of satin,
duty emanates
without anyone saying "at last."

There, no hope,
no *orietur*,[103]
science and patience,
torture is a certainty.

---

103. Latin for "[the sun] shall rise."

Elle est retrouvée.
Quoi? — L'Éternité.
C'est la mer allée
Avec le soleil.

Âge d'or

Quelqu'une des voix
Toujours angélique
— Il s'agit de moi, —
Vertement s'explique:

Ces mille questions
Qui se ramifient
N'amènent, au fond,
Qu'ivresse et folie;

Reconnais ce tour
Si gai, si facile:
Ce n'est qu'onde, flore,
Et c'est ta famille!

Puis elle chante. O
Si gai, si facile,
Et visible à l'œil nu . . .
— Je chante avec elle, —

Reconnais ce tour
Si gai, si facile,
Ce n'est qu'onde, flore,
Et c'est ta famille! . . . etc . . .

Et puis une Voix
— Est-elle angélique! —
Il s'agit de moi,
Vertement s'explique;

Et chante à l'instant
En sœur des haleines:
D'un ton Allemand,
Mais ardente et pleine:

Le monde est vicieux;
Si cela t'étonne!

It has been found again!
What? Eternity.
It's the sea that has departed
with the sun.

Golden Age

Some one of the voices,
one that's always angelic
—the subject is me—
is giving a sharp tongue-lashing:

These thousand questions
which ramify
produce, when you come down to it,
only drunkenness and madness;

recognize this stunt
so merry, so easy;
it is only water, flora,
and it's your family!

Then she sings. Oh,
so merry, so easy,
and visible to the naked eye . . .
—I sing along with her,—

Recognize this stunt
so merry, so easy;
it is only water, flora,
and it's your family! (etc.)

And then a voice
—how angelic it is!—
the subject is me—
gives a sharp tongue-lashing;

and instantly sings,
a sister to our breath:
in a German tone,
but ardently and in full voice:

"The world is full of vice;
should that surprise you?!

Vis et laisse au feu
L'obscure infortune.

O! joli château!
Que ta vie est claire!
De quel Âge es-tu,
Nature princière
De notre grand frère! etc . . .

Je chante aussi, moi:
Multiples sœurs! Voix
Pas du tout publiques!
Environnez-moi
De gloire pudique . . . etc . . .

Jeune ménage

La chambre est ouverte au ciel bleu-turquin,
Pas de place: des coffrets et des huches!
Dehors le mur est plein d'aristoloches
Où vibrent les gencives des lutins.

Que ce sont bien intrigues de génies
Cette dépense et ces désordres vains!
C'est la fée africaine qui fournit
La mûre, et les résilles dans les coins.

Plusieurs entrent, marraines mécontentes,
En pans de lumière dans les buffets,
Puis y restent! le ménage s'absente
Peu sérieusement, et rien ne se fait.

Le marié a le vent qui le floue
Pendant son absence, ici, tout le temps.
Même des esprits des eaux, malfaisants,
Entrent vaguer aux sphères de l'alcôve.

La nuit, l'amie oh! la lune de miel
Cueillera leur sourire et remplira

Live, and leave obscure
ill luck to the fire!"

O pretty château!
How bright your life is!
Of what age are you,
princely nature
of our elder brother? (etc.)

I'm singing, too:
multiple sisters! Voices
not at all public!
Surround me
with modest glory. . . . (etc.)

Young Couple

The room is open to the slate-blue[104] sky;
no space: foot lockers and bread bins!
Outside, the wall is full of birthworts[105]
in which the goblins' gums vibrate.

How truly they're intrigues of genies,
this meaningless expense and this disorder!
It's the African fairy who supplies
the mulberry, and the netting in the corners.

Several of them, discontented godmothers, enter
the sideboards in flashes of light,
then stay there! The couple are out,
frivolously, and nothing gets done.

The husband has the wind to cheat on him here
while he's away, all the time.
Even water sprites, malevolent ones,
come in and roam around the orbits of the bedroom.

The night, the friendly night, oh, the honey moon
will gather their smile and will fill

---

104. Or: "dark blue." Or: "turquoise."   105. Climbing plants popularly thought to
possess the property of easing childbirth.

De mille bandeaux de cuivre le ciel.
Puis ils auront affaire au malin rat.

— S'il n'arrive pas un feu follet blême,
Comme un coup de fusil, après des vêpres.
— O spectres saints et blancs de Bethléem,
Charmez plutôt le bleu de leur fenêtre!

"Plates-bandes d'amarantes . . ."

Bruxelles,
Boulevard du Régent.

Juillet

Plates-bandes d'amarantes jusqu'à
L'agréable palais de Jupiter.
— Je sais que c'est Toi qui, dans ces lieux,
Mêles ton Bleu presque de Sahara!

Puis, comme rose et sapin du soleil
Et liane ont ici leurs jeux enclos,
Cage de la petite veuve! . . .
                              Quelles
Troupes d'oiseaux, ô iaio, iaio! . . .

— Calmes maisons, anciennes passions!
Kiosque de la Folle par affection.
Après les fesses des rosiers, balcon
Ombreux et très bas de la Juliette.

— La Juliette, ça rappelle l'Henriette,
Charmante station du chemin de fer,
Au cœur d'un mont, comme au fond d'un verger
Où mille diables bleus dansent dans l'air!

Banc vert où chante au paradis d'orage,
Sur la guitare, la blanche Irlandaise.
Puis, de la salle à manger guyanaise,
Bavardage des enfants et des cages.

the sky[106] with a thousand copper headbands.
Then they'll have to deal with the sly rat.[107]

—If a pale will-o'-the-wisp doesn't arrive
like a rifle shot, after vespers.
—O holy, white ghosts of Bethlehem,
rather than that, cast a spell on the blue of their window!

"Flower Beds of Amaranth . . ."[108]

July

Brussels,
Boulevard du Régent.

Flower beds of amaranth all the way to
Jupiter's charming palace.[109]
—I know it's you, Jupiter, who, in these places,
blends-in your blue almost like that of the Sahara!

Then, since the rose and the fir of the sun
and the liana have their enclosed playgrounds here,
cage of the little "widow"![110]
                               What
troops of birds, oh, iaio, iaio! . . .

—Calm houses, bygone passions!
Kiosk of the woman who went mad with love.
After the props[111] of the rosebushes, the balcony,
shady and very low, of Juliet.

—Juliet reminds me of Henriette,
a delightful stop on the railroad,
in the heart of a hill, as if at the far end of an orchard
where a thousand blue devils dance in the air!

Green bench on which to the paradise of storm
the white Irishwoman sings, with guitar accompaniment.
Then, from the Guianese dining room,
the chattering of children and of cages.

---

106. Or: "[bed] tester."   107. One scholar thinks this means an unsuccessful copulation.   108. Some editors take the word "Bruxelles" to be the title.   109. Perhaps the Palais des Académies.   110. This may designate a type of African sparrow, or may allude sarcastically to Verlaine.   111. Or: "beds."

Fenêtre du duc qui fais que je pense
Au poison des escargots et du buis
Qui dort ici-bas au soleil.
                    Et puis
C'est trop beau! trop! Gardons notre silence.

— Boulevard sans mouvement ni commerce,
Muet, tout drame et toute comédie,
Réunion des scènes infinie,
Je te connais et t'admire en silence.

"Est-elle almée? . . ."

Est-elle almée? . . . aux premières heures bleues
Se détruira-t-elle comme les fleurs feues . . .
Devant la splendide étendue où l'on sente
Souffler la ville énormément florissante!

C'est trop beau! c'est trop beau! mais c'est nécessaire
— Pour la Pêcheuse et la chanson du Corsaire,
Et aussi puisque les derniers masques crurent
Encore aux fêtes du nuit sur la mer pure!

Fêtes de la faim

          Ma faim, Anne, Anne,
          Fuis sur ton âne.

Si j'ai du *goût,* ce n'est guères
Que pour la terre et les pierres.
Dinn! dinn! dinn! dinn! je pais l'air,
Le roc, les Terres, le fer.

Tournez, les faims! paissez, faims,
          Le pré des sons!
L'aimable et vibrant venin
          Des liserons;

You, the duke's[112] window, you make me think
of the poison of the snails and of the boxwood
which sleeps down here in the sun.
                                And, besides,
it's too beautiful! Too much so! Let's keep silent.

Boulevard without traffic or commerce,
mute, every drama and every comedy,
infinite meeting place of theatrical scenes,
I know you and I admire you in silence.

"Is She an Almeh? . . ."

Is she an Almeh?[113] . . . In the first blue hours
will she destroy herself like the deceased flowers . . .
in front of the splendid expanse where you can feel
the enormously prosperous city breathing?!

It's too beautiful! It's too beautiful! but it's necessary
—for the fisherwoman and the song of the corsair,
and also because the last masquers still
believed in the nocturnal parties on the pure sea!

Feasts of Hunger

            My hunger, Anne, Anne,[114]
            flee on your donkey!

If I have an appetite, it's for hardly
anything else than earth and stones.
Ding, ding, ding, ding! I graze on air,
rock, soils, iron.

Turn, my hungers! Graze, hungers,
      on the pasture of sounds!
the charming, vibrant venom
      of the bindweeds;

---

112. Maybe the Duke of Arenberg, whose palace was on the Boulevard du Régent.
113. Egyptian dancing girl.   114. Almost any Frenchman would be reminded of the
sister Anne whom the heroine repeatedly addresses by name in Perrault's "Bluebeard."

Les cailloux qu'un pauvre brise,
Les vieilles pierres d'églises,
Les galets, fils des déluges,
Pains couchés aux vallées grises!

Mes faims, c'est les bouts d'air noir;
    L'azur sonneur;
— C'est l'estomac qui me tire.
    C'est le malheur.

Sur terre ont paru les feuilles:
Je vais aux chairs de fruits blettes,
Au sein du sillon je cueille
La doucette et la violette.

      Ma faim, Anne, Anne!
      Fuis sur ton âne.

"Qu'est-ce pour nous, mon cœur . . ."

Qu'est-ce pour nous, mon cœur, que les nappes de sang
Et de braise, et mille meurtres, et les longs cris
De rage, sanglots de tout enfer renversant
Tout ordre; et l'Aquilon encor sur les débris;

Et toute vengeance? Rien! . . . — Mais si, toute encor,
Nous la voulons! Industriels, princes, sénats:
Périssez! puissance, justice, histoire: à bas!
Ça nous est dû. Le sang! le sang! la flamme d'or!

Tout à la guerre de la vengeance, à la terreur,
Mon esprit! Tournons dans la morsure: Ah! passez,
Républiques de ce monde! Des empereurs,
Des régiments, des colons, des peuples, assez!

Qui remuerait les tourbillons de feu furieux,
Que nous et ceux que nous nous imaginons frères?
À nous, romanesques amis: ça va nous plaire.
Jamais nous ne travaillerons, ô flots de feux!

Europe, Asie, Amérique, disparaissez.
Notre marche vengeresse a tout occupé,
Cités et campagnes! — Nous serons écrasés!
Les volcans sauteront! Et l'Océan frappé . . .

the rocks that a poor man breaks,
the old stones of churches,
the shingles, sons of the floods,
loaves lying in gray valleys!

My hungers are scraps of black air;
    the ringing azure;
—they're my stomach griping.
    They're misfortune.

On earth the leaves have appeared:
I go to the flesh of overripe fruit,
in the bosom of the furrow I pick
lamb's-lettuce and violets.

    My hunger, Anne, Anne,
    flee on your donkey!

"What Are They to Us, My Heart . . ."

What are they to us, my heart, the sheets of blood
and of embers, and a thousand murders, and the long cries
of rage, the sobs of every hell overturning
all order; and the north wind still on the ruins;

and all vengeance? Nothing! . . .—But yes, all that vengeance,
we still want it! Industrialists, princes, senates:
perish! Power, justice, history: down with them!
That's owed us. Blood! Blood! The golden flame!

Devote yourself entirely to the war for vengeance, to terror,
my mind! Let's turn around in the jaws that bite us: ah, pass away,
republics of this world! Emperors,
regiments, colonists, nations—enough of them!

Who would stir up the whirlwinds of furious fire,
if not us and those whom we imagine to be our brothers?
Come to our aid, romantically minded friends: we shall like that.
We shall never do labor, O streams of fire!

Europe, Asia, America, disappear!
Our avenging march has occupied everything,
cities and rural areas!—We will be crushed!
The volcanoes will erupt! and the stricken ocean . . .

Oh! mes amis! — Mon cœur, c'est sûr, ils sont des frères:
Noirs inconnus, si nous allions! Allons! allons!
O malheur! je me sens frémir, la vieille terre,
Sur moi de plus en plus à vous! la terre fond.

Ce n'est rien! j'y suis! j'y suis toujours.

"Entends comme brame . . ."

Entends comme brame
près des acacias
en avril la rame
viride du pois!

Dans sa vapeur nette,
vers Phœbé! tu vois
s'agiter la tête
de saints d'autrefois . . .

Loin des claires meules
des caps, des beaux toits,
ces chers Anciens veulent
ce philtre sournois . . .

Or ni fériale
ni astrale! n'est
la brume qu'exhale
ce nocturne effet.

Néanmoins ils restent,
— Sicile, Allemagne,
dans ce brouillard triste
et blêmi, justement!

Oh, my friends!—My heart, they're brothers, I'm sure of it:
obscure strangers, why not set out? Let's go! Let's go!
Oh, woe! I feel myself shuddering; the old earth,
the earth is dissolving onto me, I who am more and more yours!

It's nothing! I'm still here! I'm here for always.

"Hear How It Bellows . . ."

Hear how it bellows
near the acacias
in April—the verdant
branch of the pea-plant!

In its clean vapor,
toward the moon you see
them shaking their heads,
the saints of days gone by! . . .

Far from the bright millstones[115]
of the capes, from the beautiful roofs,
these dear ancients want
that sly potion. . . .

Now, the mist exhaled
by that nocturnal phenomenon
is neither ferial
nor astral!

All the same, they remain—
Sicily, Germany—
in that sad fog,
that pale fog, rightly so![116]

---

115. Or: "haystacks."   116. Editors persist in seeing a rhyme "for the eyes only" in *restent* and *justement,* but the rhyme scheme throughout the poem has been ABAB, and it may very well be that *restent / triste* and *Allemagne / justement* are assonating pairs.

Michel et Christine

Zut alors, si le soleil quitte ces bords!
Fuis, clair déluge! voici l'ombre des routes.
Dans les saules, dans la vieille cour d'honneur,
L'orage d'abord jette ses larges gouttes.

O cent agneaux, de l'idylle soldats blonds,
Des aqueducs, des bruyères amaigries,
Fuyez! plaine, déserts, prairie, horizons
Sont à la toilette rouge de l'orage!

Chien noir, brun pasteur dont le manteau s'engouffre,
Fuyez l'heure des éclairs supérieurs;
Blond troupeau, quand voici nager ombre et soufre,
Tâchez de descendre à des retraits meilleurs.

Mais moi, Seigneur! voici que mon esprit vole,
Après les cieux glacés de rouge, sous les
Nuages célestes qui courent et volent
Sur cent Solognes longues comme un railway.

Voilà mille loups, mille graines sauvages
Qu'emporte, non sans aimer les liserons,
Cette religieuse après-midi d'orage
Sur l'Europe ancienne où cent hordes iront!

Après le clair de lune! partout la lande,
Rougissant leurs fronts aux cieux noirs, les guerriers
Chevauchent lentement leurs pâles coursiers!
Les cailloux sonnent sous cette fière bande!

Et verrai-je le bois jaune et le val clair,
L'Épouse aux yeux bleus, l'homme au front rouge, ô Gaule,
Et le blanc Agneau Pascal, à leurs pieds chers,
— Michel et Christine, — et Christ! fin de l'Idylle.

Honte

Tant que la lame n'aura
Pas coupé cette cervelle,

Michel and Christine[117]

Damn it all, if the sun abandons these strands!
Flee, bright flood! Here is the shadow of the roads.
Into the willows, into the castle's old main courtyard
the storm begins by casting its heavy drops.

O hundred lambs, blond soldiers of pastoral poems,
from the aqueducts, from the thinned-out heaths
flee! Plain, deserts, grassland, horizons
wear the red garments of the storm!

Black dog, brown shepherd whose cloak is engulfed,
flee the hour of the superior lightning flashes;
yellow flock, since shadow and sulphur are swimming this way,
try to descend to better places of shelter.

But as for me, Lord! My mind is now flying
after the skies glazed with red, under the
heavenly clouds that race and fly
over a hundred Solognes[118] as long as a railway.

See there: a thousand wolves, a thousand wild seeds
being carried off (not that it doesn't love the bindweeds)
by this religious stormy afternoon
onto ancient Europe, where a hundred hordes will trek!

After the moonlight! Everywhere on the moor,
reddening their brows on the black skies, the warriors
slowly ride their pale chargers!
The pebbles ring beneath that proud band!

And will I see the yellow woods and the bright vale,
the blue-eyed bride, the red-browed man, O Gaul,
and the white Easter Lamb, at their dear feet,
—Michel and Christine,—and Christ, end of the idyll?

Shame

So long as the blade shall not have
sliced through that brain,

---

117. Title of a *vaudeville* (light comedy with music) with text by Eugène Scribe (1791–1861).   118. The Sologne is a large forested plain south of the Loire.

Ce paquet blanc, vert et gras,
À vapeur jamais nouvelle,

(Ah! Lui, devrait couper son
Nez, sa lèvre, ses oreilles,
Son ventre! et faire abandon
De ses jambes! ô merveille!)

Mais, non; vrai, je crois que tant
Que pour sa tête la lame,
Que les cailloux pour son flanc,
Que pour ses boyaux la flamme,

N'auront pas agi, l'enfant
Gêneur, la si sotte bête,
Ne doit cesser un instant
De ruser et d'être traître,

Comme un chat des Monts-Rocheux,
D'empuantir toutes sphères!
Qu'à sa mort pourtant, ô mon Dieu!
S'élève quelque prière!

Mémoire

I

L'eau claire; comme le sel des larmes d'enfance,
L'assaut au soleil des blancheurs des corps de femmes;
la soie, en foule et de lys pur, des oriflammes
sous les murs dont quelque pucelle eut la défense;

l'ébat des anges; — Non . . . le courant d'or en marche,
meut ses bras, noirs, et lourds, et frais surtout, d'herbe. Elle
sombre, ayant le Ciel bleu pour ciel-de-lit, appelle
pour rideaux l'ombre de la colline et de l'arche.

that white, green, and fatty bundle
with ever-renewed steam,

(Ah, *he* ought to cut his
nose, his lip, his ears,
his belly, and surrender
his legs, O wonder!)

But no; truly, I believe that so long
as the blade for his head,
the stones for his side,
the flame for his bowels

haven't done their job, that troublesome
boy, that so foolish animal,
won't cease for an instant
to make crafty plans and play the villain,

like a cat from the Rocky Mountains,[119]
to pollute every sphere!
Nevertheless, when he dies, O God,
let some prayer be spoken!

Memory

I

The bright water; like the salt of childhood tears,
the attack on the sun by the whiteness of women's bodies;
the silk, in a throng and of pure lily, of the royal banners
beneath the walls that were defended by some maiden;

the sport of angels;—no . . . the golden current on its way
moves its arms of grass, black, heavy, and above all cool. It,[120]
somber, having[121] the blue sky for a tester, summons
for bed curtains the shadow of the hill and the ark.

---

119. *Rocheux* may also be a humorous reference to Roche, the place in the Ardennes where Rimbaud's mother owned a family farm, and where he sometimes stayed.   120. The grass or the water?   121. *Sombre* may be the verb "sinks"; some editions print *avant* ("before") in place of *ayant* ("having").

II

Eh! l'humide carreau tend ses bouillons limpides!
L'eau meuble d'or pâle et sans fond les couches prêtes.
Les robes vertes et déteintes des fillettes
font les saules, d'où sautent les oiseaux sans brides.

Plus pure qu'un louis, jaune et chaude paupière,
le souci d'eau — ta foi conjugale, ô l'Épouse! —
au midi prompt, de son terne miroir, jalouse
au ciel gris de chaleur la Sphère rose et chère.

III

Madame se tient trop debout dans la prairie
prochaine où neigent les fils du travail; l'ombrelle
aux doigts; foulant l'ombelle; trop fière pour elle;
des enfants lisant dans la verdure fleurie

leur livre de maroquin rouge! Hélas, Lui, comme
mille anges blancs qui se séparent sur la route,
s'éloigne par-delà la montagne! Elle, toute
froide, et noire, court! après le départ de l'homme!

IV

Regret des bras épais et jeunes d'herbe pure!
Or des lunes d'avril au cœur du saint lit! Joie
des chantiers riverains à l'abandon, en proie
aux soirs d'août qui faisaient germer ces pourritures!

Qu'elle pleure à présent sous les remparts! l'haleine
des peupliers d'en haut est pour la seule brise.
Puis, c'est la nappe, sans reflets, sans source, grise:
un vieux, dragueur, dans sa barque immobile, peine.

V

Jouet de cet œil d'eau morne, je n'y puis prendre,
ô canot immobile! oh! bras trop courts! ni l'une
ni l'autre fleur: ni la jaune qui m'importune,
là; ni la bleue, amie à l'eau couleur de cendre.

II

Ah, the moist glassy plane spreads out its limpid broths!
The water furnishes the ready layers with pale, bottomless gold.
The girls' green, washed-out dresses
depict willows, from which the birds hop without bridles.

Purer than a gold coin, young, hot eyelid,
the marsh-marigold—your marriage vow of fidelity, O bride!—
in the prompt noon, from its dull mirror, envies
the dear pink sphere in the sky gray with heat.

III

Madame is standing too erect in the nearby
meadow where the threads[122] of labor snow down; her parasol
in her hand; treading the umbel; too proud for her own good;
children reading in the blossoming greenery

their book bound in red morocco! Alas, *he*, like
a thousand white angels parting ways on the road,
goes far off beyond the mountains! She, all
cold, and dark, runs after the man who has departed!

IV

A longing for the thick young arms of pure grass!
Gold of April moons in the heart of the holy bed! Joy
of the neglected riverside shipyards, a prey
to the August evenings which made this rottenness germinate!

Let her weep now below the ramparts! The breath
of the poplars above provides the only breeze.
Then, there's the sheet of water, without reflections or source, gray:
an old man, dragnet-fishing, motionless in his boat, labors.

V

Plaything of this dismal water-eye, I cannot seize,
O motionless boat, oh, too-short arms, either one
flower or the other: neither the yellow one that solicits me,
there, nor the blue one, friend to the ash-colored water.

---

122. Probably not: "sons." Possibly spiderwebs.

Ah! la poudre des saules qu'une aile secoue!
Les roses des roseaux dès longtemps dévorées!
Mon canot, toujours fixe; et sa chaîne tirée
Au fond de cet œil d'eau sans bords, — à quelle boue?

"O saisons, ô châteaux . . ."

O saisons, ô châteaux,
Quelle âme est sans défauts?

O saisons, ô châteaux,

J'ai fait la magique étude
Du Bonheur, que nul n'élude.

O vive lui, chaque fois
Que chante son coq gaulois.

Mais! je n'aurai plus d'envie,
Il s'est chargé de ma vie.

Ce Charme! il prit âme et corps,
Et dispersa tous efforts.

Que comprendre à ma parole?
Il fait qu'elle fuie et vole!

O saisons, ô châteaux!

Et, si le malheur m'entraîne,
Sa disgrâce m'est certaine.

Il faut que son dédain, las!
Me livre au plus prompt trépas!

— O Saisons, ô Châteaux!
Quelle âme est sans défauts?

Ah, the dust of the willows, shaken by a wing!
the reed roses long since devoured!
My boat, constantly stationary; and its cable tugged
to the bottom of this marginless water-eye—to what mud?

"O Seasons, O Castles . . ."

O seasons, O castles,
what soul is free of defects?

O seasons, O castles,

I have made the magical study
of happiness, which no one eludes.

Oh, long may it live, each time
that its Gallic cock crows!

But I won't have any more desires,
it has resumed responsibility for my life.

That charm! It took on a soul and a body
and scattered every effort.

How are my words to be understood?
It makes them flee and fly!

O seasons, O castles!

And if misfortune inveigles me,
its disfavor toward me is assured.

Without fail, alas, its disdain
will consign me to the promptest death!

—O seasons, O castles!
What soul is free of defects?

ALPHABETICAL LIST
OF FRENCH TITLES OF VERSE POEMS

ALPHABETICAL LIST OF FRENCH
FIRST LINES OF VERSE POEMS[1]

---

1. This list does not include the variant versions of some of the poems as printed in
Une saison en enfer.

A CATALOG OF SELECTED
DOVER BOOKS
IN ALL FIELDS OF INTEREST

A CATALOG OF SELECTED DOVER
BOOKS IN ALL FIELDS OF INTEREST

CONCERNING THE SPIRITUAL IN ART, Wassily Kandinsky. Pioneering work by father of abstract art. Thoughts on color theory, nature of art. Analysis of earlier masters. 12 illustrations. 80pp. of text. 5⅜ x 8½.   23411-8

ANIMALS: 1,419 Copyright-Free Illustrations of Mammals, Birds, Fish, Insects, etc., Jim Harter (ed.). Clear wood engravings present, in extremely lifelike poses, over 1,000 species of animals. One of the most extensive pictorial sourcebooks of its kind. Captions. Index. 284pp. 9 x 12.   23766-4

CELTIC ART: The Methods of Construction, George Bain. Simple geometric techniques for making Celtic interlacements, spirals, Kells-type initials, animals, humans, etc. Over 500 illustrations. 160pp. 9 x 12. (Available in U.S. only.)   22923-8

AN ATLAS OF ANATOMY FOR ARTISTS, Fritz Schider. Most thorough reference work on art anatomy in the world. Hundreds of illustrations, including selections from works by Vesalius, Leonardo, Goya, Ingres, Michelangelo, others. 593 illustrations. 192pp. 7⅛ x 10¼.   20241-0

CELTIC HAND STROKE-BY-STROKE (Irish Half-Uncial from "The Book of Kells"): An Arthur Baker Calligraphy Manual, Arthur Baker. Complete guide to creating each letter of the alphabet in distinctive Celtic manner. Covers hand position, strokes, pens, inks, paper, more. Illustrated. 48pp. 8¼ x 11.   24336-2

EASY ORIGAMI, John Montroll. Charming collection of 32 projects (hat, cup, pelican, piano, swan, many more) specially designed for the novice origami hobbyist. Clearly illustrated easy-to-follow instructions insure that even beginning papercrafters will achieve successful results. 48pp. 8¼ x 11.   27298-2

THE COMPLETE BOOK OF BIRDHOUSE CONSTRUCTION FOR WOOD-WORKERS, Scott D. Campbell. Detailed instructions, illustrations, tables. Also data on bird habitat and instinct patterns. Bibliography. 3 tables. 63 illustrations in 15 figures. 48pp. 5¼ x 8½.   24407-5

BLOOMINGDALE'S ILLUSTRATED 1886 CATALOG: Fashions, Dry Goods and Housewares, Bloomingdale Brothers. Famed merchants' extremely rare catalog depicting about 1,700 products: clothing, housewares, firearms, dry goods, jewelry, more. Invaluable for dating, identifying vintage items. Also, copyright-free graphics for artists, designers. Co-published with Henry Ford Museum & Greenfield Village. 160pp. 8¼ x 11.   25780-0

HISTORIC COSTUME IN PICTURES, Braun & Schneider. Over 1,450 costumed figures in clearly detailed engravings—from dawn of civilization to end of 19th century. Captions. Many folk costumes. 256pp. 8⅜ x 11¾.   23150-X

STICKLEY CRAFTSMAN FURNITURE CATALOGS, Gustav Stickley and L. & J. G. Stickley. Beautiful, functional furniture in two authentic catalogs from 1910. 594 illustrations, including 277 photos, show settles, rockers, armchairs, reclining chairs, bookcases, desks, tables. 183pp. 6½ x 9¼. 23838-5

AMERICAN LOCOMOTIVES IN HISTORIC PHOTOGRAPHS: 1858 to 1949, Ron Ziel (ed.). A rare collection of 126 meticulously detailed official photographs, called "builder portraits," of American locomotives that majestically chronicle the rise of steam locomotive power in America. Introduction. Detailed captions. xi+ 129pp. 9 x 12. 27393-8

AMERICA'S LIGHTHOUSES: An Illustrated History, Francis Ross Holland, Jr. Delightfully written, profusely illustrated fact-filled survey of over 200 American lighthouses since 1716. History, anecdotes, technological advances, more. 240pp. 8 x 10¾. 25576-X

TOWARDS A NEW ARCHITECTURE, Le Corbusier. Pioneering manifesto by founder of "International School." Technical and aesthetic theories, views of industry, economics, relation of form to function, "mass-production split" and much more. Profusely illustrated. 320pp. 6⅛ x 9¼. (Available in U.S. only.) 25023-7

HOW THE OTHER HALF LIVES, Jacob Riis. Famous journalistic record, exposing poverty and degradation of New York slums around 1900, by major social reformer. 100 striking and influential photographs. 233pp. 10 x 7⅞. 22012-5

FRUIT KEY AND TWIG KEY TO TREES AND SHRUBS, William M. Harlow. One of the handiest and most widely used identification aids. Fruit key covers 120 deciduous and evergreen species; twig key 160 deciduous species. Easily used. Over 300 photographs. 126pp. 5⅜ x 8½. 20511-8

COMMON BIRD SONGS, Dr. Donald J. Borror. Songs of 60 most common U.S. birds: robins, sparrows, cardinals, bluejays, finches, more–arranged in order of increasing complexity. Up to 9 variations of songs of each species.
Cassette and manual 99911-4

ORCHIDS AS HOUSE PLANTS, Rebecca Tyson Northen. Grow cattleyas and many other kinds of orchids–in a window, in a case, or under artificial light. 63 illustrations. 148pp. 5⅜ x 8½. 23261-1

MONSTER MAZES, Dave Phillips. Masterful mazes at four levels of difficulty. Avoid deadly perils and evil creatures to find magical treasures. Solutions for all 32 exciting illustrated puzzles. 48pp. 8¼ x 11. 26005-4

MOZART'S DON GIOVANNI (DOVER OPERA LIBRETTO SERIES), Wolfgang Amadeus Mozart. Introduced and translated by Ellen H. Bleiler. Standard Italian libretto, with complete English translation. Convenient and thoroughly portable–an ideal companion for reading along with a recording or the performance itself. Introduction. List of characters. Plot summary. 121pp. 5¼ x 8½. 24944-1

TECHNICAL MANUAL AND DICTIONARY OF CLASSICAL BALLET, Gail Grant. Defines, explains, comments on steps, movements, poses and concepts. 15-page pictorial section. Basic book for student, viewer. 127pp. 5⅜ x 8½. 21843-0

THE CLARINET AND CLARINET PLAYING, David Pino. Lively, comprehensive work features suggestions about technique, musicianship, and musical interpretation, as well as guidelines for teaching, making your own reeds, and preparing for public performance. Includes an intriguing look at clarinet history. "A godsend," *The Clarinet,* Journal of the International Clarinet Society. Appendixes. 7 illus. 320pp. 5⅜ x 8½. 40270-3

HOLLYWOOD GLAMOR PORTRAITS, John Kobal (ed.). 145 photos from 1926-49. Harlow, Gable, Bogart, Bacall; 94 stars in all. Full background on photographers, technical aspects. 160pp. 8⅜ x 11¼. 23352-9

THE ANNOTATED CASEY AT THE BAT: A Collection of Ballads about the Mighty Casey/Third, Revised Edition, Martin Gardner (ed.). Amusing sequels and parodies of one of America's best-loved poems: Casey's Revenge, Why Casey Whiffed, Casey's Sister at the Bat, others. 256pp. 5⅜ x 8½. 28598-7

THE RAVEN AND OTHER FAVORITE POEMS, Edgar Allan Poe. Over 40 of the author's most memorable poems: "The Bells," "Ulalume," "Israfel," "To Helen," "The Conqueror Worm," "Eldorado," "Annabel Lee," many more. Alphabetic lists of titles and first lines. 64pp. 5³⁄₁₆ x 8¼. 26685-0

PERSONAL MEMOIRS OF U. S. GRANT, Ulysses Simpson Grant. Intelligent, deeply moving firsthand account of Civil War campaigns, considered by many the finest military memoirs ever written. Includes letters, historic photographs, maps and more. 528pp. 6⅛ x 9¼. 28587-1

ANCIENT EGYPTIAN MATERIALS AND INDUSTRIES, A. Lucas and J. Harris. Fascinating, comprehensive, thoroughly documented text describes this ancient civilization's vast resources and the processes that incorporated them in daily life, including the use of animal products, building materials, cosmetics, perfumes and incense, fibers, glazed ware, glass and its manufacture, materials used in the mummification process, and much more. 544pp. 6¹⁄₈ x 9¼. (Available in U.S. only.) 40446-3

RUSSIAN STORIES/RUSSKIE RASSKAZY: A Dual-Language Book, edited by Gleb Struve. Twelve tales by such masters as Chekhov, Tolstoy, Dostoevsky, Pushkin, others. Excellent word-for-word English translations on facing pages, plus teaching and study aids, Russian/English vocabulary, biographical/critical introductions, more. 416pp. 5⅜ x 8½. 26244-8

PHILADELPHIA THEN AND NOW: 60 Sites Photographed in the Past and Present, Kenneth Finkel and Susan Oyama. Rare photographs of City Hall, Logan Square, Independence Hall, Betsy Ross House, other landmarks juxtaposed with contemporary views. Captures changing face of historic city. Introduction. Captions. 128pp. 8¼ x 11. 25790-8

AIA ARCHITECTURAL GUIDE TO NASSAU AND SUFFOLK COUNTIES, LONG ISLAND, The American Institute of Architects, Long Island Chapter, and the Society for the Preservation of Long Island Antiquities. Comprehensive, well-researched and generously illustrated volume brings to life over three centuries of Long Island's great architectural heritage. More than 240 photographs with authoritative, extensively detailed captions. 176pp. 8¼ x 11. 26946-9

NORTH AMERICAN INDIAN LIFE: Customs and Traditions of 23 Tribes, Elsie Clews Parsons (ed.). 27 fictionalized essays by noted anthropologists examine religion, customs, government, additional facets of life among the Winnebago, Crow, Zuni, Eskimo, other tribes. 480pp. 6⅛ x 9¼. 27377-6

CATALOG OF DOVER BOOKS

FRANK LLOYD WRIGHT'S DANA HOUSE, Donald Hoffmann. Pictorial essay of residential masterpiece with over 160 interior and exterior photos, plans, elevations, sketches and studies. 128pp. 9¼ x 10¾. 29120-0

THE MALE AND FEMALE FIGURE IN MOTION: 60 Classic Photographic Sequences, Eadweard Muybridge. 60 true-action photographs of men and women walking, running, climbing, bending, turning, etc., reproduced from rare 19th-century masterpiece. vi + 121pp. 9 x 12. 24745-7

1001 QUESTIONS ANSWERED ABOUT THE SEASHORE, N. J. Berrill and Jacquelyn Berrill. Queries answered about dolphins, sea snails, sponges, starfish, fishes, shore birds, many others. Covers appearance, breeding, growth, feeding, much more. 305pp. 5¼ x 8¼. 23366-9

ATTRACTING BIRDS TO YOUR YARD, William J. Weber. Easy-to-follow guide offers advice on how to attract the greatest diversity of birds: birdhouses, feeders, water and waterers, much more. 96pp. 5³⁄₁₆ x 8¼. 28927-3

MEDICINAL AND OTHER USES OF NORTH AMERICAN PLANTS: A Historical Survey with Special Reference to the Eastern Indian Tribes, Charlotte Erichsen-Brown. Chronological historical citations document 500 years of usage of plants, trees, shrubs native to eastern Canada, northeastern U.S. Also complete identifying information. 343 illustrations. 544pp. 6½ x 9¼. 25951-X

STORYBOOK MAZES, Dave Phillips. 23 stories and mazes on two-page spreads: Wizard of Oz, Treasure Island, Robin Hood, etc. Solutions. 64pp. 8¼ x 11. 23628-5

AMERICAN NEGRO SONGS: 230 Folk Songs and Spirituals, Religious and Secular, John W. Work. This authoritative study traces the African influences of songs sung and played by black Americans at work, in church, and as entertainment. The author discusses the lyric significance of such songs as "Swing Low, Sweet Chariot," "John Henry," and others and offers the words and music for 230 songs. Bibliography. Index of Song Titles. 272pp. 6½ x 9¼. 40271-1

MOVIE-STAR PORTRAITS OF THE FORTIES, John Kobal (ed.). 163 glamor, studio photos of 106 stars of the 1940s: Rita Hayworth, Ava Gardner, Marlon Brando, Clark Gable, many more. 176pp. 8⅜ x 11¼. 23546-7

BENCHLEY LOST AND FOUND, Robert Benchley. Finest humor from early 30s, about pet peeves, child psychologists, post office and others. Mostly unavailable elsewhere. 73 illustrations by Peter Arno and others. 183pp. 5⅜ x 8½. 22410-4

YEKL and THE IMPORTED BRIDEGROOM AND OTHER STORIES OF YIDDISH NEW YORK, Abraham Cahan. Film Hester Street based on *Yekl* (1896). Novel, other stories among first about Jewish immigrants on N.Y.'s East Side. 240pp. 5⅜ x 8½. 22427-9

SELECTED POEMS, Walt Whitman. Generous sampling from *Leaves of Grass.* Twenty-four poems include "I Hear America Singing," "Song of the Open Road," "I Sing the Body Electric," "When Lilacs Last in the Dooryard Bloom'd," "O Captain! My Captain!"—all reprinted from an authoritative edition. Lists of titles and first lines. 128pp. 5³⁄₁₆ x 8¼. 26878-0

THE BEST TALES OF HOFFMANN, E. T. A. Hoffmann. 10 of Hoffmann's most important stories: "Nutcracker and the King of Mice," "The Golden Flowerpot," etc. 458pp. 5⅜ x 8½. 21793-0

FROM FETISH TO GOD IN ANCIENT EGYPT, E. A. Wallis Budge. Rich detailed survey of Egyptian conception of "God" and gods, magic, cult of animals, Osiris, more. Also, superb English translations of hymns and legends. 240 illustrations. 545pp. 5⅜ x 8½. 25803-3

FRENCH STORIES/CONTES FRANÇAIS: A Dual-Language Book, Wallace Fowlie. Ten stories by French masters, Voltaire to Camus: "Micromegas" by Voltaire; "The Atheist's Mass" by Balzac; "Minuet" by de Maupassant; "The Guest" by Camus, six more. Excellent English translations on facing pages. Also French-English vocabulary list, exercises, more. 352pp. 5⅜ x 8½. 26443-2

CHICAGO AT THE TURN OF THE CENTURY IN PHOTOGRAPHS: 122 Historic Views from the Collections of the Chicago Historical Society, Larry A. Viskochil. Rare large-format prints offer detailed views of City Hall, State Street, the Loop, Hull House, Union Station, many other landmarks, circa 1904-1913. Introduction. Captions. Maps. 144pp. 9⅜ x 12¼. 24656-6

OLD BROOKLYN IN EARLY PHOTOGRAPHS, 1865-1929, William Lee Younger. Luna Park, Gravesend race track, construction of Grand Army Plaza, moving of Hotel Brighton, etc. 157 previously unpublished photographs. 165pp. 8⅞ x 11¾. 23587-4

THE MYTHS OF THE NORTH AMERICAN INDIANS, Lewis Spence. Rich anthology of the myths and legends of the Algonquins, Iroquois, Pawnees and Sioux, prefaced by an extensive historical and ethnological commentary. 36 illustrations. 480pp. 5⅜ x 8½. 25967-6

AN ENCYCLOPEDIA OF BATTLES: Accounts of Over 1,560 Battles from 1479 B.C. to the Present, David Eggenberger. Essential details of every major battle in recorded history from the first battle of Megiddo in 1479 B.C. to Grenada in 1984. List of Battle Maps. New Appendix covering the years 1967-1984. Index. 99 illustrations. 544pp. 6½ x 9¼. 24913-1

SAILING ALONE AROUND THE WORLD, Captain Joshua Slocum. First man to sail around the world, alone, in small boat. One of great feats of seamanship told in delightful manner. 67 illustrations. 294pp. 5⅜ x 8½. 20326-3

ANARCHISM AND OTHER ESSAYS, Emma Goldman. Powerful, penetrating, prophetic essays on direct action, role of minorities, prison reform, puritan hypocrisy, violence, etc. 271pp. 5⅜ x 8½. 22484-8

MYTHS OF THE HINDUS AND BUDDHISTS, Ananda K. Coomaraswamy and Sister Nivedita. Great stories of the epics; deeds of Krishna, Shiva, taken from puranas, Vedas, folk tales; etc. 32 illustrations. 400pp. 5⅜ x 8½. 21759-0

THE TRAUMA OF BIRTH, Otto Rank. Rank's controversial thesis that anxiety neurosis is caused by profound psychological trauma which occurs at birth. 256pp. 5⅜ x 8½. 27974-X

A THEOLOGICO-POLITICAL TREATISE, Benedict Spinoza. Also contains unfinished Political Treatise. Great classic on religious liberty, theory of government on common consent. R. Elwes translation. Total of 421pp. 5⅜ x 8½. 20249-6

MY BONDAGE AND MY FREEDOM, Frederick Douglass. Born a slave, Douglass became outspoken force in antislavery movement. The best of Douglass' autobiographies. Graphic description of slave life. 464pp. 5⅜ x 8½. 22457-0

FOLLOWING THE EQUATOR: A Journey Around the World, Mark Twain. Fascinating humorous account of 1897 voyage to Hawaii, Australia, India, New Zealand, etc. Ironic, bemused reports on peoples, customs, climate, flora and fauna, politics, much more. 197 illustrations. 720pp. 5⅜ x 8½. 26113-1

THE PEOPLE CALLED SHAKERS, Edward D. Andrews. Definitive study of Shakers: origins, beliefs, practices, dances, social organization, furniture and crafts, etc. 33 illustrations. 351pp. 5⅜ x 8½. 21081-2

THE MYTHS OF GREECE AND ROME, H. A. Guerber. A classic of mythology, generously illustrated, long prized for its simple, graphic, accurate retelling of the principal myths of Greece and Rome, and for its commentary on their origins and significance. With 64 illustrations by Michelangelo, Raphael, Titian, Rubens, Canova, Bernini and others. 480pp. 5⅜ x 8½. 27584-1

PSYCHOLOGY OF MUSIC, Carl E. Seashore. Classic work discusses music as a medium from psychological viewpoint. Clear treatment of physical acoustics, auditory apparatus, sound perception, development of musical skills, nature of musical feeling, host of other topics. 88 figures. 408pp. 5⅜ x 8½. 21851-1

THE PHILOSOPHY OF HISTORY, Georg W. Hegel. Great classic of Western thought develops concept that history is not chance but rational process, the evolution of freedom. 457pp. 5⅜ x 8½. 20112-0

THE BOOK OF TEA, Kakuzo Okakura. Minor classic of the Orient: entertaining, charming explanation, interpretation of traditional Japanese culture in terms of tea ceremony. 94pp. 5⅜ x 8½. 20070-1

LIFE IN ANCIENT EGYPT, Adolf Erman. Fullest, most thorough, detailed older account with much not in more recent books, domestic life, religion, magic, medicine, commerce, much more. Many illustrations reproduce tomb paintings, carvings, hieroglyphs, etc. 597pp. 5⅜ x 8½. 22632-8

SUNDIALS, Their Theory and Construction, Albert Waugh. Far and away the best, most thorough coverage of ideas, mathematics concerned, types, construction, adjusting anywhere. Simple, nontechnical treatment allows even children to build several of these dials. Over 100 illustrations. 230pp. 5⅜ x 8½. 22947-5

THEORETICAL HYDRODYNAMICS, L. M. Milne-Thomson. Classic exposition of the mathematical theory of fluid motion, applicable to both hydrodynamics and aerodynamics. Over 600 exercises. 768pp. 6⅛ x 9¼. 68970-0

SONGS OF EXPERIENCE: Facsimile Reproduction with 26 Plates in Full Color, William Blake. 26 full-color plates from a rare 1826 edition. Includes "The Tyger," "London," "Holy Thursday," and other poems. Printed text of poems. 48pp. 5¼ x 7. 24636-1

OLD-TIME VIGNETTES IN FULL COLOR, Carol Belanger Grafton (ed.). Over 390 charming, often sentimental illustrations, selected from archives of Victorian graphics—pretty women posing, children playing, food, flowers, kittens and puppies, smiling cherubs, birds and butterflies, much more. All copyright-free. 48pp. 9¼ x 12¼. 27269-9

CATALOG OF DOVER BOOKS

PERSPECTIVE FOR ARTISTS, Rex Vicat Cole. Depth, perspective of sky and sea, shadows, much more, not usually covered. 391 diagrams, 81 reproductions of drawings and paintings. 279pp. 5⅜ x 8½. 22487-2

DRAWING THE LIVING FIGURE, Joseph Sheppard. Innovative approach to artistic anatomy focuses on specifics of surface anatomy, rather than muscles and bones. Over 170 drawings of live models in front, back and side views, and in widely varying poses. Accompanying diagrams. 177 illustrations. Introduction. Index. 144pp. 8⅜ x11¼. 26723-7

GOTHIC AND OLD ENGLISH ALPHABETS: 100 Complete Fonts, Dan X. Solo. Add power, elegance to posters, signs, other graphics with 100 stunning copyright-free alphabets: Blackstone, Dolbey, Germania, 97 more—including many lower-case, numerals, punctuation marks. 104pp. 8⅛ x 11. 24695-7

HOW TO DO BEADWORK, Mary White. Fundamental book on craft from simple projects to five-bead chains and woven works. 106 illustrations. 142pp. 5⅜ x 8.
20697-1

THE BOOK OF WOOD CARVING, Charles Marshall Sayers. Finest book for beginners discusses fundamentals and offers 34 designs. "Absolutely first rate . . . well thought out and well executed."–E. J. Tangerman. 118pp. 7¾ x 10⅝. 23654-4

ILLUSTRATED CATALOG OF CIVIL WAR MILITARY GOODS: Union Army Weapons, Insignia, Uniform Accessories, and Other Equipment, Schuyler, Hartley, and Graham. Rare, profusely illustrated 1846 catalog includes Union Army uniform and dress regulations, arms and ammunition, coats, insignia, flags, swords, rifles, etc. 226 illustrations. 160pp. 9 x 12. 24939-5

WOMEN'S FASHIONS OF THE EARLY 1900s: An Unabridged Republication of "New York Fashions, 1909," National Cloak & Suit Co. Rare catalog of mail-order fashions documents women's and children's clothing styles shortly after the turn of the century. Captions offer full descriptions, prices. Invaluable resource for fashion, costume historians. Approximately 725 illustrations. 128pp. 8⅜ x 11¼. 27276-1

THE 1912 AND 1915 GUSTAV STICKLEY FURNITURE CATALOGS, Gustav Stickley. With over 200 detailed illustrations and descriptions, these two catalogs are essential reading and reference materials and identification guides for Stickley furniture. Captions cite materials, dimensions and prices. 112pp. 6½ x 9¼. 26676-1

EARLY AMERICAN LOCOMOTIVES, John H. White, Jr. Finest locomotive engravings from early 19th century: historical (1804–74), main-line (after 1870), special, foreign, etc. 147 plates. 142pp. 11⅜ x 8¼. 22772-3

THE TALL SHIPS OF TODAY IN PHOTOGRAPHS, Frank O. Braynard. Lavishly illustrated tribute to nearly 100 majestic contemporary sailing vessels: Amerigo Vespucci, Clearwater, Constitution, Eagle, Mayflower, Sea Cloud, Victory, many more. Authoritative captions provide statistics, background on each ship. 190 black-and-white photographs and illustrations. Introduction. 128pp. 8⅞ x 11¾.
27163-3

LITTLE BOOK OF EARLY AMERICAN CRAFTS AND TRADES, Peter Stockham (ed.). 1807 children's book explains crafts and trades: baker, hatter, cooper, potter, and many others. 23 copperplate illustrations. 140pp. 4⅝ x 6. 23336-7

VICTORIAN FASHIONS AND COSTUMES FROM HARPER'S BAZAR, 1867–1898, Stella Blum (ed.). Day costumes, evening wear, sports clothes, shoes, hats, other accessories in over 1,000 detailed engravings. 320pp. 9⅜ x 12¼. 22990-4

GUSTAV STICKLEY, THE CRAFTSMAN, Mary Ann Smith. Superb study surveys broad scope of Stickley's achievement, especially in architecture. Design philosophy, rise and fall of the Craftsman empire, descriptions and floor plans for many Craftsman houses, more. 86 black-and-white halftones. 31 line illustrations. Introduction 208pp. 6½ x 9¼. 27210-9

THE LONG ISLAND RAIL ROAD IN EARLY PHOTOGRAPHS, Ron Ziel. Over 220 rare photos, informative text document origin (1844) and development of rail service on Long Island. Vintage views of early trains, locomotives, stations, passengers, crews, much more. Captions. 8⅞ x 11¾. 26301-0

VOYAGE OF THE LIBERDADE, Joshua Slocum. Great 19th-century mariner's thrilling, first-hand account of the wreck of his ship off South America, the 35-foot boat he built from the wreckage, and its remarkable voyage home. 128pp. 5⅜ x 8½. 40022-0

TEN BOOKS ON ARCHITECTURE, Vitruvius. The most important book ever written on architecture. Early Roman aesthetics, technology, classical orders, site selection, all other aspects. Morgan translation. 331pp. 5⅜ x 8½. 20645-9

THE HUMAN FIGURE IN MOTION, Eadweard Muybridge. More than 4,500 stopped-action photos, in action series, showing undraped men, women, children jumping, lying down, throwing, sitting, wrestling, carrying, etc. 390pp. 7⅞ x 10⅝. 20204-6 Clothbd.

TREES OF THE EASTERN AND CENTRAL UNITED STATES AND CANADA, William M. Harlow. Best one-volume guide to 140 trees. Full descriptions, woodlore, range, etc. Over 600 illustrations. Handy size. 288pp. 4½ x 6⅜. 20395-6

SONGS OF WESTERN BIRDS, Dr. Donald J. Borror. Complete song and call repertoire of 60 western species, including flycatchers, juncoes, cactus wrens, many more–includes fully illustrated booklet. Cassette and manual 99913-0

GROWING AND USING HERBS AND SPICES, Milo Miloradovich. Versatile handbook provides all the information needed for cultivation and use of all the herbs and spices available in North America. 4 illustrations. Index. Glossary. 236pp. 5⅜ x 8½. 25058-X

BIG BOOK OF MAZES AND LABYRINTHS, Walter Shepherd. 50 mazes and labyrinths in all–classical, solid, ripple, and more–in one great volume. Perfect inexpensive puzzler for clever youngsters. Full solutions. 112pp. 8⅛ x 11. 22951-3

PIANO TUNING, J. Cree Fischer. Clearest, best book for beginner, amateur. Simple repairs, raising dropped notes, tuning by easy method of flattened fifths. No previous skills needed. 4 illustrations. 201pp. 5⅜ x 8½. 23267-0

HINTS TO SINGERS, Lillian Nordica. Selecting the right teacher, developing confidence, overcoming stage fright, and many other important skills receive thoughtful discussion in this indispensible guide, written by a world-famous diva of four decades' experience. 96pp. 5⅜ x 8½. 40094-8

THE COMPLETE NONSENSE OF EDWARD LEAR, Edward Lear. All nonsense limericks, zany alphabets, Owl and Pussycat, songs, nonsense botany, etc., illustrated by Lear. Total of 320pp. 5⅜ x 8½. (Available in U.S. only.) 20167-8

VICTORIAN PARLOUR POETRY: An Annotated Anthology, Michael R. Turner. 117 gems by Longfellow, Tennyson, Browning, many lesser-known poets. "The Village Blacksmith," "Curfew Must Not Ring Tonight," "Only a Baby Small," dozens more, often difficult to find elsewhere. Index of poets, titles, first lines. xxiii + 325pp. 5⅝ x 8¼. 27044-0

DUBLINERS, James Joyce. Fifteen stories offer vivid, tightly focused observations of the lives of Dublin's poorer classes. At least one, "The Dead," is considered a masterpiece. Reprinted complete and unabridged from standard edition. 160pp. 5³⁄₁₆ x 8¼. 26870-5

GREAT WEIRD TALES: 14 Stories by Lovecraft, Blackwood, Machen and Others, S. T. Joshi (ed.). 14 spellbinding tales, including "The Sin Eater," by Fiona McLeod, "The Eye Above the Mantel," by Frank Belknap Long, as well as renowned works by R. H. Barlow, Lord Dunsany, Arthur Machen, W. C. Morrow and eight other masters of the genre. 256pp. 5⅜ x 8½. (Available in U.S. only.) 40436-6

THE BOOK OF THE SACRED MAGIC OF ABRAMELIN THE MAGE, translated by S. MacGregor Mathers. Medieval manuscript of ceremonial magic. Basic document in Aleister Crowley, Golden Dawn groups. 268pp. 5⅜ x 8½. 23211-5

NEW RUSSIAN-ENGLISH AND ENGLISH-RUSSIAN DICTIONARY, M. A. O'Brien. This is a remarkably handy Russian dictionary, containing a surprising amount of information, including over 70,000 entries. 366pp. 4½ x 6⅛. 20208-9

HISTORIC HOMES OF THE AMERICAN PRESIDENTS, Second, Revised Edition, Irvin Haas. A traveler's guide to American Presidential homes, most open to the public, depicting and describing homes occupied by every American President from George Washington to George Bush. With visiting hours, admission charges, travel routes. 175 photographs. Index. 160pp. 8¼ x 11. 26751-2

NEW YORK IN THE FORTIES, Andreas Feininger. 162 brilliant photographs by the well-known photographer, formerly with *Life* magazine. Commuters, shoppers, Times Square at night, much else from city at its peak. Captions by John von Hartz. 181pp. 9¼ x 10¾. 23585-8

INDIAN SIGN LANGUAGE, William Tomkins. Over 525 signs developed by Sioux and other tribes. Written instructions and diagrams. Also 290 pictographs. 111pp. 6⅛ x 9¼. 22029-X

ANATOMY: A Complete Guide for Artists, Joseph Sheppard. A master of figure drawing shows artists how to render human anatomy convincingly. Over 460 illustrations. 224pp. 8⅜ x 11¼. 27279-6

MEDIEVAL CALLIGRAPHY: Its History and Technique, Marc Drogin. Spirited history, comprehensive instruction manual covers 13 styles (ca. 4th century through 15th). Excellent photographs; directions for duplicating medieval techniques with modern tools. 224pp. 8⅜ x 11¼. 26142-5

DRIED FLOWERS: How to Prepare Them, Sarah Whitlock and Martha Rankin. Complete instructions on how to use silica gel, meal and borax, perlite aggregate, sand and borax, glycerine and water to create attractive permanent flower arrangements. 12 illustrations. 32pp. 5⅜ x 8½. 21802-3

EASY-TO-MAKE BIRD FEEDERS FOR WOODWORKERS, Scott D. Campbell. Detailed, simple-to-use guide for designing, constructing, caring for and using feeders. Text, illustrations for 12 classic and contemporary designs. 96pp. 5⅜ x 8½. 25847-5

SCOTTISH WONDER TALES FROM MYTH AND LEGEND, Donald A. Mackenzie. 16 lively tales tell of giants rumbling down mountainsides, of a magic wand that turns stone pillars into warriors, of gods and goddesses, evil hags, powerful forces and more. 240pp. 5⅜ x 8½. 29677-6

THE HISTORY OF UNDERCLOTHES, C. Willett Cunnington and Phyllis Cunnington. Fascinating, well-documented survey covering six centuries of English undergarments, enhanced with over 100 illustrations: 12th-century laced-up bodice, footed long drawers (1795), 19th-century bustles, 19th-century corsets for men, Victorian "bust improvers," much more. 272pp. 5⅝ x 8¼. 27124-2

ARTS AND CRAFTS FURNITURE: The Complete Brooks Catalog of 1912, Brooks Manufacturing Co. Photos and detailed descriptions of more than 150 now very collectible furniture designs from the Arts and Crafts movement depict davenports, settees, buffets, desks, tables, chairs, bedsteads, dressers and more, all built of solid, quarter-sawed oak. Invaluable for students and enthusiasts of antiques, Americana and the decorative arts. 80pp. 6½ x 9¼. 27471-3

WILBUR AND ORVILLE: A Biography of the Wright Brothers, Fred Howard. Definitive, crisply written study tells the full story of the brothers' lives and work. A vividly written biography, unparalleled in scope and color, that also captures the spirit of an extraordinary era. 560pp. 6⅛ x 9¼. 40297-5

THE ARTS OF THE SAILOR: Knotting, Splicing and Ropework, Hervey Garrett Smith. Indispensable shipboard reference covers tools, basic knots and useful hitches; handsewing and canvas work, more. Over 100 illustrations. Delightful reading for sea lovers. 256pp. 5⅜ x 8½. 26440-8

FRANK LLOYD WRIGHT'S FALLINGWATER: The House and Its History, Second, Revised Edition, Donald Hoffmann. A total revision–both in text and illustrations–of the standard document on Fallingwater, the boldest, most personal architectural statement of Wright's mature years, updated with valuable new material from the recently opened Frank Lloyd Wright Archives. "Fascinating"–*The New York Times*. 116 illustrations. 128pp. 9¼ x 10¾. 27430-6

PHOTOGRAPHIC SKETCHBOOK OF THE CIVIL WAR, Alexander Gardner. 100 photos taken on field during the Civil War. Famous shots of Manassas Harper's Ferry, Lincoln, Richmond, slave pens, etc. 244pp. 10⅝ x 8¼.   22731-6

FIVE ACRES AND INDEPENDENCE, Maurice G. Kains. Great back-to-the-land classic explains basics of self-sufficient farming. The one book to get. 95 illustrations. 397pp. 5⅜ x 8½.   20974-1

SONGS OF EASTERN BIRDS, Dr. Donald J. Borror. Songs and calls of 60 species most common to eastern U.S.: warblers, woodpeckers, flycatchers, thrushes, larks, many more in high-quality recording.   Cassette and manual 99912-2

A MODERN HERBAL, Margaret Grieve. Much the fullest, most exact, most useful compilation of herbal material. Gigantic alphabetical encyclopedia, from aconite to zedoary, gives botanical information, medical properties, folklore, economic uses, much else. Indispensable to serious reader. 161 illustrations. 888pp. 6½ x 9¼. 2-vol. set. (Available in U.S. only.)   Vol. I: 22798-7
Vol. II: 22799-5

HIDDEN TREASURE MAZE BOOK, Dave Phillips. Solve 34 challenging mazes accompanied by heroic tales of adventure. Evil dragons, people-eating plants, blood-thirsty giants, many more dangerous adversaries lurk at every twist and turn. 34 mazes, stories, solutions. 48pp. 8¼ x 11.   24566-7

LETTERS OF W. A. MOZART, Wolfgang A. Mozart. Remarkable letters show bawdy wit, humor, imagination, musical insights, contemporary musical world; includes some letters from Leopold Mozart. 276pp. 5⅜ x 8½.   22859-2

BASIC PRINCIPLES OF CLASSICAL BALLET, Agrippina Vaganova. Great Russian theoretician, teacher explains methods for teaching classical ballet. 118 illus-trations. 175pp. 5⅜ x 8½.   22036-2

THE JUMPING FROG, Mark Twain. Revenge edition. The original story of The Celebrated Jumping Frog of Calaveras County, a hapless French translation, and Twain's hilarious "retranslation" from the French. 12 illustrations. 66pp. 5⅜ x 8½.   22686-7

BEST REMEMBERED POEMS, Martin Gardner (ed.). The 126 poems in this superb collection of 19th- and 20th-century British and American verse range from Shelley's "To a Skylark" to the impassioned "Renascence" of Edna St. Vincent Millay and to Edward Lear's whimsical "The Owl and the Pussycat." 224pp. 5⅜ x 8½.   27165-X

COMPLETE SONNETS, William Shakespeare. Over 150 exquisite poems deal with love, friendship, the tyranny of time, beauty's evanescence, death and other themes in language of remarkable power, precision and beauty. Glossary of archaic terms. 80pp. 5³⁄₁₆ x 8¼.   26686-9

THE BATTLES THAT CHANGED HISTORY, Fletcher Pratt. Eminent historian profiles 16 crucial conflicts, ancient to modern, that changed the course of civiliza-tion. 352pp. 5⅜ x 8½.   41129-X

THE WIT AND HUMOR OF OSCAR WILDE, Alvin Redman (ed.). More than 1,000 ripostes, paradoxes, wisecracks: Work is the curse of the drinking classes; I can resist everything except temptation; etc. 258pp. 5⅜ x 8½. 20602-5

SHAKESPEARE LEXICON AND QUOTATION DICTIONARY, Alexander Schmidt. Full definitions, locations, shades of meaning in every word in plays and poems. More than 50,000 exact quotations. 1,485pp. 6½ x 9¼. 2-vol. set.
Vol. 1: 22726-X
Vol. 2: 22727-8

SELECTED POEMS, Emily Dickinson. Over 100 best-known, best-loved poems by one of America's foremost poets, reprinted from authoritative early editions. No comparable edition at this price. Index of first lines. 64pp. 5³⁄₁₆ x 8¼. 26466-1

THE INSIDIOUS DR. FU-MANCHU, Sax Rohmer. The first of the popular mystery series introduces a pair of English detectives to their archnemesis, the diabolical Dr. Fu-Manchu. Flavorful atmosphere, fast-paced action, and colorful characters enliven this classic of the genre. 208pp. 5³⁄₁₆ x 8¼. 29898-1

THE MALLEUS MALEFICARUM OF KRAMER AND SPRENGER, translated by Montague Summers. Full text of most important witchhunter's "bible," used by both Catholics and Protestants. 278pp. 6⅝ x 10. 22802-9

SPANISH STORIES/CUENTOS ESPAÑOLES: A Dual-Language Book, Angel Flores (ed.). Unique format offers 13 great stories in Spanish by Cervantes, Borges, others. Faithful English translations on facing pages. 352pp. 5⅜ x 8½. 25399-6

GARDEN CITY, LONG ISLAND, IN EARLY PHOTOGRAPHS, 1869–1919, Mildred H. Smith. Handsome treasury of 118 vintage pictures, accompanied by carefully researched captions, document the Garden City Hotel fire (1899), the Vanderbilt Cup Race (1908), the first airmail flight departing from the Nassau Boulevard Aerodrome (1911), and much more. 96pp. 8⅞ x 11¾. 40669-5

OLD QUEENS, N.Y., IN EARLY PHOTOGRAPHS, Vincent F. Seyfried and William Asadorian. Over 160 rare photographs of Maspeth, Jamaica, Jackson Heights, and other areas. Vintage views of DeWitt Clinton mansion, 1939 World's Fair and more. Captions. 192pp. 8⅞ x 11. 26358-4

CAPTURED BY THE INDIANS: 15 Firsthand Accounts, 1750-1870, Frederick Drimmer. Astounding true historical accounts of grisly torture, bloody conflicts, relentless pursuits, miraculous escapes and more, by people who lived to tell the tale. 384pp. 5⅜ x 8½. 24901-8

THE WORLD'S GREAT SPEECHES (Fourth Enlarged Edition), Lewis Copeland, Lawrence W. Lamm, and Stephen J. McKenna. Nearly 300 speeches provide public speakers with a wealth of updated quotes and inspiration–from Pericles' funeral oration and William Jennings Bryan's "Cross of Gold Speech" to Malcolm X's powerful words on the Black Revolution and Earl of Spenser's tribute to his sister, Diana, Princess of Wales. 944pp. 5⅜ x 8⅜. 40903-1

THE BOOK OF THE SWORD, Sir Richard F. Burton. Great Victorian scholar/adventurer's eloquent, erudite history of the "queen of weapons"–from prehistory to early Roman Empire. Evolution and development of early swords, variations (sabre, broadsword, cutlass, scimitar, etc.), much more. 336pp. 6⅛ x 9¼. 25434-8

CATALOG OF DOVER BOOKS

AUTOBIOGRAPHY: The Story of My Experiments with Truth, Mohandas K. Gandhi. Boyhood, legal studies, purification, the growth of the Satyagraha (nonviolent protest) movement. Critical, inspiring work of the man responsible for the freedom of India. 480pp. 5⅜ x 8½. (Available in U.S. only.)   24593-4

CELTIC MYTHS AND LEGENDS, T. W. Rolleston. Masterful retelling of Irish and Welsh stories and tales. Cuchulain, King Arthur, Deirdre, the Grail, many more. First paperback edition. 58 full-page illustrations. 512pp. 5⅜ x 8½.   26507-2

THE PRINCIPLES OF PSYCHOLOGY, William James. Famous long course complete, unabridged. Stream of thought, time perception, memory, experimental methods; great work decades ahead of its time. 94 figures. 1,391pp. 5⅜ x 8½. 2-vol. set.
Vol. I: 20381-6 Vol. II: 20382-4

THE WORLD AS WILL AND REPRESENTATION, Arthur Schopenhauer. Definitive English translation of Schopenhauer's life work, correcting more than 1,000 errors, omissions in earlier translations. Translated by E. F. J. Payne. Total of 1,269pp. 5⅜ x 8½. 2-vol. set.   Vol. 1: 21761-2 Vol. 2: 21762-0

MAGIC AND MYSTERY IN TIBET, Madame Alexandra David-Neel. Experiences among lamas, magicians, sages, sorcerers, Bonpa wizards. A true psychic discovery. 32 illustrations. 321pp. 5⅜ x 8½. (Available in U.S. only.)   22682-4

THE EGYPTIAN BOOK OF THE DEAD, E. A. Wallis Budge. Complete reproduction of Ani's papyrus, finest ever found. Full hieroglyphic text, interlinear transliteration, word-for-word translation, smooth translation. 533pp. 6½ x 9¼.   21866-X

MATHEMATICS FOR THE NONMATHEMATICIAN, Morris Kline. Detailed, college-level treatment of mathematics in cultural and historical context, with numerous exercises. Recommended Reading Lists. Tables. Numerous figures. 641pp. 5⅜ x 8½.   24823-2

PROBABILISTIC METHODS IN THE THEORY OF STRUCTURES, Isaac Elishakoff. Well-written introduction covers the elements of the theory of probability from two or more random variables, the reliability of such multivariable structures, the theory of random function, Monte Carlo methods of treating problems incapable of exact solution, and more. Examples. 502pp. 5⅜ x 8½.   40691-1

THE RIME OF THE ANCIENT MARINER, Gustave Doré, S. T. Coleridge. Doré's finest work; 34 plates capture moods, subtleties of poem. Flawless full-size reproductions printed on facing pages with authoritative text of poem. "Beautiful. Simply beautiful."—*Publisher's Weekly.* 77pp. 9¼ x 12.   22305-1

NORTH AMERICAN INDIAN DESIGNS FOR ARTISTS AND CRAFTSPEOPLE, Eva Wilson. Over 360 authentic copyright-free designs adapted from Navajo blankets, Hopi pottery, Sioux buffalo hides, more. Geometrics, symbolic figures, plant and animal motifs, etc. 128pp. 8⅜ x 11. (Not for sale in the United Kingdom.)   25341-4

SCULPTURE: Principles and Practice, Louis Slobodkin. Step-by-step approach to clay, plaster, metals, stone; classical and modern. 253 drawings, photos. 255pp. 8⅛ x 11.   22960-2

THE INFLUENCE OF SEA POWER UPON HISTORY, 1660–1783, A. T. Mahan. Influential classic of naval history and tactics still used as text in war colleges. First paperback edition. 4 maps. 24 battle plans. 640pp. 5⅜ x 8½.   25509-3

THE STORY OF THE TITANIC AS TOLD BY ITS SURVIVORS, Jack Winocour (ed.). What it was really like. Panic, despair, shocking inefficiency, and a little heroism. More thrilling than any fictional account. 26 illustrations. 320pp. 5⅜ x 8½.
20610-6

FAIRY AND FOLK TALES OF THE IRISH PEASANTRY, William Butler Yeats (ed.). Treasury of 64 tales from the twilight world of Celtic myth and legend: "The Soul Cages," "The Kildare Pooka," "King O'Toole and his Goose," many more. Introduction and Notes by W. B. Yeats. 352pp. 5⅜ x 8½.
26941-8

BUDDHIST MAHAYANA TEXTS, E. B. Cowell and others (eds.). Superb, accurate translations of basic documents in Mahayana Buddhism, highly important in history of religions. The Buddha-karita of Asvaghosha, Larger Sukhavativyuha, more. 448pp. 5⅜ x 8½.
25552-2

ONE TWO THREE . . . INFINITY: Facts and Speculations of Science, George Gamow. Great physicist's fascinating, readable overview of contemporary science: number theory, relativity, fourth dimension, entropy, genes, atomic structure, much more. 128 illustrations. Index. 352pp. 5⅜ x 8½.
25664-2

EXPERIMENTATION AND MEASUREMENT, W. J. Youden. Introductory manual explains laws of measurement in simple terms and offers tips for achieving accuracy and minimizing errors. Mathematics of measurement, use of instruments, experimenting with machines. 1994 edition. Foreword. Preface. Introduction. Epilogue. Selected Readings. Glossary. Index. Tables and figures. 128pp. 5⅜ x 8½.
40451-X

DALÍ ON MODERN ART: The Cuckolds of Antiquated Modern Art, Salvador Dalí. Influential painter skewers modern art and its practitioners. Outrageous evaluations of Picasso, Cézanne, Turner, more. 15 renderings of paintings discussed. 44 calligraphic decorations by Dalí. 96pp. 5⅜ x 8½. (Available in U.S. only.)
29220-7

ANTIQUE PLAYING CARDS: A Pictorial History, Henry René D'Allemagne. Over 900 elaborate, decorative images from rare playing cards (14th–20th centuries): Bacchus, death, dancing dogs, hunting scenes, royal coats of arms, players cheating, much more. 96pp. 9¼ x 12¼.
29265-7

MAKING FURNITURE MASTERPIECES: 30 Projects with Measured Drawings, Franklin H. Gottshall. Step-by-step instructions, illustrations for constructing handsome, useful pieces, among them a Sheraton desk, Chippendale chair, Spanish desk, Queen Anne table and a William and Mary dressing mirror. 224pp. 8⅛ x 11¼.
29338-6

THE FOSSIL BOOK: A Record of Prehistoric Life, Patricia V. Rich et al. Profusely illustrated definitive guide covers everything from single-celled organisms and dinosaurs to birds and mammals and the interplay between climate and man. Over 1,500 illustrations. 760pp. 7½ x 10⅛.
29371-8